KEYS TO THE ENCOUNTER

A Library of Congress Resource Guide
for the Study of the Age of Discovery

KEYS TO THE ENCOUNTER

LIBRARY
OF CONGRESS
RESOURCE
GUIDE

KEYS TO THE ENCOUNTER

A LIBRARY OF CONGRESS
RESOURCE GUIDE
FOR THE STUDY OF
THE AGE OF DISCOVERY

LOUIS DE VORSEY, JR.

LIBRARY OF CONGRESS Washington 1992

Copyright © 1991 Chapters 1–6 by Louis de Vorsey, Jr.

Library of Congress Cataloging-in-Publication Data

De Vorsey, Louis.
    Keys to the encounter: a Library of Congress resource guide for the study of the Age of Discovery / by Louis De Vorsey, Jr.
        p.   cm.
    Includes bibliographical references and index.
    ISBN 0-8444-0692-9
—— —— Copy 3 Z663 .K49 1991
    1. America—Discovery and exploration. 2. Columbus, Christopher.
3. Indians—First contact with Europeans. 4. America—Discovery and exploration—Bibliography—Catalogs. 5. Columbus, Christopher—Bibliography—Catalogs. 6. Indians—First contact with Europeans—Bibliography—Catalogs. 7. America—Discovery and exploration—Sources—Bibliography—Catalogs. 8. Indians—First contact with Europeans—Sources—Bibliography—Catalogs. 9. Library of Congress—Catalogs. I. Title.
E101.D48 1991   91-16735
016.9701—dc20   CIP

Designed by Adrianne Onderdonk Dudden

COVER: *Chart of the Gulf of Maine, drawn by Samuel de Champlain (see page 54).*

FRONTISPIECE: *Illustration from the codex "Relacion . . . de la provincia de Michoacán" (see page 89).*

For sale by the Superintendent of Documents
      U.S. Government Printing Office
      Washington, D.C. 20402

CONTENTS

CHAPTER ONE

CHAPTER TWO

CHAPTER THREE

CHAPTER FOUR

CHAPTER FIVE

CHAPTER SIX

This globe of the earth was made in about 1615. The globe's world map gores were printed in the shop of Jodocus Hondiüs, one of the great map and atlas producers of the late sixteenth and early seventeenth centuries. Hondiüs was Flemish and began his career in Ghent before settling in London in the early 1580s. Since Jodocus Hondiüs died in 1612 it is probable that the map on this globe was produced under the supervision of his son who succeeded him in the business (Geography and Map Division).

FOREWORD

In three buildings on Capitol Hill, the Library of Congress now houses almost 100 million items. On its shelves and in its cases are books, manuscripts, maps, prints, photographs, posters, motion pictures, TV tapes, sound recordings, and much else. It is this rich array of resources that we invite you to explore: the knowledge therein can be mined only when someone actively seeks it out.

It is the obligation of the Library of Congress to make known what we have. We do so largely by creating extensive cataloging information, some of it in machine-readable tape, cartridge, or CD-ROM, some on microfiche or cards. We supplement this cataloging and bibliographic data in various ways. Among them is a new series of illustrated guides to our resources for the study of particular subjects. Each guide will describe such resources in all formats—from books to film to prints—throughout the Library.

We have now embarked on this new series with the book you are now holding. *Keys to the Encounter* has been written by a scholar, Louis De Vorsey, Jr., who has both deep knowledge of the Age of Discovery and long familiarity with the Library of Congress. Professor De Vorsey offers a stimulating tour of both subject and sources, accompanied by numerous illustrations, all of which are drawn from our collections.

Keys to the Encounter will be followed by guides to our holdings in African American history and culture, Native American studies, and World War II. Others are planned. They will all have a similar format and design; we intend to produce a coherent array of resource guides to which a researcher may refer.

In this book one reads about encounters between civilizations. Another kind of encounter is the one between a researcher and a library. We hope that your encounter with the Library of Congress, whether it is to undertake the study of the Age of Discovery or any other subject, will prove both useful and pleasant. We will strive to make it so.

James H. Billington
The Librarian of Congress

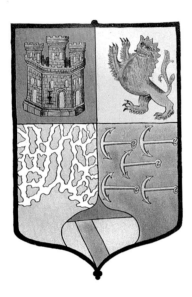

Columbus's Coat of Arms (three versions). In recognition of his great discovery Columbus was made a nobleman and granted arms as a visible symbol of his rank. In the letters patent conferring his rank and arms, dated May 20, 1493, the following was specified: "You may place above your arms a castle and a lion . . . viz. the gold castle on a green field in the upper quarter of the shield . . . on the dexter hand and in the other upper quarter . . . a purple lion rampant with green tongue on a white field, and . . . below . . . some gold islands in waves of the sea . . . and in the other quarter below . . . your own arms which you are accustomed to bear." Although we can be sure that Columbus had banners and waistcloths, emblazoned with his arms, dressing his ships no original copy has survived in any form. By 1502, when he compiled his Book of Privileges, he made a number of changes in the original design of his arms, as can be seen here in the colored facsimiles prepared by Henry Harrisse. Included also is a third version of Columbus's arms which was engraved to appear in Oviedo's La Historia General . . . [Seville, 1535]. Notice that this engraving adds a small globe and cross above a helmet (Rare Book and Special Collections Division).

PREFACE

In this book I attempt to provide an interesting narrative covering the Age of Discovery and its principal personalities and events during the period from roughly 1450 to 1580. It was clear at the outset that such a narrative would require a fresh perspective, one that would be suitable for the era of international observances of the Quincentenary of Columbus's voyage of 1492–93. The Columbian Quincentenary promises to stimulate new concerns with that Age and its consequences for the world at large.

The world of the 1990s is a world made up of one hundred and fifty-odd sovereign states. Only a handful of territorial fragments remain on the world political map as reflections of the bygone era of colonial empires. In many instances the schedule for their release is in place and political pressures are propelling the others toward the seemingly inevitable and universal goal of national sovereignty.

The major problem with the former "tried and true" perspective on the Age of Discovery is revealed in the term itself. It is a perspective that concentrates on the story of the *discovery* of a world that existed beyond the limited horizon of fifteenth- and sixteenth-century Europeans. In a word, it is a Europocentric story written by Europeans. At its worst, the *discovery* story serves as a justification of colonialism. At its best, it is insulting to the millions of indigenous people who flourished in the lands and continents encountered. By implication, they and their cultures were made relevant only through European discovery and even then only insofar as they impinged on essentially European affairs and accomplishments.

Rather than another iteration of such a perspective, this book focuses on the intercultural encounters that unfolded as groups of Europeans and the indigenous peoples of the Americas discovered one another. Although almost always recorded in written form by the European participants, many accounts reveal the indigenes to have been as richly human as their chroniclers. The fact that their cultures were alien and their languages unintelligible to the Europeans in no way made them inferior in humanity, intelligence, wit, and sophistication. The impact wrought by European weapons of war and disease soon took their toll, however, and whole cultures were annihilated in their wake. The fact that many if not most of their survivors have chosen not to celebrate the Columbian Quincentenary is understandable when seen in this light. When surveyed, a majority of Native Americans indicated that the Quincentenary should be described as commemorating 500 years of Native People's resistance to colonization. Some chose to call it the anniversary of a massacre.

A further purpose of this book is to demonstrate the breadth and richness of Age of Discovery research materials in the holdings of the Library of Congress. In part the sixty-odd illustrations illuminating my chapters form a selective visual catalog of a small part of those holdings. A comprehensive, but by no means exhaustive, view of the Library's holdings bearing on this historical epoch can be gained from the appendix, Researching the Age of Discovery in the Library of Congress. In this compilation several of the Library's divisions are singled out and described in terms of their holdings and facilities. I thought such descriptions could ease the tasks of the Age of Discovery readers and researchers and the librarians assisting them.

Some readers may be surprised to find divisions such as Prints and Photographs, Motion Picture, Broadcasting, and Recorded Sound, and the Archive of Folk Culture included in this research guide. They are included because I feel their holdings can tell us even more than traditional documentary sources about how the events and personalities of the Age of Discovery entered into and continue to resound in our contemporary culture.

As I proceeded in my research, I found that a chronology listing the key events and personalities contributing to the Age of Discovery was helpful. With that in mind I decided to include it here. It is selective and utilitarian and not presumed to be in any way complete or definitive. The reader should keep this in mind as interest in the Age of Discovery carries him or her beyond this book.

When I concluded my research and began writing I avoided excessive paraphrasing and allowed the explorers, chroniclers, and scribes who wrote the record to speak for themselves.

In my own reading over the years I had sometimes felt cheated when I had later read the originals of paraphrased extracts of historical documents. Often the richness, color, and immediacy of the originals were more important, in my judgment, than a particular author's paraphrased key point of a statement or description.

Whenever possible quoted extracts were taken from generally available published texts. In the Notes section following the chapters full bibliographic citations to those sources are provided.

ACKNOWLEDGMENTS

I wish to acknowledge the generous assistance and encouragement received from many individuals as I prepared the manuscript of this book. John R. Hébert, Coordinator of An Ongoing Voyage, the Library of Congress's Quincentenary Program, is to be thanked for linking my research interests with that ambitious effort and the Library's new series of published resource guides. Once that link was forged he was unstinting in his often creative and always valuable advice and assistance, first in my research and then by critiquing and correcting manuscript drafts. The Library's Director of Publishing, Dana Pratt, and Senior Editor, Iris Newsom, are similarly thanked for their confidence and efforts in making this first resource guide available in time for use as the Quincentenial era begins.

Several librarians in Library of Congress divisions where I worked were gracious enough to share materials that they had been preparing to assist readers in anticipation of the increased interest in Christopher Columbus and the Age of Discovery that the Quincentenary would bring. Their work was indispensable as I compiled the appendix, Researching the Age of Discovery in the Library of Congress. They are Rosemary F. Plakas, Rare Book and Special Collections Division, Richard W. Stephenson, Geography and Map Division, Everette E. Larson, Hispanic Division, Patrick G. Loughney, Motion Picture, Broadcasting, and Recorded Sound Division, and Anthony P. Mullan and Patrick Frazier, General Reading Rooms Division.

While I worked in the Library of Congress, the Geography and Map Division extended generous hospitality by providing a workplace and staff support. While everyone in that division made me feel welcome the following individuals rendered frequent and valuable assistance: Kathryn L. Engstrom, Charlotte A. Houtz, Ralph E. Ehrenberg, James A. Flatness, Ronald E. Grim, John A. Wolter and Richard W. Stephenson.

In other Library of Congress divisions the following staff members made contributions which are much appreciated: Mary M. Wolfskill and Charles J. Kelly, Manuscript Division, Judith A. Gray, American Folklife Center, Jon Newsom, Music Division, Rubens Medina and T. Daniel Burney, Law Library, Mary M. Ison and Bernard F. Reilly, Prints and Photographs Division, and Andrew J. Cosentino, Office of Interpretive Programs.

Closer to home, the reference librarians at the University of Georgia libraries have been equally generous and unstinting in their response to my almost daily calls upon their time and talents. They are sincerely thanked for their many services.

Colleagues at the University of Georgia to whom I am particularly indebted are Prof. James S. Fisher, Head of the Department of Geography, and Prof. Charles Hudson of the Department of Anthropology and Linguistics. Department of Geography staff members are thanked for responding so cheerfully to my many requests. Of that group of friendly and helpful people, Audrey Hawkins and Donna Bowman are deserving of special mention for converting my longhand scrawls to a clean typescript.

Finally, my deepest appreciation is for my wife, Rosalyn, who patiently read and criticized my work from beginning to end. Without her enthusiastic support and unflagging assistance this book would never have seen the light of day.

Capt. John Smith's Map of Virginia first published in 1612. Longtime curator of maps at the Library of Congress, Philip Lee Phillips was only one of the many experts to praise this map. Phillips wrote in 1907, "of all the Virginia maps the most interesting is that made by Captain John Smith under the most trying conditions owing to the enmity of the savage tribes. If we knew nothing of the famous Captain but what is conveyed to us in his map of Virginia it would alone entitle him to rank preeminently among great explorers and cartographers." A long-enduring vestige of the hope for an easy passage to the Pacific Ocean, first suggested by Verrazano in 1524, is shown by Smith in the form of a water body just above the letters NIA in VIRGINIA. Take careful note of the small maltese crosses along the courses of the rivers. As the legend explains, everything that is shown beyond the crosses "is by relation" meaning that Indian informants and maps were the sources for what is on the inner portions of the map (Geography and Map Division).

ABOUT THE AUTHOR

Before entering Montclair State College, Louis De Vorsey grew up and attended local schools in Lyndhurst, New Jersey. Upon the conferring of his baccalaureate (cum laude) he won a graduate assistantship in the Department of Geography of Indiana University. For the second and final year of his M.A. program he was awarded an Indiana University Fellowship.

Completing his M.A. studies, De Vorsey entered the U.S. Navy Officer Candidate School at Newport, Rhode Island, where he earned a commission as an Aviation Ground Officer. Ensign De Vorsey attended specialized training courses in both tactical and strategic photographic intelligence. Thus trained, De Vorsey served with Heavy Photographic Squadron 61 and became qualified as a photo and radar navigator. His last year of active duty saw him in the position of Photographic Intelligence Training and Scheduling Officer on the staff of the Pacific Fleet Air Intelligence Training Center in California. He retired from the Naval Reserve with the rank of Commander.

While maintaining his commission in the U.S. Naval Reserve, De Vorsey left active service to resume his academic studies first at the University of Stockholm and then at University College, London. With the successful defense of his dissertation, in 1965, he received the Ph.D. degree in Historical Geography from the University of London.

De Vorsey held full-time faculty positions at East Carolina University and the University of North Carolina at Chapel Hill before joining the geography faculty of the University of Georgia. In 1987 he assumed the position of Professor Emeritus of Geography which he continues to hold at the University of Georgia.

In the course of his career, Dr. De Vorsey has received two prestigious honor awards from the Association of American Geographers; in 1975 the Award for Meritorious Contributions to the Field of Geography and, in 1983, the Honor Award in Applied Geography, were conferred at the Association's annual meetings. The University of Georgia Research Foundation awarded him its Medal for Research Creativity in the Social Sciences in 1980.

Dr. De Vorsey has served as an expert witness in several cases involving local, state, federal, and international boundary lines. In original actions argued before the U.S. Supreme Court he has testified on behalf of the United States (3) and the states of Georgia and Massachusetts. In the World Court case between Canada and the United States concerning their boundary in the Gulf of Maine and Atlantic Ocean, he supervised a major historical-geographical research effort under contract to the U.S. Department of State and served as a Legal Consultant to the U.S. litigation team.

Among the books written or edited by Dr. De Vorsey are: *The Indian Boundary in the Southern District of North America, DeBrahm's Report of the General Survey in the Southern District of North America, The Atlantic Pilot, The Georgia South Carolina Boundary: A Problem in Historical Geography, In the Wake of Columbus: Islands and Controversy, Rights to Oceanic Resources: Deciding and Drawing Maritime Boundaries,* and *A Panorama of Georgia.*

This impression of the fortified Indian town Hochelaga, that Jacques Cartier described in 1535, was published in Gian Battista Ramusio's book, Delle Navigationi aet Viaggi, that appeared in 1606. The engraver has attempted to depict the populous village Cartier described as "circular and . . . completely enclosed by a wooden palisade in three tiers like a pyramid." Within the wooden palisade Cartier found "some fifty houses . . . each of fifty or more paces in length, and twelve or fifteen in width, built completely of wood and covered in and bordered up with large pieces of the bark and rind of trees . . . which are well and cunningly lashed after their manner." Within each of these large houses many Indian families lived in common. Notice that "Monte Real" is shown just to the left of Hochelaga. This is the hill which Cartier climbed to view the rapids blocking the St. Lawrence River to the west. The modern Canadian metropolis, Montreal, now covers this area (Rare Book and Special Collections Division).

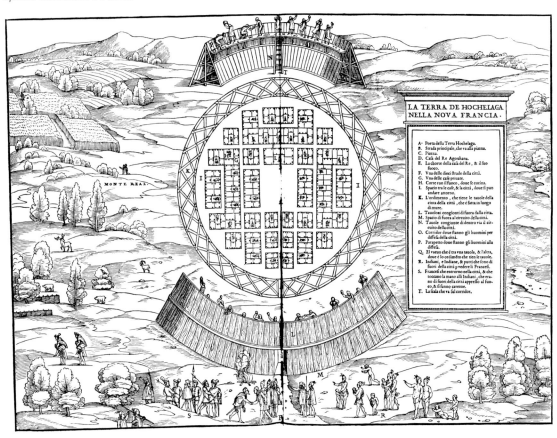

THE LIBRARY OF CONGRESS
Quincentenary Program—An Ongoing Voyage

The dramatic meeting of two separate and complex worlds occurred on October 12, 1492, when Columbus unwittingly sailed three ships into the Bahamas and into the history books. As a result of this historic landfall, the inhabitants of the Americas found themselves in the midst of unexpected cultural interaction, while Europe tried quickly to explain and to grasp the cultural and geographic breadth of what it had encountered.

The Library of Congress Quincentenary Program examines the events leading up to and following that complex encounter. This major interpretive program features exhibitions, publications, film series, scholarly programs, and educational outreach efforts.

An Ongoing Voyage, The Library of Congress's Quincentenary Program, has been planned to raise interest in the significant happenings surrounding Christopher Columbus's historic voyage of 1492 and the ensuing 500 years of development in the Americas. The Program seeks to broaden our understanding of the activities, influences, and contributions of the period through a cohesive and internationally significant interpretive program. That program projects the Library's unique resources and cultural identity and sponsors scholarship based on the vast resources of the Library to support fresh interpretations regarding the meaning of the Quincentenary.

The Library's Quincentenary Program, begun in the spring of 1989, is dedicated to the creative use of the Library's collections and specialists. Highlights of the Program include the major 1992 exhibition 1492: An Ongoing Voyage; *The Hispanic World 1492–1902*, a survey of microfilm and other photographic holdings in U.S. institutions of archival documents from Spain; research guides to Columbus and the age of exploration (this publication) and to Native American materials in the Library of Congress; facsimiles of key documents in the Library of Congress's collections; the 1990 Educator's Insti-

tute for secondary school social science teachers; and an hour-long film of Columbus, *Christopher Columbus: The Ongoing Voyage* prepared by the Library's Global Library Project.

A number of bibliographic tools have been and are being produced through the Library's Quincentenary Program or with its auspices. In addition, significant research materials devoted to the Quincentenary period have been acquired. For example, the Spanish national commission for the Quincentenary gave to the Library of Congress a collection of more than four hundred recent Spanish publications on Quincentenary themes; that collection, titled "Biblioteca Quinto Centenario," includes facsimiles of fifteenth- and sixteenth-century documents, among them copies of Columbus's letters and his book of prophecies.

A survey of U.S. collections containing archival documents from Spain has been prepared through the Quincentenary Program. *The Hispanic World 1492–1902: A Guide to Photoreproduced Manuscripts from Spain in the Collections of the United States, Guam, and Puerto Rico*, by Guadalupe Jiménez Codinach, will be a Library of Congress bilingual publication. Information from more than fifty U.S. institutions is provided.

1492: An Ongoing Voyage, an exhibition on display from August 12 to December 31, 1992, explores the issues related to the meeting that took place between two previously separated parts of the world—America and the Mediterranean—and the immediate consequences of the 1492 Columbus voyage. On view will be documents that show the complexity and the variety of cultures in the Mediterranean and America immediately before and after contact, as well as examples of the continuity and the deep radical changes that occurred in American societies as a result of the European arrival, conquest, and cultural impositions. The exhibition director is Barbara Loste. John Hébert is the curator and the guest curators are Ida Altman (University of

New Orleans) and John Fleming (Princeton University). An accompanying catalog, *1492: An Ongoing Voyage,* will appear at the time of the exhibition. The work, with contributions from John Fleming, Ida Altman, and James Lockhart, is a collection of articles on the themes of the Quincentenary, i.e., the Mediterranean world circa 1492, America before Columbus, and the meeting of two worlds—America and the Mediterranean, 1492–1600. The book will be richly illustrated with documents—maps, manuscripts, prints, rare book images—from the Library's collections.

A series of guides are being compiled to provide access to the Library's materials on Columbus and the age of exploration and Native America. This guide takes a broad view of the initial period of contact between America and Europe. The Native American guide, concentrating on Indian societies in the United States encompasses a much longer period (to the twentieth century) but for a limited geographical area. Both publications will be available through the Library of Congress.

At the time of the writing of this volume, the Quincentenary Program has developed projects to produce facsimiles of five documents from the Library of Congress collections, the 1531 Huejotzingo (Mexico) Codex, the 1540 Oztoticpac (Mexico) map, Columbus's 1502 Book of Privileges, Angelo Trevisan's 1503 account of Spanish and Portuguese explorations, and the 1562 Gutiérrez map of America.

The 1531 Huejotzingo (Mexico) Codex, in the Harkness Collection, Manuscript Division, is an illustrated document prepared by the Indian people of the community of Huejotzingo, Puebla, Mexico, in response to a legal case between Hernándo Cortés and the Spanish administration in Mexico. The Codex, on eight sheets of indigenous paper, *amatl* and maguey, provides graphic illustrations of the variety of food, clothing, and other resources demanded of the people as tribute to the Spanish crown. Possibly the first illustration of the Madonna and Child prepared in the Americas appears in this document.

The 1540 Oztoticpac (Mexico) map is a unique manuscript, on *amatl.* Produced as a result of land litigation among the Indian people of Oztoticpac, Texcoco, Mexico, the map contains, in Nahuatl, references to land holdings of a native family and the various crops that were grown on the land. The intricate accounting system and other graphic symbols used by the people of the region appear; of utmost importance is the documentation of various fruit trees and orchards in the farms of the family. The grafting of European fruit trees onto native root stock is displayed. That information is noteworthy since it represents the earliest graphic representation of such an exchange between two distinct parts of the world, Europe and America. The map is located in the Library's Geography and Map Division.

In 1502, in preparation for his fourth and final voyage to America, Christopher Columbus asked scribes in Seville, Spain, to record those privileges that he had been granted by the crowns of Spain on matters related to his voyages and later administration of the lands that he claimed. These agreements provided Columbus with a record that he believed was necessary for his own welfare and that of his family. Four exact copies of this collection of agreements were prepared in 1502, of which the Library has one of the three on vellum. This precious historical legacy, referred to as Columbus's Book of Privileges, is located in the Library's Manuscript Division.

The successful voyage of Columbus to America in 1492 and those that he and other European explorers concluded during the last decade of the fifteenth century stirred interest throughout the Mediterranean world. While the achievement of reaching the east by sailing west brought about, without expectation, contact with a vast landmass unrecorded in contemporary European memory, it also brought with it concern on the part of the various states of the Mediterranean world regarding access and control of trade networks. Venetian businessmen sought the latest information about Spanish and Portuguese explorations in the Western Atlantic and in 1503 Angelo Trevisan, a representative of Venice in Spain, prepared a description of such exploration. The Library's Trevisan Codex (1503), written in a clear Venetian dialect, is a manuscript record of Columbus's first three voyages and of the 1500 Portuguese voyage along the coast of Brazil. The document is located in the Library's Rare Book and Special Collections Division.

The Diego Gutiérrez map of 1562, entitled "Americae sive quartae orbis partis nova et exactissima descriptio," is the largest known map of the Western Hemisphere printed up to that time. The map identifies the eastern coast of North America, all of Central and South America, and portions of the western coasts of Europe and Africa. A gift of Lessing J. Rosenwald and located in the Library's Geography and Map Division, the Library's copy is one of two extant. Gutiérrez was a chart and instrument maker as well as a pilot who was active in Spain from the early sixteenth century, where he was established with the pilots and the cosmographers of the House of Trade in Seville.

Through the 1990 Educator's Institute (July 1990), exhibitions in 1992 and 1994, a documentary study of Italian Americans in the U.S. West, potential film series, a conference on the music of the Americas in the summer of 1992, and other programs of outreach and enrichment, the Library of Congress has proposed an ambitious and varied program for the commemoration of the 500th anniversary of Columbus's historic voyage.

John R. Hébert
Coordinator
The Quincentenary Program

CHAPTER ONE

INTRODUCTION

The Age of Discovery,

Focus and Perspective

Miranda: . . . How beauteous mankind is!
O brave new world, That
hath such people in't!
Prospero: 'Tis new to thee.

The Tempest, William Shakespeare

It would be surprising if Fernando Raul Colomb is not thinking about his namesake, Christopher Columbus, on October 12, 1995. This is the day that Professor Colomb will throw the control switches activating Argentina's sophisticated new SETI radiotelescope receivers. SETI is the acronym for a worldwide effort known as "Search for Extraterrestrial Intelligence" sponsored by the Planetary Society.

The Planetary Society boasts a membership of 125,000 scientists in over seventy countries around the globe. The Society shipped the two SETI receivers to Argentina's Institute for Radioastronomy back in 1990. Professor Colomb's role in the official opening ceremony in 1995 is based on his position as Director of the Institute rather than his surname being that of the Admiral of the Ocean Sea, but the coincidence is sure to attract the attention of journalists covering the events outside Buenos Aires on Columbus Day, 1995.

Before the opening of the Argentinian SETI array, practically the whole effort aimed at detecting radio signals that may provide evidence of intelligent life forms beyond our solar system was located in the Northern Hemisphere. Professor Colomb and his colleagues at Argentina's Institute for Radioastronomy will extend that search to the skies visible in the Southern Hemisphere.

Like the NASA scientists connected with the Magellan space probe and countless others involved with programs designed to extend humankind's frontiers of knowledge, Professor Colomb and his colleagues in Argentina are seen as contemporary players in the drama of world discovery that began over five hundred years ago. The earliest "acts" in that drama are usually called the Age of Discovery. This book is about people living in that exciting period.

The Age of Discovery has received searching attention from a legion of historians as have most of the important periods or epochs chosen to mark humankind's march through time. For this reason it is not surprising to find that the dates and names employed to define that age have varied widely from one expert to another. Indeed some, like Harvard's late J. H. Parry, felt the need to adopt a different name for the Age of Discovery altogether. For his magisterial treatment of the period "between the middle of the fifteenth century and the late seventeenth" he chose the title *The Age of Reconnaissance*.[1] In a recent more modest contribution, designed for use as a supplement with college-level history students, Dan O'Sullivan chose to title his book *The Age of Discovery 1400–1550*.[2]

In spite of their differences in dating and naming the Age of Discovery, Parry and O'Sullivan are in close harmony with their fellow historians in their approach to the events of that period of human experience. O'Sullivan's first sentence is clear on this point. He left no room for doubt when he wrote, "the theme of this book is the sensationally rapid opening up of the world by European explorers in the fifteenth and early sixteenth centuries." Published twenty years earlier, Parry's book similarly set out "to tell in outline the story of European geographical exploration, trade and settlement outside the bounds of Europe in the fifteenth, sixteenth and seventeenth centuries; to define the factors which stimulated expansion and made it possible; and to describe briefly the consequences which followed from it." Both books, it should be added, are successful in accomplishing what their authors set out to do.

Clearly, however, both books share a common point of view best described as Europocentric. Indeed, they should be seen as typcial

of scores, even hundreds, of books by some of the most esteemed and influential historical writers. The Age of Discovery has come to represent the first stage in a grand historical perspective that tends to view the past five centuries in terms that can be said to add up to the story of the "Europeanization of the World." That this should be the case is in no way surprising. It was, after all, the Europeans who sailed forth to initiate the encounters with the peoples of the Americas. As one student of early culture contact observed, "Europeans invariably assumed, and it never seemed to have been questioned, that Europe was the centre of the world and of civilization, that its culture was older than any other cultures, that America was a new continent and that her people were relatively recent immigrants."[3] Age of Discovery history, it can be concluded, reflects the Europocentric bias of the society that initiated and wrote it.

In this narrative an attempt will be made to lessen that bias by shifting our historical perspective slightly to an angle more fully revealing of what occurred in the Americas during the Age of Discovery. That age is defined here as roughly the period from Columbus's birth to the time of Drake's circumnavigation, in the late sixteenth century. Following Drake's return in 1580, the coastal outlines of South and North America were charted from Tierra del Fuego to Frobisher Bay and Oregon, and discovery as an impulse for European involvement with the Americas gave way to colonization and economic exploitation.

Rather than "Discovery" alone we will focus on a series of human encounters that, when combined, can be viewed as marking the onset of the Age of World Encounter. This will not be an easy undertaking because the encounters took place between markedly different and unequally equipped participants. They were the Western Europeans who, while groping for new routes to Asia in the fifteenth century, stumbled into a populous world that they were certain did not exist and encountered the Native American peoples who came to be called, albeit erroneously, Indians.

Estimates of the number of people inhabiting the Americas at the time of the first encounters vary from a conservative ten million to a generous two hundred million. At the present time many experts appear to feel comfortable with estimates indicating that there were as many as forty million Native Americans at the time of the earliest encounters with the Europeans.[4] This was also a time when all of Western Europe from Italy to Iceland and Portugal to Austria numbered only slightly over forty million. The descendants of those original Native Americans form important communities and population components that today spread from the southern extremities of South America to the most northern reaches of the circum-Arctic world from Greenland across Canada to Alaska. The story of their ancestors' role in the encounters of the Age of Discovery is no less important or interesting than that of the Europeans who came to their lands first as groping explorers and a short time later as aggressive conquerors and acquisitive colonists.

By shifting our focus from European "Discovery" to one of "Encounters" between disparate peoples, the Native Americans are allowed to reveal themselves as the intelligent and resourceful humans they were. Remarkably, this is true even when viewed through the dark and distorted lens provided by the accounts written by the Europeans. When this shift is accomplished there can be no doubt that the Native Americans were major players in the historical dramas formed by their encounters with the Europeans of the fifteenth and sixteenth centuries.

To some native groups the Europeans appeared as superhuman fulfillments of ancient prophecies. This is not surprising when we reflect on their arrival in ships that appeared to be moving islands carried along by the winds captured in cloth sails as large as Indian farm plots. To others, however, European would-be conquerors were quickly perceived as invaders and unwelcome violaters of sacred precincts. While still other Indian leaders sought to rally the Europeans' military power to their own ongoing geopolitical agendas. In at least one instance the Europeans astonished their Indian hosts who thought them to be deceased friends and loved ones returned from the dead.

Historians and anthropologists concerned with cultural exchange have suggested that our understanding of the encounters taking place between native people and Europeans in the fifteenth through the eighteenth centuries can be aided by a simple, three-part encounter typology. In this typology encounters are viewed as either "Contacts," "Collisions," or "Relationships."

Contacts are the initial, usually short-lived or intermittent, encounters that took place between groups of native people and European explorer-voyagers. As a consequence, Contacts were characterized by their brevity and casualness and were usually conducted through sign language and pantomime rather than spoken dialogue. Presents and goods were usually exchanged in an atmosphere of mutual goodwill but not in conditions suggesting barter or trade. In terms of the demeanor shown by the parties engaged in Contacts a great diversity can be observed. Native people are often revealed as exhibiting a broad spectrum of responses extending from extreme shyness to an almost smothering hospitality and generosity to the Europeans. By and large the Europeans were guarded and cautious but tended toward friendliness and kindness rather than brutality in Contact situations.

Overt hostility on the part of native people in New World Contact episodes was extremely rare. When it occurred it was probably an indication that the natives had experienced prior unrecorded contact with Europeans and, needless to say, had suffered in some manner or other.

An excellent example of the difference in behavior of Indians being contacted for the first time from that of Indians who have suffered from some prior unrecorded contact can be found in the account of Giovanni Verrazano who explored coastal North America from Georgia to Nova Scotia for the King of France in 1524.

Verrazano's description of his encounter with the Indians living around the shores of Narragansett Bay is reviewed in considerable detail in Chapter 6. It is a classic Contact encounter story with twenty canoes filled with Indians coming out from shore to meet the ship "uttering various cries of wonderment" and "then all together they raised a loud cry which meant they were joyful." Verrazano and his crew responded in kind "by imitating their gestures" and throwing "a few little bells and mirrors and many trinkets" into their canoes. As discussed in Chapter 6, Verrazano spent a good while studying the homes, agriculture, and beliefs of these Indians. His account leaves no doubt that the Indians were friendly and outgoing throughout the two weeks of his contact with them. He wrote that they looked quickly at proffered European goods such as rich textiles and steel and iron weapons and wares, but "then refuse them, laughing." Verrazano concluded "they are very generous and give away all they have."[5]

Only 50 leagues (150 miles) farther north along the New England coast, Verrazano landed again, now in the vicinity of Casco Bay, Maine. Here he met with a somewhat harsher climate and, to his eye, a less inviting landscape inhabited by a people who followed a hunting, fishing, and gathering way of life. According to Verrazano, the natives he met on the Maine coast lacked the "cultivated manners" of their farming fellows living farther south. Indeed, he described them as "full of uncouthness and vices, so barbarous that we were never able, with howsoever many signs we made them, to have any intercourse with them." From what he could learn by "going many times to their habitations," the explorer concluded that they subsisted on animals "of the chase, fish and some products which are a species of roots which the ground yields by its own self." "They do not have pulse, nor did we see any signs of cultivation," Verrazano noted. When the Europeans attempted to enter into barter, for some of the "skins of bear, lynxes, seawolves and other animals" they possessed, the Indians showed great caution. As Verrazano described:

they came to the shore of the sea upon some rock where it was very steep, and—we remaining in the small boat,—with a cord let down to us what they wished to give, continually crying on land that we should not approach, giving quickly the barter, not taking in exchange for it except knives, hooks for fishing, and sharp metal. They had no regard for courtesy, and when they had nothing more to exchange, at their departing the men made at us all the signs of contempt and shame which any brute creature could make.[6]

While one can sympathize with Verrazano's wounded sensibility, it would seem clear that these Indians had good cause to keep their distance in the described Contact encounter. It is probable that they had been cheated or otherwise suffered at the hands of unrecorded Europeans who had preceded Verrazano to these shores. According to a work by Fr. Pierre Biard published in 1616, New France had been reached by French Bretons in the year 1504, two decades before Verrazano's voyage. A Dieppe sea captain named Thomas Aubert was also credited with a voyage made in 1508 during which he captured and "brought back from there some of the Natives, whom he exhibited to the wonder and applause of France."[7] It is possible that Verrazano's "Bad People" had seen their friends or relatives taken captive by Aubert or some other

This engraving by Theodor de Bry epitomizes the Europo-centric view of a Contact encounter. Note the Indians in the background fleeing in astonishment at the sight of the oceangoing ships. In the foreground the Indians, drawn to look like naked Greek athletes, are presenting elaborately wrought European-style jewelry and chests of treasure to the resplendent armed conquerors as the symbol of Christianity is raised (Girolamo Benzoni, Americae pars quarta . . . historia . . . Occidental India [Part IV, Historia Americae sive Novi Orbis]. *Rare Book and Special Collections Division*).

visitor in a large sailing vessel. Whatever their reasons, the Casco Bay Indians showed good sense in avoiding possible kidnapping and exposure to any infectious European diseases Verrazano and his crew might have been incubating.

Although Verrazano may not have had an opportunity to observe them closely enough, it is almost certain that all of the Indians he met, even the "uncouth" residents of coastal Maine, at the very least kept oral records of important encounters, battles, or other notable events. In his great work titled *Historia General y Natural de las Indias*, the official Spanish chronicler, Gonzalo Fernandez de Oviedo y Valdes, told how Indians with no form of written records "retain the memory of their origins and ancestors." The following extract was intended as a description of the Arawak Indians who were the original inhabitants of Hispaniola. For our purposes it is suggestive of what many Indian groups outside Mexico and Andean South America may have relied on in the way of group record keeping:

their only books are their songs, which they call *areitos* and which they pass from generation to generation . . . they sing their history relating how their caciques (chiefs) died, who and how many they were, and other things they do not want to forget . . . when they perform these songs they do not forget their heroic deeds. These songs remain in their memory rather then in books; . . .[8]

Verrazano's low opinion of the Indians living around Casco Bay could be seen as similar to the way in which the Micmac Indians of Canada's Gaspé Peninsula responded to the overtures made by the first party of Frenchmen they encountered. According to the missionary, Father Le Clercq, the Micmacs involved in the contact "mistook the bread which was given them for a piece of birch tinder" and, when wine was proffered, became convinced that their visitors were "cruel and inhuman, since in their amusements . . . they drank blood without repugnance."[9]

Clearly what these few widely spaced Contact encounters and accounts from the sixteenth century demonstrate is that there is no predictable or stereotypical Indian response to the Europeans. As historian James Axtell has taken pains to point out, "the natives no less than the Europeans were divided by politics, gender, age, rank, and status."[10] Axtell continued, "they met Europeans at different times in different places under different circumstances," all of which colored their responses to the encounters. As he further pointed out "the perception of a young Iroquois girl whose first white person was a gentle missionary walking alone and unarmed into her village was obviously different from that of an older Micmac warrior who

was greeted by cannon shot from the first sailing ship he ever saw." To glean the maximum insight and understanding from the dramatic encounters that took place during the Age of Discovery, Axtell's admonitions concerning Indian responses should be kept in the forefront of our attention.

Before leaving the topic of Contact encounter characteristics, it should be added that native groups often showed a sense of awe and wonder at the arrival and appearance of European visitors in their midst. For one thing, the scale of European seagoing ships far outsized even the largest Indian craft. To the Indians, the size of the ships with their billowing white sails suggested floating islands with close-hanging clouds. European landing ceremonies and trappings such as unfurled royal banners or ensigns carried by bearded, white-skinned strangers clad in gilded armor and helmets who sang and spoke in unintelligible tongues, heightened the exotic nature of their exciting arrival from distant horizons.

Most awesome of all, however, was the discharge of European cannon. Even sophisticated, battle-hardened Aztecs were almost petrified by the discharge of Cortés's cannon. Montezuma's messengers, returning from an embassy to Cortés, frightened their emperor by telling him of the Spaniards' cannon:

how it resounded like thunder when it went off. Indeed, it overpowered one: it deafened our ears. And when it discharged, something like a round pellet came from within. Fire went scattered forth; sparks showered forth. And its smoke smelled very foul; it had a fetid odor which, verily wounded the head. And when [the pellet] struck [a] mountain, [it was] as if it fell apart and crumbled. And when it struck a tree, it splintered, seeming to vanish as if someone blew it away.[11]

Needless to say, the Europeans lost an opportunity to profit from the Indians' sense of awe and wonderment. Cortés was one of many Europeans who seized upon existing native myths

European horses and fighting dogs were used to terrorize and control the Indians. To be "thrown to the dogs" was tantamount to a death sentence for unfortunate Indians in many Conflict encounters. Notice the ponderous size of the primitive firearm, called an arquebus, being carried by the Spanish soldiers. Its heavy weight required use of the supporting staff they are holding. Even with the support, the arquebus was a notoriously inaccurate weapon. Its noise and smoke, however, caused real fear among the Indians (Girolamo Benzoni, Americae pars quarta . . . historia . . . Occidental India [Part IV, Historia Americae sive Novi Orbis]. *Rare Book and Special Collections Division*).

Once they learned how effective the Europeans were at warfare, the Indians enlisted them as allies in their own conflicts. In this engraving a force of arquebus-wielding French are turning the tide of battle for Chief Outina in a conflict with his rival, Chief Potanou. The French commander was furious when Outina allowed his defeated enemies to escape with their lives. Other ethnohistorical evidence suggests that the formalized grouping of Indians in an open phalanx around their chief during battle did take place in the Southeast (Theodor de Bry, Florida. *Rare Book and Special Collections Division*).

predicting "that men should come from distant parts where the sun rises, to subjugate the country." As Cortés wrote, "they believed us to be those of whom their gods had spoken."[12]

The key attributes of Contact encounters were their casualness, limited duration, and generally amicable nature. Regrettably the history of the Age of Discovery reveals that Contact encounters all too quickly became Collisions. Encounter Collisions took place everywhere white men from Europe penetrated and began to threaten native societies.

The reasons for Contact encounters evolving to Collision are many and varied. A common thread in most, however, appears to be the overweening ethnocentricism of the Europeans. As the encounter record of the Age of Discovery is reviewed the Europeans appear to have been almost oblivious to the impact their actions were having on the native societies in either physical, psychological, or moral terms. In case after case the vulnerable native group was threatened with loss of cultural integrity and physical well-being, if not annihilation, through the actions of white interlopers on their islands and shores.

In terms of physical threat and annihilation, island dwellers were at greatest risk. On the mainlands native groups could retreat to remote refuge areas, but on islands it was difficult to hide from European horsemen and savage dogs. Tourists and visitors who have been to Caribbean islands do not need to be told that the descendants of Africans and not American Indians now dominate in their populations. Within a little over a decade following Columbus's first landing in 1492, the growing shortage of Indian laborers on Hispaniola had led to the importation of African slaves to work in the island's mines and fields. As they were colonized the other islands followed suit.

The catastrophic loss of life among Native American societies was not entirely the result of direct actions such as warfare and abuse by the Europeans. As mentioned in Chapter 4, most Indians died as a result of the introduction of infectious Old World diseases to which they had no natural immunity. Fatal epidemics of diseases like smallpox, measles, and influenza deserve consideration as a special category of Collision encounter because of the indirectness of their introduction, transmission, and spread.

Attention is called to the quotation selected to head Chapter 5. It is taken from the biography of Christopher Columbus that is attributed to his son Ferdinand. The sentiment reflected in this quotation, bizarre as it is to the reader of today, was certainly not confined to the Admiral of the Ocean Sea and his son but was widely shared by Europeans of their era. It reads:

But the Lord wished to punish the Indians, and so visited them with such shortage of food and such a variety of plagues that he reduced their number by two thirds, that it might be made clear that such wonderful conquests proceeded from His supreme hand and not from our strength or intelligence or the cowardice of the Indians; for even admitting the superiority of our men, it is obvious that the numerical preponderance of the Indians would have nullified this advantage.

The ethnocentricism of the Europeans mentioned above can be seen to elevate to the plane of divine preordination in this and many similar statements written by participants in numerous Collision encounters.

Collision encounters were not, however, preordained. In some cases Contact encounters were followed by what is termed Relationship. In the literature of cultural encounter Relationship is usually defined as a prolonged series of reciprocal contacts on the basis of political equilibrium or stalemate between the parties involved. More often than not, Relationship depended on supply and demand between the groups. On the European side it was usually maintained and cultivated by merchants and traders supplying European goods for the more valuable and durable New World products.

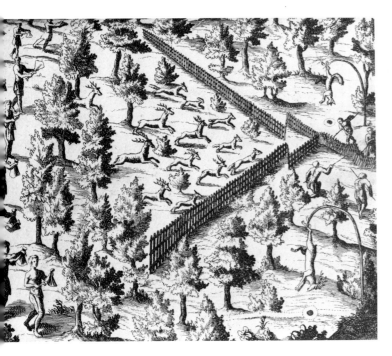

The Canadian fur trade is often cited as an example of a long-term Relationship encounter. This engraving was prepared to illustrate Samuel de Champlain's description of how the Iroquois drove deer into a "triangular enclosure . . . made of great wooden stakes eight or nine feet in height" so that they could be killed. Champlain reported that the Indians caught 120 deer in the trap during the 38 days he was with them. Deer hide, known as buckskin, was an important element in the fur trade along with the fur (Samuel de Champlain, Voyages Et Descouvertures Faites En La Novelle France . . . 1618, vol. III. Paris: 1632. *Rare Book and Special Collections Division).*

Perhaps the best known Relationship encounter in the New World was the centuries-long fur trade of New France. Indian trappers and middlemen were linked with the French in a network of continental scope. When Britain defeated France and gained control of Canada the system was maintained and extended by merging with the Hudson Bay Company. Important vestiges of the fur trade Relationship encounter continue to influence the lives of many thousands of Native Americans and European Canadians today.

Of the three types of encounters the one that is most frequently discussed in the following chapters of this book is the Contact encounter. In some cases the journals and narratives of the discoverers and explorers permit us to follow encounters from Contact to Conflict. The first of these involved the crew members from Columbus's wrecked flagship the *Santa Maria*. The *Santa Maria* sank on the north coast of Hispaniola on Christmas Day, 1492. Unable to accommodate the whole expedition on his two remaining smaller ships, Columbus left thirty-nine crewmen in a fortified settlement he named Navidad. By the time Columbus returned from Spain, in 1493, Navidad had been destroyed and its garrison killed by local Indians. As discussed in Chapter 5, the Spaniards seem to have provided more than ample provocation for such a drastic solution to the Conflict encounter on the part of the Indians.

The final point to be made concerning encounters as a focus when studying the Age of Discovery is that the impacts of those encounters often echo in the world of the moment. All too often the stress marring the relationships of culturally different groups in today's Western Hemisphere can be traced back to the ignorance, insensitivity, and rampant ethnocentricism of Age of Discovery encounters. This is an historical heritage that can be regretted but not escaped.

In this engraved view of Europeans in plumed, wide-brimmed hats, and fur-clad Indians wearing feathers in their hair, Theodor de Bry has captured the essential ingredients of an encounter that could lead to a Relationship between the two contrasting cultures. The Europeans have responded to the Indians' invitation to trade for their furs which was made by waving a hide on a staff. Note the staff and fur lying on the beach in the foreground and the Indian still waving one from his dugout canoe near the center of the scene. More furs can be seen draped over and lying in front of the Indian houses. The Europeans are offering knives and strings of shell beads in exchange for the furs. When such a mutually satisfactory relationship existed over a long period of time it is spoken of as an "Encounter Relationship" (Theodor de Bry, America, Part XIII, Rare Book and Special Collections Division).

CHAPTER TWO

WORLDS APART

European World Views

Before Columbus

Columbus, one might say, did not discover America; he discovered the land-mass upon which America was to be constructed. He did not discover a new world, but his successors created one.

The Conquerors and the Conquered,
John H. Parry and Robert G. Keith

If we could join a party of imaginary visitors from another corner of the universe, voyaging through the solar system in the year 1492, would planet earth look any different than it looks in the photographs taken by modern astronauts? "Probably not" is the answer most experts would give to this question. From a vantage point in space the gleaming blue and white 1992 image of "spaceship earth" would be little or no different from one taken in 1492 or any time in the historic past.

LANDMASSES A REALITY— CONTINENTS A DISCOVERY

Once the broken, swirling, white cloud layers are penetrated, the blue color is found to be reflecting from the nearly three-fourths of the earth's crust covered by water. Closer approach reveals green or dun-colored areas where the crust heaves above the water in the form of four huge, unevenly distributed landmasses. Today we are taught to think of these landmasses in terms of seven arbitrary divisions called continents. As every school-age child knows the seven continents are Antarctica, Australia, Asia, Africa, Europe, and North and South America. As we will find, however, at least four of these names did not exist in 1492—they are themselves products of the Age of Discovery. The world of Columbus and his fellows was made up of Asia, Africa, and Europe.

A moment of reflection, aided by a study of a globe, will affirm the physical fact that the bulk of the earth's land surfaces form four markedly irregular landmasses. By far the largest of the landmasses is Afro-Eurasia, composed of the connected "continents," Europe, Asia, and Africa. Afro-Eurasia embraces considerably more than one-half of the total land area of the earth. In the literature of the Age of Discovery Afro-Eurasia is often referred to as the Old World.

Some idea of Afro-Eurasia's incredible size and resultant significance in human history was provided by the English political geographer, Sir Halford J. Mackinder, who termed it the "World Island," in his seminal geopolitical essay *Democratic Ideals and Reality*. In that book Mackinder proposed a dictum that continues to

ABOVE: *The earth, photographed by an astronaut aboard the Apollo 17 spacecraft from about 25,000 miles out in space. The swirling white masses are clouds in the atmosphere, made up of condensed water vapor, and the dominant blue color is reflected from the water of the world ocean. Heaving up and above sea level are three green and dun-colored landmasses that cover less than one-third of the earth's surface and provide the living space for humankind (Geography and Map Division).*

LEFT: *When this armillary sphere was assembled by Caspar Vopell, in 1542, Europeans accepted the earth-centered Aristotelian cosmology that Ptolemy had followed. Armillary spheres consist of several metal rings representing the celestial equator, the ecliptic, and other great circles of the astronomer's celestial sphere. Since the earth was believed to be spherical and at the center of the universe, Vopell and other instrument makers often placed a small-diameter globe at the center of their armillary spheres. It was not until the work of Nicolas Copernicus was finally accepted, about a century later, that the Europeans abandoned the idea of a geocentric universe (Geography and Map Division).*

fuel discussions among world military strategists more than seventy years after he first published it in 1919. Every student of geopolitics will recall Mackinder's argument that ran: Who rules East Europe commands the Heartland; Who rules the Heartland commands the World Island; and Who rules the World Island commands the World.[1] In the present era, marked by the rejection of monolithic Soviet-style communism and control in Eastern Europe, Mackinder's words lack some of the threat they seemed to promise during the chilly years of the Cold War of the fifties, sixties, and seventies.

The combined areas of North and South America are linked by the narrow Isthmus of Panama to form the world's second largest landmass. In much of the literature involved with the Age of Discovery, North and South America have the collective name and identity familiar to us as the New World or, at times, the Western Hemisphere. With less than half the area, it is not surprising to find that Mackinder reduced North and South America along with Australia to mere satellites on the periphery of his Afro-Eurasian World Island. Antarctica, in spite of its area being almost twice that of Australia, lacks a permanent human population and so played no significant part in Mackinder's geopolitical view of the world. Eluding the efforts of early explorers, the physical reality of the Antarctic landmass played no role in the period of discovery with which we are concerned. Theoretical constructs that argued for the presence of some balancing landmass in the Southern Hemisphere were, however, current and not without influence in the years before and after 1580.

Of course Mackinder's ideas are mentioned here only to help in forming our view of the world of today and the world as it was believed to be five centuries ago. The landmasses existed as physical realities. Continents, however, did not exist in the way that they are understood today. This is because the people living in the fif-

teenth century, whether in American Indian societies or in the empires, kingdoms, or caliphates of Afro-Eurasia, were operating with severely restricted views of the planet they inhabited. No one at that time knew or even suspected that the earth's surface was formed of the two great and two lesser landmasses separated by broad intervening oceans. This knowledge was the slowly won product of the Age of Discovery. To appreciate the significance and impact of Columbus's 1492 voyage, the reader must keep in the forefront of his mind the "fact" that the Americas simply did not exist in the minds of fifteenth-century Europeans!

At quite another scale, the physical world has dramatically changed since 1492. When we look more closely at selected areas of our dynamic planet significant physical changes can be detected. Coastal configurations in Scandinavia and northern North America, for example, have changed as the earth's crust has continued its post-ice sheet rebound following the melting of the great continental glaciers. In more southerly regions, rising world sea level has similarly changed the details of coast, island, and inlet outlines. Lakes and inlets have been silted in to become marsh or swamp in some places while in others volcanic outpourings, avalanches, or the growth of mountain glaciers have dammed valleys and inlets to form new lakes. In North and South America the character and extent of the plant and animal associations that covered the land in 1492 have undergone truly profound change. Vast areas of woodland and prairie have given way to clearing for monoculture-dominated farming and commercial grazing. In South America this process continues, apparently unabated by the shrill warnings of ecologists and environmental action groups, in the form of the relentless burning of tropical rain forests. Some American animal, bird, and fish species, present in almost unbelievable numbers at the time of Columbus, are now extinct, and lists of endangered species continue to lengthen.

The environmental changes that have taken place since the fifteenth century have been major topics for research in several of the sciences since the days of George P. Marsh, Charles Darwin, and Sir Charles Lyell in the last century. More recently, a number of historians have been investigating the manifold environmental changes associated with the global encounter of peoples resulting from the events set in motion during the Age of Discovery. A leader in this historiographic movement is Alfred W. Crosby, whose book *The Columbian Exchange Biological and Cultural Consequences of 1492* was published just twenty years before the Columbus Quincentenary year. In 1986 Professor Crosby followed with a second, more broadly based study titled *Ecological Imperialism the Biological Expansion of Europe, 900–1900.* Books like these have opened whole new vistas for study and added a welcome new dynamism to the way Age of Discovery events are now viewed. The encounters and exchanges that took place in that age are increasingly recognized as keys to understanding global changes they initiated. Many of those changes are ongoing and continue to shape the destiny of humankind as we move toward an increasingly uncertain future as passengers sharing "spaceship earth."

As might be expected, much has been written concerning the world view or world awareness of the European, Arab, and Chinese and other Old World societies in the midfifteenth century. Some understanding of what Christopher Columbus and others of his period knew and thought about the larger world around them is essential as we attempt to appreciate more thoroughly the assumptions and motivations underlying the major decisions and events that led to the dramatic human encounters of the Age of Discovery. What is seriously lacking, however, is an equally extensive literature to il-

luminate the world views of the multitude of American Indian societies forming the other parties to those encounters. That lack will be addressed in the next chapter where Native American world views will be discussed.

COLUMBUS'S WORLD VIEW IN 1492

H. G. Wells is well known as a novelist-pioneer in the writing of science fiction. As the scholar of today searches the pages of history he or she often envies the Time Traveller, the protagonist of Wells's *The Time Machine,* who operated a machine that could transport him bodily through time. How satisfying it would be to go back and quiz a person like Christopher Columbus and clear up the multitude of questions that the historical records leave unanswered. "Will you please tell us when and where you were born?", might well be the first question put to this man who has been claimed as a Genoese Italian, Greek, Jew, Majorcan, and Galician and called by one recent author "a riddle wrapped in a mystery inside an enigma." Time travel, however, remains in the purview of science fiction.

Wells, prolific author that he was, also undertook ambitious projects in the realm of nonfiction. In one of these, *The Outline of History,* he included a chapter devoted to "The Renascence of Western Civilization." In that discussion he wrote that "all over Europe in the fifteenth century merchants and sailors were speculating about new ways to the East."[2] What Wells went on to emphasize was the shift in Europe's outlook and world view from one centered on the Mediterranean Sea and its surrounding Afro-Eurasian Old World, to one that came to be centered increasingly on the Atlantic and ultimately the New World. It was a period during which, in Europe, "land ways" gave way to "sea ways." While it would be wrong to claim that Columbus alone caused this shift, it is clear that he played a pivotal role in the historical shift that was beginning to gain momentum at about the time he was born.

Probably born in Genoa, one of Europe's important Mediterranean ports, in 1451, Columbus was a product of the intellectual climate of his time. It was a time of transition, with intellectual tides flowing (but sometimes ebbing) out of the mind-numbing authoritarian religiosity of the Middle Ages toward the increasingly secular and materialistic humanism and empiricism the Renaissance produced. As Columbus made clear, in a letter written to Ferdinand and Isabela, his adopted Spanish sovereigns, in 1501:

From a very Young age I began to follow the sea and have continued to do so to this day. This art of navigation incites those who pursue it to enquire into the secrets of this world. I have passed more than forty years in this business and have traveled to every place where there is navigation up to the present time. I have had dealings and conversation with learned men, priests, and laymen, Latins and Greeks, Jews and Moors, and many other sects. I found Our Lord very favorable to this my desire, and to further it He granted me the gift of knowledge. He made me skilled in seamanship, equipped me abundantly with the sciences of astronomy, geometry, and arithmetic, and taught my mind and hand to draw this sphere and upon it the cities, rivers, mountains, islands, and ports, each in its proper place. During this time I have made it my business to read all that was written on geography, history, philosophy, and the other sciences. Thus Our Lord revealed to me that it was feasible to sail from here to the Indies, and placed in me a burning desire to carry out this plan. Filled with this fire, I come to Your Highnesses . . .[3]

From this letter and other writings that have endured, we can reconstruct a reasonable profile of Christopher Columbus's world view and the intellectual underpinnings on which it was based. At the outset, it can be seen clearly that Columbus, like most educated Europeans of his day, believed the earth was a sphere. The spherical nature of the earth was, after all, the linchpin of his grand enterprise to sail west on the ocean sea from Spain to the riches of the Orient.

To any observant seaman the sphericity of the earth was easily proved by the way that objects on shore or other ships were revealed as one approached or sailed away from them. What was far from easy to prove from casual observation, however, was the true size of the sphere on which we lived. Once away from land the ocean sea seemed boundless and, to the knowledge of fifteenth-century Europeans, it had never been crossed. There were authorities in the classical past who had employed elegant methods to find the earth's circumference and, thanks to their understanding of trigonometry, arrived at amazingly accurate estimates.

It is clear that Columbus was largely self-taught but not given to self-doubt or rigorous testing of his assumptions once they had formed in his mind. While he may have used the term *sciences* in describing his reading and study it is not hard to conclude that his research pattern was less than scientific and took the form of finding authorities that would support his basic assumptions rather than gathering data with which those assumptions could be tested. Given the age in which he lived this characteristic is in no way surprising.

Limited space will not allow a thorough review of all the sources and authorities Columbus employed to structure his scheme to sail westward to reach the eastern shore of Asia. There are already a large number of available books that treat that facet of the Columbus story. There are, however, at least two crucial assumptions reached by Columbus that cannot be omitted in even a brief overview. They deal with his ideas concerning the circumference of the earth and the resulting value of a degree of longitude and the west to east distance across the Eurasian landmass from Western Europe to the Orient and Japan. As his son Ferdinand put it, "he assumed and knew on the authority of approved writers that a large part of this sphere had already been navigated and there remained to be discovered only the space which extended from the eastern end of India, known to Ptolemy and Marinus, eastward to the Cape Verde and Azores Islands, the westernmost land discovered . . ." That undiscovered space, Columbus believed, "could not be more than the third part of the great circle [circumference] of the sphere." In Columbus's world view the sphere of the earth was 10 percent smaller than Ptolemy thought it to be and about 25 percent smaller than it truly was. This came about because he accepted an ancient value of 56⅔ short Italian miles for the length of a degree of longitude at the equator rather than the correct value of approximately 69 statute miles. On such a small earth his scheme to sail west from Europe's fringing islands to Japan and the fringing islands of Asia could be presented as within the operating range of the ships available and therefore worthy of backing and support.

PTOLEMY AND EUROPEAN WORLD VIEWS

The Ptolemy Columbus relied on was Claudius Ptolemy, the second-century A.D. author of *Geographia,* a work considered to be the scientific foundation of the disciplines we know as cartography and geodesy. As Ptolemy was quick to point out he owed much to even earlier thinkers such as Marinus of Tyre. No one, however, had ever approached the challenge of mapping the earth with his vigor and scientific rigor. His *Geographia* deserves its place high on the list of landmarks in the history of science. Originally written in Greek, *Geographia,* sometimes characterized as "a complete cartographer's handbook," described a method for producing maps

of the earth's curved surface on a plane. Also included were tables giving the locations of over eight thousand places of the known world in terms of their latitude and longitude.

Like so many writings of the Classical Age, *Geographia* was almost unknown in Western Europe until the general revival of learning that began toward the end of the fourteenth century. It was a Byzantine scholar, living in Italy's Renaissance center, Florence, in the early 1400s, who was responsible for translating Ptolemy's *Geographia* into Latin. The names on the twenty-seven maps which are found with most surviving manuscript copies of *Geographia* were also Latinized at this time. Once it became available in Latin, European scholars began to correct errors and improve the maps of regions familiar to them. In due course *tabulae novellae* or "modern maps" were added to expanded and improved versions of *Geographia.* Ptolemy's maps had such a profound influence on Renaissance cartography in Europe that his name alone came to mean a book of maps and geographical information. One of the "rare treasures" of the Library of Congress is its collection of forty-seven editions of Ptolemy, which date from 1475 to 1867. Pictured here is the beautiful Ptolemaic map of the known or "habitable" world that appears in the Library's 1482 Ulm edition. The first Ptolemy to be printed outside of Italy, the Ulm edition maps were also the first to be printed from woodblocks. The twelve decorative heads with puffed cheeks surrounding the map depict the directions of the winds. Notice that the Indian Ocean is shown to be an enclosed sea, a larger "Mediterranean" or sea within the land. This belief was shattered when the Portuguese rounded the Cape of Good Hope before the decade ended.

Most important to Columbus, however, was the Ptolemaic concept that held the west to east extent of the habitable world, or "oecumene," to be 180 degrees or one-half the earth's circum-

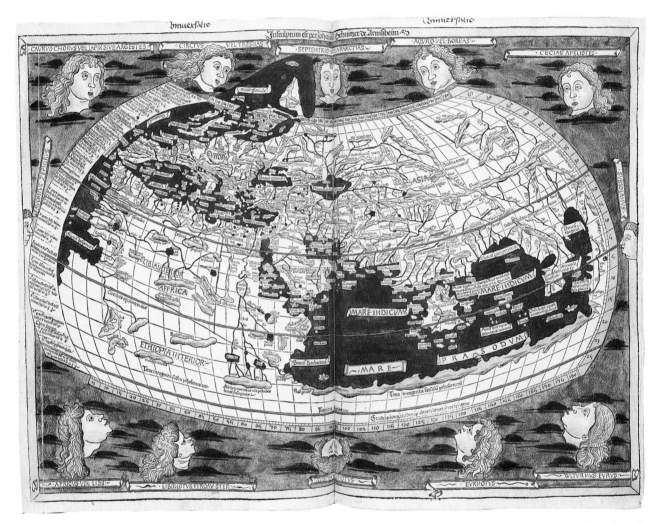

Map of the inhabited world or "oecumene" of Claudius Ptolemy printed in Ulm, Germany, in 1482. The Ptolemaic world view dates from the second century A.D., when Claudius Ptolemy compiled his great work Geographia (Cosmographia). *So great was Ptolemy's influence in Europe during the Renaissance that the word Ptolemy became the term used for any book of maps and geographical data. To a considerable degree the Ptolemaic world view summarized in this 1482 map was the world view held by most Europeans on the eve of Columbus's voyages and the onset of the Age of Discovery (Geography and Map Division).*

ference. This greatly exaggerated the extent of the known world from the western coast of Europe to the eastern coast of China but left too wide an extent of ocean for Columbus's liking. Rejecting this aspect of the Ptolemaic world view, Columbus chose to accept Cardinal Pierre d'Ailly's estimate that the Eurasian landmass covered 225 degrees of longitude. Reckoning that the cardinal had been unaware of Marco Polo's discoveries in the Far East, Columbus took it upon himself to add another 28 degrees to bring the land area extent to a total of 253 degrees. To further enhance the plausibility of his scheme, Columbus estimated that Cipangu (Japan) lay another 30 degrees off the coast of Asia toward Europe. This left an ocean covering only 77 degrees of longitude between the shores of Spain and the island of Cipangu (Japan). From this total the would-be discoverer subtracted another 9 degrees because his oceanic voyage would actually commence when he departed the westernmost of the Canary Islands. When he completed his calculations, Columbus could assure his listeners that a voyage of only 68 degrees of longitude on a conveniently miniaturized world separated him from the unimaginable wealth of Cipangu (Japan), India, and Cathay. Columbus chose his authorities and selected his evidence with skill and care, but could he make such a scheme succeed?

THE ECUMENICAL TRADITION IN EUROPEAN CARTOGRAPHY

At the time of the rediscovery and translation of Ptolemy's *Geographia*, European cartography and geography were, in large measure, the handmaidens of the medieval theology then dominating Christendom. Theologians, steeped as they were in biblical lore, were deeply concerned with the origin, shape, movement, and peopling of the earth. In view of this it is small surprise to

find that the first European map to be printed is the small woodcut included here. Called a "T-O" map, it is representative of a cartographic evolution reaching far back to the disk maps of the Romans known as "Orbis Terrarum."

These were maps the Romans constructed to show the known world as it extended out and away from the Mediterranean basin. The early Christian church, spreading as it did through the lands of the Roman Empire, adopted the Orbis Terrarum concept for its world cartographic framework. Asia, as the seat of the Gar-

Known as a "T-O" map, this example holds the honor of being the first map used to illustrate a printed book. It appeared in the 1472 Augsburg, Germany, edition of Etymologiae, a treatise written in the seventh century by Isidore of Seville. It is a type of map that summarizes the world view sanctioned by the early Christian church. The three continents, Asia, Europa, and Africa, surrounded by the boundless world ocean (Mare Oceanum) comprise what is often called the European tripartite world. Asia, as the seat of the Holy Land and Garden of Eden, was always shown at the top of the T-O maps. Because of this "Oriens," or east, was similarly always at the top of the map. We still "orient" our maps, although now with a secular north rather than a spiritual east at the top (Rare Book and Special Collections Division).

Far more maplike than the medieval T-O cartograms, were a category of world maps known as mappae mundi. *This example is owned by Hereford Cathedral in England and dates from about 1290 A.D.* Mappae mundi *were compiled from a wide variety of sources and can be regarded as graphic summaries of both the sacred and secular geographical lore of the Middle Ages. In some respects they resemble the maps of Native Americans. Exaggeration, for example, calls attention to interesting or important places. Palestine, as the seat of the Holy Land, was often greatly exaggerated as well as centrally located on* mappae mundi *(Facsimile, Geography and Map Division).*

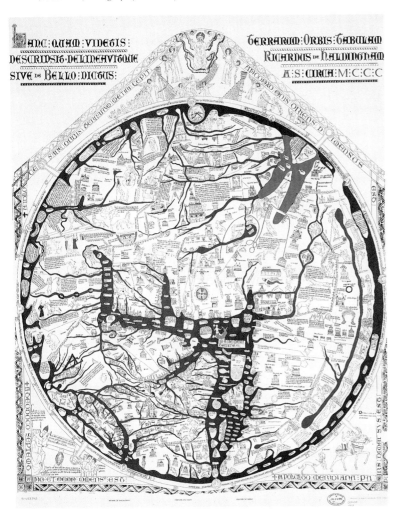

den of Eden and Holy Land, was invariably shown at the top of T-O maps with Africa invariably below and to the right with Europe facing Africa across the Mediterranean Sea. Around the whole of the habitable world washed the all-embracing world ocean. As the photograph shows, Asia was to the east, or "Oriens" in Latin, hence we, to this day, "orient" our maps, but now with a secular north rather than a spiritual east at the top. The biblical account of the post-flood peopling of the world by Noah's sons, "Sem," "Cham," and "Jafeth" in Asia, Africa, and Europe is also a part of the story suggested here. Some might argue that T-O maps are correctly to be classified as religious diagrams or schematics more useful in guiding the faithful's thoughts and prayers than their feet or ships.

The basic three-continent, known world surrounded by the Ocean Sea, pattern of the T-O map schematics, such as the one illustrated here from the Library of Congress's 1472 edition of the work titled *Etymologiae* by Isidore of Seville, was repeated on the other great class of medieval maps known to scholars as *mappae mundi.* Usually rich in detail and adornment the *mappae mundi* attempted to show the known world of the medieval Europeans with some degree of accuracy while retaining the spiritual messages of the T-O maps. One of the largest and best known of the *mappae mundi* is the world map owned by Hereford Cathedral in England. The recent threat that church authorities might offer it for sale to gain funds needed to preserve the cathedral's fabric brought world media attention and cries of anguish from all quarters in England. Drawn on vellum, possibly prepared from an ox hide, the Hereford map is about 5 feet 3 inches long by 4 feet 6 inches wide. Its content is based on a wide variety of sources and it can be regarded as a summary of the sacred and secular geographical lore of the Middle Ages. The Ebsdorf *mappae mundi,* also pictured here, is a facsimile of a similar thirteenth-century map once hanging in a German monastery. Regrettably the original was destroyed in World War II. Fortunately this facsimile was published before it was lost.

Passionate Catholic that he was, Columbus was heir to the writings of Cardinal d'Ailly and Isidore of Seville as well as, "Bede, Strabo, and the master of scholastic history, with St. Ambrose and Scotus, and all the learned theologians," all of whom he found to "agree that the earthly paradise is in the east, ect."[4] During his third voyage Columbus kept a journal which was sent to Ferdinand and Isabela when he reached Hispaniola. After skirting the coast of Trinidad and the South American mainland and tasting the fresh water issuing from the delta of the Orinoco River, Columbus began to suspect the true extent of his latest discovery went beyond additional islands to something quite extraordinary. He concluded that the water body now known as the Gulf of Paria on the coast of Venezuela was close to the biblical earthly paradise. The authority of *mappae mundi* was called upon in explaining this to his monarchs:

I do not find, nor have ever found, any account by the Romans or Greeks, which fixes in a positive manner the site of the terrestrial paradise, neither have I seen it given in any mappe-monde, laid down from authentic sources. Some placed it in Ethiopia, at the sources of the Nile, but others traversing all these countries, found neither the temperature nor the altitude of the sun correspond with their ideas respecting it; nor did it appear that the overwhelming waters of the deluge had been there. Some pagans pretended to adduce arguments to establish that it was in the Fortunate Islands, now called the Canaries, etc.[5]

EUROPE'S PORTOLAN CHART TRADITION

In addition to what has been termed the religious or ecumenical tradition of European cartography, Columbus and his fellow mariners were heirs to maps of another and far more practical type. This branch of cartography developed in response to the needs occasioned by the increasing tempo of trade and commerce which began to characterize the shores of the Mediterranean Sea in the late twelfth and early thirteenth centuries. To serve the navigators charged with transporting valuable cargoes and ships over increasingly greater distances a distinctive type of sea chart was developed. Known today as "portolan" charts they took their name from the term *portolani* which originally meant books of written lists or tables of sailing directions and information on tides, harbors, landmarks, and other important navigation details. Recent research has shown that the charts were drawn to accompany the *portolani* and clarify the otherwise confusing spatial relationships of the descriptive data the books contain.

When the magnetic compass came into use the portolan charts were adapted for its employment in navigation over longer distances beyond the sight of land. The most striking visual features of almost all existing portolans are the numerous wind roses and emanating rhumb lines or loxodromes that crisscross the watery areas of the charts and the hundreds of names of ports, headlands, and harbors written perpendicular to the coastlines. The lines appear to have been used by navigators in plotting compass headings to be steered in the days before parallel rulers became popular. The portolan chart pictured here shows the Black Sea and Mediterranean Sea plus part of the Red Sea, appropriately colored, as well as the Atlantic shores of Western Europe and Northern Africa. The original was drawn on vellum in 1559 by Mateus Prunes, a prominent chart maker on the island of Majorca. Although most portolans were prepared as working charts for use at sea some, like this handsomely decorated example, were made for merchants and political leaders. We are fortunate because these cartographic treasures were preserved in libraries and archives whereas most of the working portolans were worn out or lost at sea. Readers are able to obtain an excellent facsimile copy of this rare and beautiful chart for closer study. It is one of several historical maps available at reasonable cost through the "Facsimiles of Cartographic Treasures" from the Library of Congress's publication project.

There can be no doubt that Columbus was intimately familiar with and utilized portolan charts similar to this one by Prunes. While no universally accepted examples of charts drawn by Columbus are known to have survived it can be said with certainty that he prepared charts which, in all probability, were in the style of portolan charts. Many scholars, including Samuel Eliot Morison, have accepted an unsigned sketch map of the north coast of Haiti as the only surviving map drawn by Christopher Columbus.[6] More recently, however, Robert H. Fuson termed this map, from the Duke of Alba's collection, "a later forgery."[7] Clearly the Alba map of northern Haiti is deserving of further investigation.

In the log of his first voyage, prepared for Ferdinand and Isabela, Columbus wrote "I propose to make a new chart for navigation, on which I will set down all the sea and lands of the Ocean Sea, in the correct locations and with their correct bearings." In addition to a sea chart he also promised "to compile a book and shall map everything by latitude and longitude."[8] In promising to record his discoveries by latitude and longitude Columbus was moving away from the tradition of the portolan chart and navigation as it was practiced in the Mediterranean. At the time Columbus was writing, Mediterranean navigators relied on a method of dead reckoning which depended on the magnetic compass and the estimation of ship's speed underway. Columbus was, however, drawing on the system that Ptolemy recommended for the mapping of the world. This may also be a further in-

dication that Columbus was a latitude sailor rather than the dead reckoner that Samuel Eliot Morison and others, have made him out to be.[9] Proponents of "Columbus was a latitude sailor" arguments point out that the navigators of northern Europe in Columbus's day routinely sailed more or less squared courses along meridian and latitude lines. It may be that Columbus employed latitude sailing techniques in his system of navigation but the evidence for this is still debatable.

FROM MEDITERRANEAN TO ATLANTIC

Probably the most important factor, outside of the church's dogma, operating to shape the world view of Columbus and other Western Europeans was the shift in the power balance of the Mediterranean world. Shortly after Marco Polo's return from China, in 1295, the power balance in the Mediterranean basin tipped sharply against the interests of the Europeans and Christen-

Portolan chart of the Black and Mediterranean Seas and Atlantic Ocean, off North Africa and Western Europe, drawn by the Majorcan cartographer Mateus Prunes in 1559. Most portolan charts were less elegant than this richly illustrated example. They were developed to serve the navigation needs of Mediterranean mariners. Portolan charts were drawn on vellum prepared from the skin of a goat or sheep. The shape of the skin can be made out in this photograph of the original. At the skin's neck, cartographer Prunes drew a "wind head" face with puffed cheeks named "Ponente" (west) to represent the west wind. Just below the wind head are drawings of a bishop holding a small ship and the Virgin and child surrounded by angels carrying a crown and playing a variety of musical instruments. The figure to the right is holding a large sword over a crowned head. Both real and mythical islands are shown in the Atlantic. Other vignettes feature a number of kings and other rulers as well as several great cities. Of particular interest are the vignettes representing Genoa and Venice at the top of the Italian "boot" (Geography and Map Division).

dom. The capture of Acre in northern Palestine by the Sultan of Egypt eliminated the last of the many Christian strongholds won during the Crusades. An awareness of the strength of Islam was thrust on the Europeans, as first Egypt, and then the Ottoman Empire, gained control of the trade routes to the sources of Far Eastern commodities, particularly spices, on which the Europeans had come to rely. Food preservation and preparation in that unrefrigerated age demanded spices as essentials, not luxuries for the favored few. The so-called "spice trade" involved many other exotic products such as drugs, scents, and dyestuffs, in addition to the products still known as spices. Italian merchant republics, dominated by Venice and Genoa, entered into trading alliances with the Moslem powers and became profiteering middle men in commercial links with the East. The windfall profits reaped by Italians fueled the system of art patronage that characterized the Renaissance.

As these pressures developed in the Europe-Mediterranean-Middle East trading system, important events were transpiring on the Atlantic front of Europe. Technological advances pioneered by Mediterranean navigators made safe oceanic sailing far from land a reality. The compass, astrolabe, and sea charts aboard improved ships, which could sail almost into the wind, were the basic tools needed for exploring the far reaches of the globe. All had been perfected in the Mediterranean, and were at hand when the Spanish and Portuguese led the way into the Atlantic.

Portugal was particularly well suited to adopt programs of Atlantic exploration. A long Atlantic coastline provided numerous ports so vital in the sea link between northwestern Europe and the Mediterranean. Genoese merchants and navigators formed important and influential communities in those ports and their capital contributed to the growth of the Portuguese merchant fleet.

Aided by their Genoese and northern guests, the Portuguese began to probe the Atlantic off their shores and those of northern Africa. Prince Henry, immortalized with the title "Navigator," played a truly extraordinary role in these developments. As the third son of his royal father, Henry had little hope of ever assuming the throne, and seemed destined for an army career. He led the military campaign which succeeded in driving the Moors from Ceuta, in 1415, and thereby planted the first seed of what was to become a vast Portuguese empire in Africa.

Prince Henry's encounters with the Moors probably gave him good opportunities to absorb their geographical lore and add it to his own European understanding of world geography. He was instrumental in mounting expeditions that discovered and colonized the Madeiras and the Azores Islands in 1425 and 1439. Oceanic discovery and exploration were not hit-or-miss undertakings to Henry. On the contrary, he set up a highly organized international center at Sagres for gathering geographical intelligence and training navigators. From this "think tank" command center at Europe's southwestern tip, he conducted a program of discovery and exploration which culminated, after his death, in the rounding of Africa and the forging of regular trade between Portugal and India and beyond.

By the time Columbus sailed under the banner of Portugal's enemy-neighbor, Spain, the Madeiras had become integrated into the economies of Europe and Africa. As Atlantic island expert T. Bentley Duncan wrote, "the island was the prototype of that momentous and tragic social and economic system of sugar and slavery that was to be repeated, on a far larger scale, in the West Indies and Brazil."[10] Only seventy years after first settlement, Madeira was the world's greatest sugar producer and an important center of commerce and navigation.

ISLANDS IN THE WEST
SEND SIGNALS

Many maps of Columbus's day showed more than the explored islands of the Atlantic off the coasts of Western Europe and Africa. Along with the Azores, Canary, and Cape Verde groups there were shown many legendary islands. Columbus reasoned that some of these islands existed and would be useful as stepping stones on his route to Asia. One of the legends he mentioned dealt with the island shown on many maps and named Antillia, which, Columbus believed, was west of the Azores and contained "Seven Cities, settled by the Portuguese at the time the Moors conquered Spain . . . in the year A.D. 714."[11]

Columbus also claimed to have heard firsthand reports from Atlantic navigators who had sighted land or seen good evidence of it to the west of the known island groups. Such evidence included "a piece of wood ingeniously carved, but not with iron," pieces of cane "so thick that one joint held nine decanters of wine," and, on one of the Azores islands, "dead bodies with broad faces and different in appearance from the Christians" had been flung up by the sea.[12] Given the nature of the great gyre formed by the clockwise circulation of Atlantic surface waters, reports of such tantalizing hints of lands in the west were probably based on fact.

CHRISTOPHER COLUMBUS AND
MARTIN BEHAIM

The world that Columbus and his European fellows knew was little different from the habitable world or oecumene known to Ptolemy almost thirteen centuries before. Travelers' reports, especially the book by Marco Polo that circulated widely in manuscript form throughout Europe

Martin Behaim is less well known than Christopher Columbus but shared a similar world view in 1492. As a German in the service of the King of Portugal, Behaim was well acquainted with most of the theories, information, and ideas that Columbus drew on to support his plan to sail west across the Atlantic to Japan and Asia. Returning home to his native Nuremberg in 1490, Behaim joined with a local artist in producing a globe of the world for the city council (F. W. Ghillany, Geschichte Des Seefahress Ritter Martin Behaim . . . (Nuremberg: 1853), Geography and Map Division).

from the end of the thirteenth century, had greatly heightened interest in places like China and Japan. "Of all the accounts of Asia written by medieval European travellers," J. H. Parry wrote, "the *Travels* of Marco Polo is the best, the most complete and the most informative."[13] Marco Polo was cited by Columbus as one who "journeyed far beyond the eastern lands described by Ptolemy and Marinus."[14] From the descriptions of the East recorded by Polo and others, Columbus felt that it could be argued that "India neighbors on Africa and Spain," a further confirmation of the correctness of his plan to sail west to reach the East.

Needless to say, Christopher Columbus was not alone in sifting through and synthesizing the geographic information provided by the maps, documents, and legends current in Europe during the second half of the fifteenth century. Another person with similar interests and similar access to data was a merchant and native of Nuremberg named Martin Behaim. Like Columbus, Behaim was convinced that the earth was one-quarter smaller than its true size and that the exaggerated width of Ptolemy's Eurasian landmass left only 3,000 miles of ocean separating the Canary Islands from the island of "Cipangu" or Japan as it is now known.[15]

Behaim first visited Portugal in 1480 as a merchant connected to the then flourishing trade with the Low Countries. By convincing members of the court that he was proficient in astronomy, he was able to gain a position as an adviser on navigation matters to King John. During his decade in Portugal Behaim probably took part in one or more voyages south along the African coast. Returning to his home city in 1490, he worked with the painter Georg Glockendon to produce a terrestrial globe of the world for the Nuremberg city council. It is the earliest globe in existence and rests as a treasure in the German National Museum of that city.

The photograph included here is of an eigh-

teenth-century German engraving of the world shown on Martin Behaim's "erdapfel" or earth-apple as he termed the globe. Had Columbus constructed a globe or world map on the eve of his 1492 voyage there can be little doubt that it would have been very similar or essentially identical to Behaim's.

The significance of Martin Behaim's globe and the world view it portrays cannot be overstated. With this world map in view Columbus's voyage, sponsored by the Spanish monarchs in 1492, became a feasible scheme. Notice how it departs from the Ptolemaic world view by showing the eastern extent of Asia flanked by a grand arc of large and small islands. No longer is the Indian Ocean closed off, although Africa retains a strong Ptolemaic "twist" to the east. Most important of all notice the large island "Cipangu Insula"; this represents Japan. It should come as no great surprise to learn that Columbus insisted that Cuba was Japan when he reached that large island in 1492.

PRE-COLUMBIAN CONTACTS BETWEEN THE OLD AND THE NEW WORLDS

Perhaps the most amazing fact of all to be discovered about Columbus and Behaim in the year 1492 is that they, and apparently all other concerned Europeans, were not including Vinland in their world views. As we have seen there was no dearth of speculation about legendary Atlantic islands such as Antillia, St. Brendan's, and even Atlantis but no mention of the Helluland, Markland, and the Norsemen's Vinland. This omission of the Viking voyages and discoveries is all the more surprising when seen in the light of Columbus's claim to have voyaged 100 leagues beyond the island of "Tile" or Tule, as Iceland was then called.[16]

In our own period, plagued as we often are

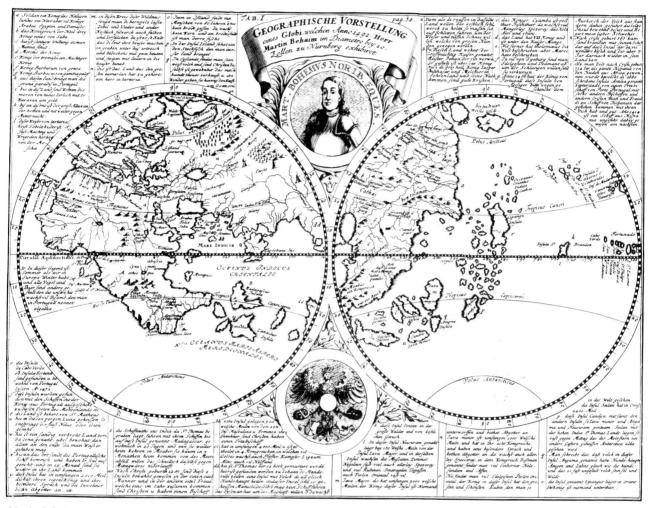

Martin Behaim completed his globe of the world at about the time Columbus was preparing to set out on his first voyage. The world view it portrayed came very close to reflecting Columbus's ideas concerning what he expected to encounter on the eastern coast of Asia. This first engraving of Behaim's world map was published by J. G. Doppelmayer in 1730. Notice the large island stretching south from the Tropic of Cancer (Tropicus Cancri) in the right-hand hemisphere; it is named "Cipangu Insula" and represents Japan, Columbus's intended landfall in 1492. Notice also that the Indian Ocean is no longer shown as enclosed by land as it was on the 1482 Ptolemaic map. Behaim's globe was referred to as his "erdapfel" or earth-apple (Rare Book and Special Collections Division).

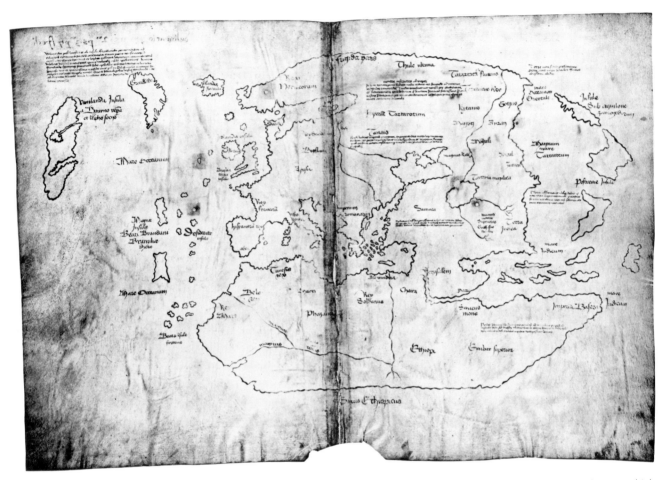

Yale's Vinland Map from a photograph in the Geography and Map Division. A still-simmering debate concerns the authenticity of this map which is touted as "The Oldest Known Map Showing American Lands" by its proponents. The pickle-shaped landmass to the west of a recognizable Greenland is named "Vinlandia Insula" and is inscribed with a Latin caption stating "discovered by Bjarni and Leif in company." To some experts the most startling aspect of the Vinland Map is not that a large island named Vinland appears, but rather the incredibly good outline of Greenland that it presents. Critics of the map's genuineness point to Greenland as "proof" that the map is a fairly recent forgery. The jury of scholarly opinion is, however, still divided on the question (Geography and Map Division).

by "media overload," hardly a month or two goes by without a news release concerning some new evidence or theory touching on a "pre-Columbian" discovery of the New World. Many of these verge on the bizarre and compete for column space with reports of U.F.O. sightings and landings. Some, however, present stimulating hypotheses and kindle debates that add novelty and verve to Age of Discovery topics and research questions.

A still-simmering debate of this sort concerns the map owned by Yale University that is called the Vinland Map. Amid fanfare and hype more commonly associated with the launching of a new line of automobiles or brand of beer, Yale University Press chose the day before Columbus's official birthday in October 1965, to announce publicly their scholarly tome, *The Vinland Map and the Tartar Relation*. It was a handsome, well-illustrated volume, containing secretly prepared extended essays by three internationally recognized scholars who were concerned with the map Yale had added to the Beinecke Library's collection. The Vinland Map was presented to the world as "the earliest known and indisputable cartographic representation of any part of the Americas."[17]

The Vinland Map was revealed, through a two-page photograph, to be an elliptically shaped world map, in a simplified *mappae mundi* style, that included several large islands in the Mare Oceanum to the west of Europe. The westernmost island was named "Vinlandia Insula" and inscribed with the Latin text for "discovered by Bjarni and Leif in company." Closely argued essays based on painstaking scholarly analyses of the Vinland Map and the document with which it had once been bound, the "Tartar Relation," reached the conclusion that both the map and document had been copied in Europe's Rhineland in about the year 1440 from even earlier originals.

There was, of course, nothing new or startling about the idea of Norsemen visiting North America 500 years before Columbus's voyage. The long-known Icelandic Sagas had been confirmed by the archaeological finds of Norwegian Helge Ingstad at L'Anse aux Meadows. At this site, on the northern tip of Newfoundland's Western Peninsula, conclusive archaeological evidence had been found proving Viking occupation during the period around 1000 A.D. Canada's historic park at the L'Anse aux Meadows was officially recognized as a World Heritage site in 1980 by the United Nations.

Nor does the historical record leave any doubt as to the energy and adventurousness of the peoples of northernmost Western Europe during the early Middle Ages. The ancestors of the peoples we now know as Swedes, Norwegians, and Danes appear to have poured forth from their northern homelands in a number of "waves" from the eighth to the eleventh centuries. Exactly what triggered their movements is not entirely clear. Some suggest that overpopulation or climatic deterioration may have been the stimulus for sea roving and migration. Others hold that political unrest, triggered by unpopular and repressive rulers, provided the impetus.

In his book, *Medieval Cities*, Henri Pirenne provided an interesting analysis:

The invasions of Norsemen had been only the first manifestation of the need of expansion felt by the Scandinavian peoples. Their overflowing energy had driven them forth, towards Western Europe and Russia simultaneously, upon adventures of pillage and conquest. They were not mere pirates. They aspired, as had the Germanic tribes before them with regard to the Roman Empire, to settle in countries more rich and fertile than was their homeland, and there to create colonies for the surplus population which their own country could no longer support. In this undertaking they eventually succeeded. To the east, the Swedes set foot along those natural routes which led from the Baltic to the Black Sea by the way of the Neva, Lake Ladoga, the Lovat, the Volchof, the Divina and the Dneiper. To the west, the Danes and the Norwegians colonized the Anglo Saxon Kingdoms north of the Humber. In France, they had ceded to them by Charles the Simple the country on the Channel which took from them the name of Normandy.[18]

The western wing of this Norse expansion surged even farther to reach and colonize the remote shores of Iceland in the ninth century. From Iceland, the next step was the island which the outlaw known as Eric the Red, in an effort to encourage others to join the settlement he pioneered, wisely chose to call "Greenland." In time, two large Norse settlements were founded on the coast of southern Greenland. The most southerly colony came to be known as the East

Settlement and the other, centered in the area of modern Godthaab about 250 kilometers to the north, was called the West Settlement.

Like their relatives in Northern Europe, the pioneers in Iceland and Greenland were pagans who worshipped the old Norse gods Odin, Freya, and Thor. According to many experts, Leif Ericson brought Christianity to Greenland from Norway in the same year he is believed to have sighted Vinland. According to interpretations of the Icelandic Sagas, Norway's Christian King Olaf converted Leif and sent him to spread Christianity to Greenland. In spite of notable reactionaries like Leif's father Eric, the pagan status quo eventually gave way before the zeal of early Christian missionaries. Churches were built and, by 1126, an ecclesiastical see was established in the East Settlement to provide for the spiritual needs of the almost ten thousand Greenland colonists.

A Latin inscription on Yale's Vinland Map, located to the north of the island named Vinland, may relate to the activities of one of the early bishops of Greenland, as well as the discovery credited to Leif Erickson. The text states:

By God's will, after a long voyage from the island of Greenland to the south toward the most distant remaining parts of the western ocean sea, sailing southward amidst the ice, the companions Bjarni and Leif Eriksson discovered a new land, extremely fertile and even having vines, the which island they named Vinland. Eric [Henricus], legate of the Apostolic See and bishop of Greenland and the neighboring regions, arrived in this truly vast and very rich land, in the name of the Almighty God, in the last year of our most blessed father Pascal, remained a long time in both summer and winter, and later returned northeastward toward Greenland and then proceeded [home to Europe?] in most humble obedience to the will of his superiors.[19]

Whatever the specific dates and details, concerning the Norse discovery of North America, are eventually found to be, one thing appears reasonably clear at this point: the Greenland colonists, and not the Viking kingdoms in Europe, provided the manpower and equipment that made such contacts a reality. Further, the remoteness and small number of Greenlanders coupled with stress on their limited resource base eventually led to their loss of contact with Europe and ultimate extinction. Many scholars have speculated on the reasons for the decline of the Greenland colonies. Although it is beyond the scope of this chapter to delve into those reasons, it is appropriate to conclude that the mystery of Vinland and its Norse colonists will only be understood when the larger mystery of the decline and extinction of the Greenland settlements is solved.

The debates concerning the authenticity of the Vinland Map are not finished, nor is the historical record of Norse contacts with North America, five centuries before those by Columbus, a completed one. At this point, it is probably best to keep an open mind on the whole subject of pre-Columbian contacts between the Old and the New Worlds. That such contacts took place seems certain. Exactly who made them, and when and where they occurred, are matters which represent research challenges to workers in a number of disciplines concerned with humankind's past. At this time, most scholars would agree that the impacts of those early contacts were probably very limited in scope compared with the revolutionary character of the impacts that flowed from the continuous European contact between the New and Old World spearheaded by Columbus.

With these facts in mind it is appropriate to ask why the publication of *The Vinland Map* in 1965 was deemed so important. Why had it, in the words of the eminent historian of discovery Wilcomb E. Washburn, writing in 1971, "set off one of the most vigorous debates ever seen in the world of historical scholarship"?[20] As Washburn further noted, circumstances surrounding the Vinland Map book had "caused the historical pot not only to boil but to run over."

Much of the scholarly heat to which Washburn alluded grew out of charges that the Vinland Map was a hoax. Even if its authenticity had not been challenged, however, the map was certain to stir debate. This was because it seemed to argue that the land the Vikings had explored beyond Greenland in the Western Atlantic was common knowledge in Europe at about the time of Columbus's birth when the evidence suggested the Vinland Map and Tartar Relation were copied. Not only did it indicate that the Viking discoveries were known, but, more importantly that the knowledge was de-

rived ultimately from information based on navigational experience and not merely on the imprecise oral traditions embodied in the Sagas.

If this was the case, the question that begs an answer is why Columbus, Behaim, and others interested in the possibility of sailing west to reach the wealth of the Far East did not include Vinland in their schemes and arguments. Could Vinland have been a part of his world view that Columbus chose to keep secret? Rather than attempting an answer here to the question of Columbus's knowledge of the Norse New World voyages, that question will be addressed in Chapter 4, "Christopher Columbus Finds the Way: First Encounters on the Islands in the Ocean Sea."

CHAPTER THREE

WORLDS APART

Native American World Views in the Age of Discovery

They imagined the world to be flat and round, like a trencher; and they in the middest.

Travels and Works, Captain John Smith

I will say at the outset that there is only one world and although we speak of the Old World and the New, this is because the latter was lately discovered by us, and not because there are two.

Royal Commentaries of the Incas,
Garcilaso de la Vega, El Inca

BERINGIA, A TWO-WAY BRIDGE

An Age of Discovery of sorts began when the first groups of Old World hunters spread across the broad, tundra-covered plain that is now the floor of the Bering Strait between Alaska and Siberia. During the last ice age, when much of the earth's water was locked up in vast continental ice sheets, world sea levels were much lower than they are today. In that period a low, tundra-clad plain, at times as much as a thousand miles wide, called Beringia, firmly joined and allowed movement between the Afro-Eurasian and North American landmasses.

Most discussions of Beringia tend to lay stress on movements of people, ideas, and influences *from* the Old World *to* the New World without due consideration of similar movements in the reverse or opposite direction. While it may be true that the impact of the Old World on the New has been greater than vice versa, it would be a mistake to fall prey to the idea that Beringia was, for some unstated reason, a one-way passage. To omit consideration of the probability of reverse flows would be unscientific at best, and insulting to the proven genius and creativity of New World peoples at worst.

It would be far more advisable to consider movements from the New World to the Old World as a logical probability in the spirit of the eighteenth-century polymath-traveler, Count

Volney. Volney had travelled widely in Europe, Africa, and Asia before coming to America. While visiting the American frontier in what is today the State of Michigan, the French scientist was introduced to a famous Miami Indian chief named Mishikinakwa, or Little Turtle. In a conversation with Little Turtle, Volney explained that the "Chinese Tartars" were strikingly similar to Indians in their appearance and that this had led to the belief that the American Indians originated in Asia. Volney continued:

I explained this theory to the chief, and laid before him a map of the contiguous parts of Asia and America. He readily recognized the Canadian lakes, and the Ohio, Wabash, etc., and the rest he eyed with an eagerness that showed it was new to him: but it is a rule in Indian manners never to betray surprise. When I showed him the communication by Behrings Straits and the Aleutian isles, "Why" said he, "should not these Tartars who are like us have gone first from the American side? Are there any proofs to the contrary? Why should not their fathers and ours have been born in our country?"

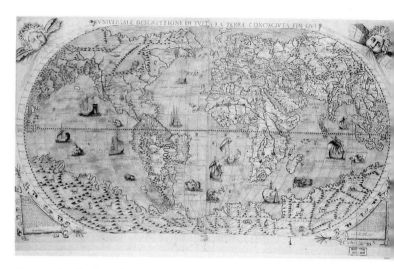

Cartographer Paolo Forlani reached back almost twenty years to the work of Giacomo Gastaldi when he engraved the copper plates for this world map dated 1565. This helps explain why he showed North America as a broad extension of Asia. It is a depiction based on theory and surmise, not exploration. But nonetheless it is a depiction that would have pleased the Miami Indian Chief Little Turtle, had it been available during his conversation with Count Volney. By the 1560s a watery separation between northeastern Siberia and Alaska called the Strait of Anian was being shown on some world maps. It appears to have developed as a theory to explain Marco Polo's description of a large gulf he claimed existed in eastern Asia. Today, the narrow body of water separating Alaska from the Soviet Union is named the Bering Strait after its discoverer, Vitus Bering. He was a Dane in the service of Russia who explored the strait in 1728 and 1732 (Geography and Map Division).

Volney obviously enjoyed Little Turtle's perspicacity and observed, "the Indians, indeed, give themselves the name of Metoktheniaka (born of the soil)." Responding to the Chief, Volney told him "I see no objection, but our *black coats* (the name given by the Indians to the missionaries) won't allow it. It is [singly] difficult to find out how any particular nation sprung up at the beginning."

Little Turtle was in no way swayed in his logic by Volney's invocation of the authority of Christian beliefs. He answered "But that is as great a difficulty to the *black coats* as to us."[1]

Their numbers may have been small but the ancestors of Little Turtle were mentally on a par with modern humans. Equipped with language, fire, and other tools the new arrivals began to explore and make North and South America their own. These people, who erroneously came to be called Indians by the Europeans, had tra- versed every region of the Americas thousands of years before they were first encountered by Columbus. While these Native Americans "discovered" and "explored" as individuals and small groups they lacked the means to record the details of their findings in writing. This was in sharp contrast to the literate Europeans they began to encounter in the late fifteenth century.

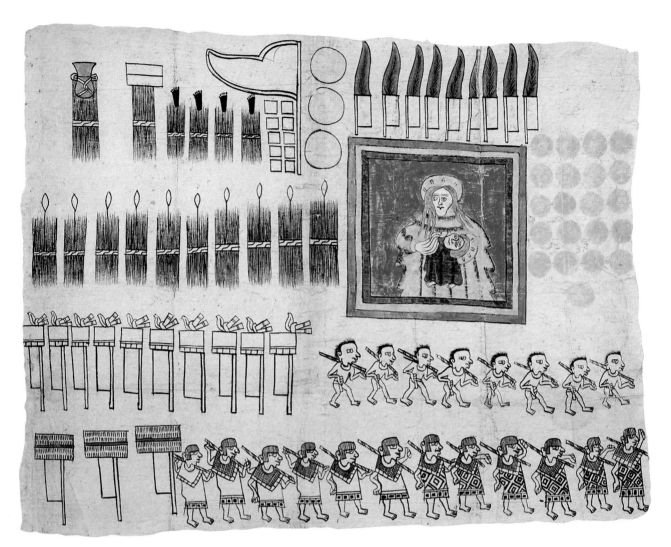

This painting, from the 1531 Huejotzingo Codex in the Harkness Collection, gives a hint of how sophisticated record keeping was among the Indians of Central Mexico at the time of their subjugation by the Spanish. The Codex is a portion of a legal action brought by Mexico's conqueror, Hernando Cortés, Marqués del Valle, against members of the first "audienca" or high court of Spain in Mexico. Among the witnesses called were a number of Indians whose testimony was illustrated by eight Indian paintings. This is painting V in the manuscript; it records the amounts of warriors' equipment and other materials that the people of Huejotzingo contributed to support an expedition of conquest in New Galicia. The Madonna and child framed in the blue rectangle represents the standard of the expedition's leader, Nuño de Guzman, and is one of the earliest native artworks devoted to Christianity. Directly under the Madonna standard are eight small figures which can be identified as slaves by the large wooden collars around their necks. They symbolize the fact that eight male slaves had been sold to pay for the gold needed in making the standard. The ten objects to the left of the male slaves represent 200 loads or 4,000 loincloths provided for Indians involved in the expedition (Manuscript Division).

RECORDING DISCOVERIES

The Western Europeans were heirs of rich systems of written language, cartography, and mathematics that allowed them to accumulate an incredibly vast corpus of detailed knowledge about the world. This corpus could be shared across great distances of both space and time. New valid and verifiable information about the nature of the world heretofore unknown or unproven, when tested and shared in detail by the wide society of interconnected, literate peoples of Afro-Eurasia constituted discovery in the sense that the word usually conveys in the term *Age of Discovery*. Only a relative handful of

American native peoples at the apex of a few Meso American and Andean polities even came near to enjoying a role in the process of "Discovery" that almost all literate or informed Europeans enjoyed in the late fifteenth century.

Far more typical were the record keeping and communication techniques of the Native Americans encountered by John Lederer when he explored the Southern Piedmont in 1670. Lederer attempted to "shew by what means the knowledge of them [the Indians] hath been conveyed from former ages to posterity." He wrote of the "three ways they supply their want of Letters: first by Counters, secondly by Emblemes or Hieroglyphics, thirdly by Tradition delivered in long Tales from father to son, which being children they are made to learn by rote."[2]

Lederer continued by explaining what he meant by "counters," "hieroglyphics," and "tradition":

For Counters they use either Pebbles, or short scantlings of straw or reeds. Where a Battel had been fought, or a Colony seated, they raise a small Pyramid of these stones, consisting of the number slain or transplanted. Their reeds and straws serve them in Religious Ceremonies: for they lay them orderly in a Circle when they prepare for Devotion or Sacrifice; and that performed, the Circle remains still; for it is Sacriledge to disturb or to touch it: the disposition and sorting of the straws and reeds, shew what kinde of Rites have there been celebrated, as Invocation, Sacrifice, Burial, etc.
    The faculties of the minde and body they commonly express by Emblems. By the figure of a Stag, they imply swiftness; by that of a Serpent, wrath; of a Lion, courage; of a Dog, fidelity; by a Swan, they signifie the *English*, alluding to their complexion, and flight over the Sea.
    An account of Time, and other things, they keep on a string or leather thong tied in knots of several colours. I took particular notice of small wheels serving for this purpose among the *Oenocks*, because I have heard that the *Mexicans* use the same. Every Nation gives his particular Ensigne or Arms: The *Sasquesahanaugh* a Tarapine, or small Tortoise; the *Akenatzy's* a Serpent; the *Nahyssanes* three arrows, etc. In this they likewise agree with the *Mexican* Indians.[3]

THE ABORIGINAL LANDSCAPE

Indian populations increased as they devised improved systems of subsistence and resource exploitation. In time, imposing earthworks, massive effigies, and mounds were raised, palisaded villages built, fields and trails hewn from the forest, fish traps were constructed in rivers, lakes, and coastal lagoons, and everywhere fire was deliberately loosed on the land to drive game, clear undergrowth, and achieve other desired alterations. Giovanni da Verrazano, whose landfall, near Cape Fear, North Carolina, was guided by Indian fires, was only one of scores of Age of Discovery visitors to North America

The use of memory aids, termed mnemonics, was widespread among Native American societies. Probably the best known of these were the Inca's knotted cord devices called quipus. They were used efficiently to keep the complex records of a vast empire. Shown here is a group of young Iroquois Indians being taught to remember and accurately recite the laws of the Five Nation Confederacy through the use of beaded belts called wampum. The engraving was published in Moeurs des Sauvages Ameriquaines . . . (Paris, 1724) by Pere Joseph François Lafitau. Notched or marked sticks and sheets of bark marked with symbols were other mnemonic devices widely used by North American Indians (Rare Book and Special Collections Division).

who drew attention to the Indians' recurrent use of fire as a tool in landscape modification and management. In Mexico and Andean America great cities were built by societies that rivalled or exceeded those of the Old World in their size and sophistication.

As their cultures evolved and their numbers grew, the Indians altered their habitat in major ways over much of the New World. The sum total of these alterations of the natural state of the continent, by the time of the first European contacts, is still to be accurately determined. One thing is clear, however, the Americas were far from being covered by a "forest primeval" when Europeans reached their shores in the fifteenth and sixteenth centuries. On the contrary, what the European explorers found and reported is best described as an Aboriginal Landscape— a landscape palimpsest already inscribed with patterns and forms reflecting the cultural use of the Indian occupants for whom it had been home for millennia. Only to the Europeans were the Americas a "New Land." In the words of John Collier, longtime U.S. Commissioner of Indian Affairs:

At the time of white arrival there was no square mile unoccupied or unused. . . . The million Indians of the United States and Alaska were formed within more than six hundred distinct societies, in geographical situations ranging from temperate oceansides to arctic ice, from humid swamps to frozen tundras, from eastern woodlands to western deserts.[4]

The accounts of early encounters between Indians and Europeans leave no doubt as to the great diversity of social and material accomplishment existing within the Indian populations. In terms of the usual indices of tangible human accomplishment, their societies appear to have represented a broad range of what some have termed *evolutionary types*. At one end of such a scale would be the socially highly stratified and materially richly endowed Aztecs and Incas, while at the other end one might place the mobile, egalitarian hunting, fishing, and gathering societies, equipped with a minimum of portable tools, shelters, and clothing. The overriding problem with such schema is that they fail to plumb the intellectual achievements and belief structures of the members of the societies they index. What were the intellectual abilities, value systems, mind sets, and world views operating on the Indian side of the encounters?

To attempt to answer this question would involve research far beyond the confines and purpose of this modest book. Rather than making such an attempt, we will be content to offer several examples of world views and understandings which indicate the diversity that existed among the Indians of the Americas during the Age of Discovery. In large measure these observations derive from their encounter experiences with the Europeans.

THE AZTECS OR MEXICA

At the outset it is striking to find how many similarities exist between the Indian and European mentality and world views. Tzvetan Todorov has drawn attention to the similarities between Columbus and Montezuma. Todorov observed that "by his mental structures, which link him to the medieval conception of knowledge, Columbus is closer to those whom he discovered than to some of his own companions: How shocked he would have been to hear it!"[5] Columbus like Montezuma, head of the Aztec Empire, lived in a world where great events were predicted "by soothsayers, revelations or by portents and other celestial signs." Nor was Columbus unusual; the contemporary historian-cleric Las Casas has a chapter in his *History of the Indies* "wherein is seen how Divine Providence

Title page from Descripción de las Indias Ocidentales, *the ninth part of Antonio de Herrera y Tordesillas's great work,* Historia General. *It is made up of fourteen maps accompanying the comprehensive narrative by Herrera, Philip II's official historiographer. The engraved interpretations of Aztec deities are copies of Indian drawings included in two of the many codices that were sent to Europe following the conquest of Mexico. Notice also the representation of the Western Hemisphere with its distorted configurations of North and South America and a theorized southern continent named "Terra Australis." The seascape scenes, on either side of the hemisphere, are a curious blend of figures from European mythology mixed with canoemen and islands with structures of apparent Indian design. The heraldic devices are those of Philip II and Herrera who included his own portrait in the lower left of the page (Geography and Map Division).*

never permits important events, either for the good of the world or for its chastisement, to occur without their having been first heralded and predicted by the saints, or by other persons, even by infidels or wicked people, and even on certain occasions by the demons themselves."[6]

Unfortunately most Indian documents including books, maps, and paintings were systematically destroyed by Cortés, his fellow conquerors, and zealous Catholic priests. Regrettable as their systematic destruction was, the Spanish were doing nothing new. The Aztecs themselves had, in similar fashion, destroyed the codices and records of the societies they had conquered. The Aztec tradition of destroying historical records of other groups is exemplified in the "Codice Matritense de la Real Academia." Translated from the Nahuatl it states:

> They preserved their history.
> But it was burned
> at the time that Itzcóatl reigned in Mexico.
> The Aztec lords decided it,
> saying:
> "It is not wise that all the people
> should know the paintings.
> The common people would be driven to ruin
> and there would be trouble,
> because these paintings contain many lies,
> for many in the pictures have been hailed
>   as gods."[7]

As a consequence little remains as evidence on which to base an authentic detailed reconstruction of Aztec or other Mexican Indian pre-Conquest world views.

We do know, however, that they were capable of constructing detailed maps of extensive areas that could be read and understood by the Spanish. In his second report to the Emperor Charles V dated October 30, 1520, Cortés described how in an interview with Montezuma:

. . . I likewise inquired . . . if there was on the coast of the Sea any river or bay into which ships could enter, and lie with safety. He answered that

Captioned "Concerning the dreams and omens of these people before the Spaniards came," this painting is one of several illustrations included in the Library of Congress codex titled "Relación de las ceremonias y ritos y población y gobierno de los indios, de la provincia de Michoacán." Michoacán is the state located to the west of the state of Mexico and Mexico City. It is still the home of the Tarascan Indians who were there at the time of European contact. Like their Aztec neighbors, the Tarascans were great believers in auguries and prophesies. The "Relación" was probably compiled between 1539 and 1541 by the Spanish missionary, Fr. Martín de Jesús de la Coruña, with the assistance of Indian informants. The original manuscript was presented to Viceroy Don Antonio de Mendoza when he visited the city of Michoacán in 1541. It is the only known survey of Tarascan government, customs, and traditions drawn from Indian sources at the time of the Conquest. The Library of Congress manuscript is an eighteenth-century copy of the "Relación" in the Library of the Escorial in Spain (Peter Force Collection, Manuscript Division).

he did not know, but that he would cause a chart of the coast to be painted, showing the rivers and bays, and that I might send Spanish to examine them, for which purpose he would despatch suitable persons with them as guides; and he did so. The next day they brought me a chart of the whole coast, painted on cloth; on which appeared a river that discharged into the sea, with a wider mouth, according to the chart, than any others; this seemed to be between the mountains called Sanmin [San Martin], which extend to a bay until then believed by the pilots to separate the land at a province called Mazalmaco . . . [8]

In another despatch Cortés told of a group of chiefs from Tabasco and Xicalango who "drew on a cloth a figure of the whole land, whereby I calculated that I could very well go over the great part of it . . . " This map appears to have extended from Mexico east of Yucatan to Honduras and Panama and served Cortés as an indispensable guide "during all his difficult travels through the almost impassable regions of Chiapas and Guatemala." [9]

While there are no documents to confirm it absolutely, there is good reason to suspect that Cortés's map of the Gulf of Mexico shown herein was based to some extent on an Indian original. It is also possible that the original Indian information was supplemented by the pilot Pineda and his fellows when they explored the coast of the Gulf for Francisco de Garay a few years before this engraving was prepared in Germany. In any event the map usually, if not correctly, attributed to Cortés is the first printed map to show the Gulf and name "Florida," and "Yucatan."

Of even more interest is the fascinating map of Mexico City, also attributed to Cortés, and first published in 1524 with the map of the Gulf in the Latin edition of his Second Letter. Like the map of the Gulf of Mexico it contains many clues suggesting it was based on an Indian original. For one thing, it is centered on the island capital of the Aztecs in a way that echoes their view of the cosmos.

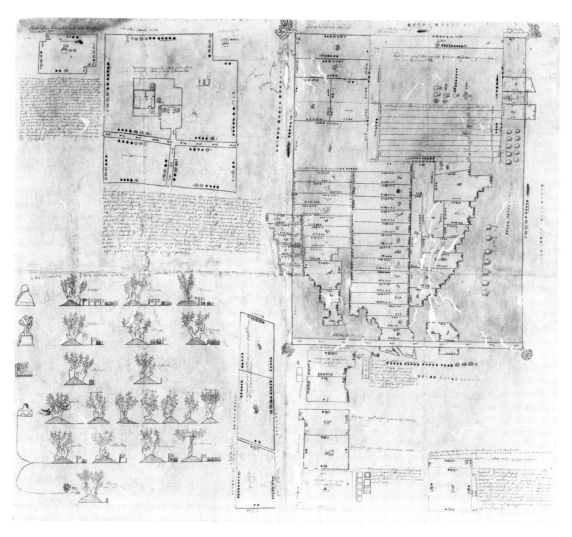

The Oztoticpac Estate Lands Map was drawn on amate paper of Indian manufacture in about 1539 or 1540. The original is in a very good state of preservation and measures about 30 by 33 inches. The map was prepared by one or more Indians skilled in drawing and aided by an interpreter who added a number of glosses in the Aztec language, Nahuatl, as well as Spanish. It concerns properties belonging to members of the Texcoco Indian nobility, including a Don Carlos Chichimecatecol and his half-brother Ixtlilxochitl. Don Carlos was executed by the Inquisition for possessing, among other things, an ancient Aztec book of paintings and an Indian calendar that set forth the "Count of fiestas of the Demon." Needless to say, the offending documents were promptly destroyed. Important to the suit concerning his estate was the orchard inventory pictured in the lower left of the map. Groves of pears, quince, apples, pomegranates, peaches and grapevines are located. A number of grafting techniques can be identified in the tree and vine symbols. The clear depiction of these horticultural practices places the Oztoticpac Estate Lands Map among the most important Indian pictorial documents which provide noteworthy economic and cultural data for Mexico's immediate post-Contact period (Geography and Map Division).

In Aztec myth and poetry their capital Tenochtitlan was portrayed as a majestic place—
the center of the universe in both horizontal
and vertical space. This revealing engraving suggests a vertical photograph taken from above the
city with a fish-eye lens. Not only does the exaggerated scale of the Great Temple enclosure
cause it to dominate the plane of the map, but it
appears also to be raised vertically above the
rest of the crowded city and the circling lake
shores beyond. In the words of Diego Durán,
the Aztec capital set in the brackish waters of
the lake now covered by the sprawl of Mexico
City was "the root, the navel, and the heart of
this whole worldly machine."

As we noted the similarities that existed be-

Maps of the Gulf of Mexico and Tenochtitlan (Mexico City), printed on a single sheet and published in 1524 with the second letter of Hernando Cortés to Charles V, the Emperor and King of Spain. There is much in both of these maps to suggest that the drawings supplied to the Nuremberg engraver who prepared the printer's woodblock were based on Aztec originals. Cortés, anxious to inform and impress Charles V, sent his lieutenant, Juan de Ribera, in 1522 to deliver samples of Aztec objets d'art and treasure to the royal court in advance of a fully laden treasure ship. Ribera also carried "numerous maps" of Aztec origin which were examined by Peter Martyr. Martyr described one Aztec map that was "thirty feet long and not quite so wide" painted on white cotton cloth, and a smaller "native painting representing the town of Temistitan [Tenochtitlan], with its temples, bridges, and lakes." There is reason to believe they were the original maps from which these were derived (Rosenwald Collection no. 654, Rare Book and Special Collections Division).

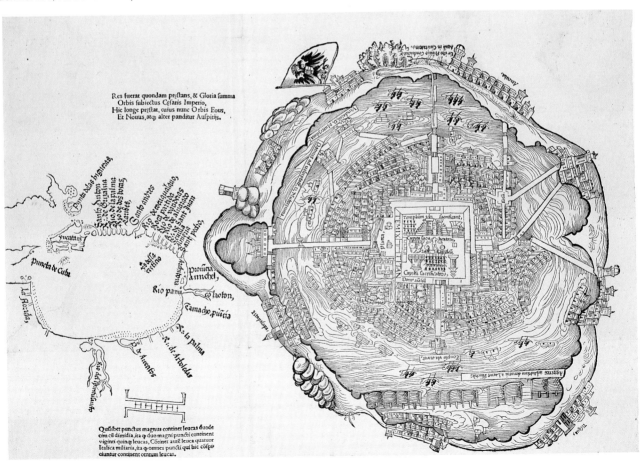

tween the mind-sets of Columbus and Montezuma above, so here we can reflect on the marked similarities existing between the Aztec and medieval European views of the universe. The European concept of a disklike tripartite world made up of Asia, Europe, and Africa, all surrounded by the endless waters of the ocean sea was shown to be epitomized in the T-O map shown in Chapter 2. Like the Europeans, the Aztecs believed that the earth was surrounded by a great expanse of water. The waters extended to the four corners and eventually rose to the heavens like an unascendable wall. Each of the four quadrants of this celestial space was in turn supported by one of the principal gods who held the heavens aloft.

This cosmic order came into being when the four creator dieties dispersed the all-flooding primordial waters, graded four roads to the center of the earth, and then lifted the sky. Predictably the Aztecs' capital, Tenochtitlan, was built at the center of the resulting four-quartered universe to receive the fullest benefit flowing from the forces and dieties of cosmic space. As Fray Diego Durán wrote, it was the navel of the cosmos.

Although many authorities have expressed the opinion that this engraved image of Tenochtitlan is "European" in its essentials there is evidence indicating that it retains many of the Indian characteristics of the lost Aztec original on which it is based. Peter Martyr was genuinely impressed when he was shown what may have been that original by Cortés's lieutenant, Juan de Ribera. In his "Fifth Decade" Martyr told of "numerous maps" Ribera brought from Mexico with other treasures for presentation to Emperor Charles V. One of these was "a native painting representing the town of Temestitan, with its temples, bridges, and lakes."[10]

Martyr's description of the architectural styles of Tenochtitlan's buildings, before their burning and destruction by Cortés and his Indian allies, suggests that the engraving retains those details from the original Indian depiction. In discussing the zoos and aviaries present in Montezuma's capital, Martyr wrote, "some day the pleasure houses will be rebuilt. They were constructed of stone from the foundations, finished with *crenaux* like a fortress."[11] The dwellings were also built with stone first stories with the upper living spaces "built by baked or sundried brick, mixed with beams." Roofs were not tiled but were protected with "a sort of bituminous earth" or tar. As can be seen from these brief descriptions, Tenochtitlan's built environment was not radically different from that found in many contemporary European urban settings. There appears to have been considerably less "Europeanizing" of the original Aztec map of Tenochtitlan than most published experts have assumed.

Even the archetypical Spanish conquistador, Cortés, admitted that the Templo Mayor or Great Temple was of such "great size and magnificence" that "no human tongue could describe it." In spite of this he continued "for . . . within the precincts, which are surrounded by a very high wall, a town of some five hundred inhabitants could easily be built." And finally he wrote: "There are as many as forty towers, all of which are so high that in the case of the largest there are fifty steps leading up the main part of it; and the most important of these towers is higher than that of the cathedral of Seville."[12]

Fray Diego Durán recounted the description of Tenochtitlan that had been given to him by "the first conquerors to arrive in this land." These "trustworthy and reliable" informants:

assured me that the day they entered the City of Mexico, when they saw the height and grandeur of the temples, they thought them castellated fortresses, splendid monuments and defenses of the city, or castles or royal dwelling places, crowned with turrets and watchtowers. Such were the glorious heights which could be seen from afar![13]

With available eye-witness testimony like this it is exceedingly difficult to deny that the so-called Cortés map, whoever its author may have been, depicts the pre-Conquest architecture and condition of Tenochtitlan.

Another unexpected bit of evidence of European-appearing crenellated towers in aboriginal Meso-America is found in Ferdinand Columbus's *Life of the Admiral*. Ferdinand described how the tatoo designs on the Indians he encountered with his father on the coast of Honduras included "lions . . . deer . . . turreted castles, and . . . a variety of other figures."[14]

THE INCAS

Like the Aztecs of Mexico, the Incas of Peru were possessed of a world view that pervaded most areas of their lives. Space limitations will permit little more than a highly selective review of a few aspects of that world view in this chapter. One of the most accessible and eloquent authorities who wrote on the Inca world view was himself half Inca. In his Foreword to *Royal Commentaries of the Incas*, historian Arnold J. Toynbee wrote of its author, Garcilaso de la Vega: "thanks to his mixed Andean-European descent and to his initiation into both his ancestral traditions— a double education, which was the privilege, or burden, of his Mestizo blood—Garcilaso was able to serve, and did serve, as an interpreter or mediator between two different cultures that had suddenly been brought into contact with each other."[15] Just as author Garcilaso de la Vega, son of an Inca princess and Spanish conqueror of noble lineage, served his own generation so he can serve the reader of today as both a product of and commentator on the climactic period of the first encounters between the culture of early sixteenth-century Spain and the Inca Empire.

Through Garcilaso we can discover that Cuzco, like the Aztec capital, was designed and built to enshrine in stone and architecture the essence of the Inca world view. In an unnecessarily apologetic tone the Mestizo author informed his European readers concerning the sophistication of Incan astronomy:

But for all their simplicity, the Incas realized that the sun completed its course in a year, which they called huata . . . The ordinary people reckoned the years by harvests. They understood also the summer and winter solstices; these were marked by large and visible signs consisting of eight towers built to the east and eight to the west of the city of Cuzco. They were arranged in sets of four: two small ones three times the height of a man stood between the two larger. The small ones were set eighteen or twenty feet apart, and at the same distance from them stood the larger, which were much higher than Spanish watchtowers. The larger towers were observatories from which the smaller could be more easily watched. The space between the small towers by which the Sun passed in rising and setting was the point of the solstices. The towers of the east corresponded with those of the west, according to whether it was the summer or winter solstice, an Inca stood at a certain point at sunrise and sunset, and watched whether the sun rose and set between the two small towers to the east and west. In this way they established the solstices in their astrology.[16]

The equinoxes also were observed "with great solemnity" by the sun-worshipping Incas.

Garcilaso described how these feast days were similarly determined through use of architecture:

To ascertain the time of the equinoxes they had splendidly carved stone columns erected in the squares or courtyards before the temples of the Sun. When the priests felt that the equinox was approaching, they took careful daily observations of the shadows cast by the columns. The columns stood in the middle of great rings filling the whole extent of the squares or spaces. Across the middle of a ring a line was drawn from east to west by a cord, the two ends being established by long experience. They could follow the approach of the equinox by the shadow of the column cast on this line, and when the shadow fell exactly along the line from sunrise and at midday the sun bathed all sides of the column and cast no shadow at all, they knew that the day was the equinox. Then they decked the columns with all the flowers and aromatic herbs they could find, and placed the throne of the Sun on it, saying on that day the Sun was seated on the column in all his full light. Consequently they especially worshipped the Sun on that day with a greater display of rejoicing and celebration than usual, and offered to him rich presents of gold, silver, precious stones, and other valuable things.[17]

The territorial growth of the empire resulted in an unforeseen benefit to the Incas' understanding of the cosmos. As Garcilaso noted:

The Inca kings and their *amautas* or philosophers discovered as they extended their provinces, that the nearer they approached the equator, the smaller was the shadow cast by the column at midday. They therefore venerated the columns more and more as they were nearer to the city of Quito, and were especially devoted to those of that city itself and in its neighborhood as far as the sea, where the sun is in a plumb-line, as bricklayers say, and shows no shadow at all at midday. For this reason they were held in the greatest veneration, it being thought that they afforded the Sun, the seat he liked best, since there he sat straight up and elsewhere on one side.[18]

Like the temples and monuments central to the Aztecs' world view and religion, the astronomical towers and columns of the Inca cities were "pulled down and broken to pieces" by the Spanish conquerors "because the Indians worshipped them idolatrously."

Inca map skills appear to have been in no way inferior to those of the Aztecs. Garcilaso de la Vega wrote of scale models that were constructed to depict accurately the geography and land-use patterns of cities and provinces. A model of Cuzco and part of its surrounding area was described as done:

in clay, pebbles, and sticks . . . to scale with the squares, large and small; the streets broad and narrow; the districts and houses, even the most obscure; and the three streams that flow through the city, marvelously executed. The countryside with high hills and low, flats and ravines, rivers and streams with their twists and turns were all wonderfully rendered, and the best cosmographers in the world could not have done it better.[19]

Cuzco, like Tenochtitlan, was planned and built as a nexus to the cosmos. Perhaps because he was a Catholic and long-time resident of Andalusia in Spain when he wrote his *Royal Commentaries*, Garcilaso de la Vega chose to secularize the motivations underlying Cuzco's pre-Conquest city plan. In a chapter he titled "The City Contained the Description of the Whole Empire," Garcilaso wrote of how "anyone who contemplated the wards and the dwellings of the numerous and varied tribes who had settled in them beheld the whole empire at once, as if in a looking glass or a cosmographic plan."[20] The "wards" making up Cuzco were divided "according to the four parts of their empire," a division that "dated back to the first Inca, Manco Cápac." As his empire grew through military victories he ordered "that the savages he had subjugated should be settled according to their places of origin, those from the east to the east, those from the west to the west, and so on."

When Cuzco was young "the dwellings of the first subjects were thus disposed in a circle within the limits of the town." As infilling took place by people of status from the outlying provinces, the location of their houses relative to one another reinforced the symbolic character of the city. As Garcilaso explained "if a chief's province was to the right of his neighbor's, he built his house to the right; if to the left, he built it to the left, and if behind, he built his house behind."

The Incas of Peru, like the North American Indians John Lederer described above, made effective use of a mnemonic device formed of colored and knotted cords called a quipu. In his *Letter to a King: A Picture History of the Inca Civi-*

lization, the Incan Indian Don Felipe Huamán Poma de Ayala included the following discussion of the quipu's use:

Both the Inca and his Council of the Realm were served by secretaries, some of whom belonged to my family in past times, and my ancestor the Incap rantin or Viceroy also had his own secretary. Such people were highly esteemed because of their ability to use the quipu. The secretaries calculated dates, recorded instructions, received information from messengers and kept in touch with their colleagues who used the quipu in all parts of the country. They accompanied the rulers and judges on important visits, recording decisions and contracts with such skill that the knots in their cords had the clarity of written letters.[21]

With such an effective mnemonic in wide use it is not surprising to find early Spaniards commenting on the absence of a written form of language in Peru similar to what they had found in Mexico.

NORTH AMERICAN INDIANS

In spite of the great diversity that characterized them, the Indians living beyond the regions of America's great empire builders appear to have shared broadly similar views of the world and cosmos in which they existed. To be sure there was "a dazzling complexity" in the belief systems that grew out of these shared outlines of the universal scheme of things. As one leading ethnohistorian has noted, "it is a complexity that has a system behind it, so that complex appearances can often be accounted for in terms of a few basic categories and principles."[22]

From the evidence available it appears that all or most Indians at the time of first European contact conceived of their world as consisting of a huge island surrounded by water. Above this world was the inverted bowl of the sky which rose at dawn and fell at dusk so that the night and day resulted. When the sun was within the

The Indian Village of Secoton, in eastern North Carolina, engraved by Theodor de Bry from a painting by John White. White was one of the company sent by Sir Walter Raleigh to establish an English colony on Roanoke Island in 1585. The engraving is close to White's original painting with the exception of details de Bry added to fill in empty areas. Certain small features, that are not distinct in the paintings, are engraved with precision and serve to enhance interpretation of White's eye-witness depiction of the Indians and their village. While White may have used his artistic license in grouping and regularizing the features and activities he pictured, nothing included here appears to be anything but accurate and true to life as he saw it. This engraving by de Bry could serve as a visual summary or icon of Indian life and the aboriginal landscape of much of Eastern North America at the time of Contact encounters. White's original paintings are in the British Library and have been published in full color (T. de Bry, Virginia, 1620, Rare Book and Special Collections Division).

vault of the sky it was day and when he or she returned to the place of beginning he or she was on the outside and night resulted.

If there is a single term that can be said to epitomize both Indian and European belief systems during the Age of Discovery it is *order*. The conscious desire to create a sense of order in what otherwise appears to be a chaotic universe seems to be a human trait that holds for all races and cultures. Like their Old World counterparts, the Native Americans believed in an upper world which had heavenlike attributes which were structured, ordered, bounded, stable, and generally of the past, and on a grander scale than the things of the here and now world around them.

Much of the ritual and symbology that entered into almost all phases of Indian life was aimed at achieving a balance between the forces of their upper world and the contrasting lower world, wherein lay a horde of threatening opposites of the upper world. It was the domain of disorder, chaos and instability, and inverted properties, inhabited by ghosts, witches, monsters, and other powerful spirits.

A rich language of metaphor and symbol was invented by the many Indian societies as they developed their collective lifeways in the varied environmental settings of the Americas. The Cherokee Indians living in southern Appalachian valleys at the time of their first encounters with the Europeans have been chosen to exemplify what has been all too briefly discussed here. Ethnologist James Mooney devoted much of his long and productive career to collecting and publishing the largely oral histories and traditions of these internationally famous Native Americans. The following Cherokee story of creation is only a fragment of the corpus his work provides the modern reader:

How the World was Made. The earth is a great island floating in a sea of water, and suspended at each of the four cardinal points by a cord hanging down from the sky vault, which is of solid rock. When the world grows old and worn out, the people will die and the cords will break and let the earth sink down into the ocean, and all will be water again. The Indians are afraid of this.

When all was water, the animals were above in [the Upper World], beyond the arch; but it was very much crowded, and they were wanting more room. They wondered what was below the water, and at last . . . "Beaver's Grandchild," the little Water-beetle, offered to go and see if it could learn. It darted in every direction over the surface of the water, but could find no firm place to rest. Then it dived to the bottom and came up with some soft mud, which began to grow and spread on every side until it became the island which we call the earth. It was afterward fastened to the sky with four cords, but no one remembers who did this.

At first the earth was flat and very soft and wet. The animals were anxious to get down, and sent out different birds to see if it was yet dry, but they found no place to alight and came back again to [the Upper World]. At last it seemed to be time, and they sent out the Buzzard and told him to go and make ready for them. This was the Great Buzzard, the father of all the buzzards we see now. He flew all over the earth, low down near the ground, and it was still soft. When he reached the Cherokee country, he was very tired, and his wings began to flap and strike the ground, and whenever they struck the earth there was a valley, and where they turned up again there was a mountain. When the animals above saw this, they were afraid that the whole world would be mountains, so they called him back, but the Cherokee country remains full of mountains to this day.

When the earth was dry and the animals came down, it was still dark, so they got the sun and set it in a track to go every day across the island from east to west, just overhead. It was too hot this way, and . . . the Red Crawfish had his shell scorched a bright red, so that his meat was spoiled; and the Cherokee do not eat it. The conjurers put the sun another hand-breadth higher in the air, but it was still too hot. They raised it another time, and another, until it was seven hand-breadths high and just under the sky arch. Then it was right, and they left it so. This is why the conjurers call the highest place . . . "the seventh height," because it is seven hand-breadths above the earth. Every day the sun goes along under this arch, and returns at night to the upper side to the starting place.

There is another world under this, and it is like ours in everything—animals, plants, and people— save that the seasons are different. The streams that come down from the mountains are the trails by which we reach this underworld, and the springs at their heads are the doorways by which we enter it, but to do this one must fast and go to water and have one of the underground people for a guide. We know that the seasons in the underworld are different from ours, because the water in the springs is always warmer in winter and cooler in summer than the outer air.

When the animals and plants were first made— we do not know by whom—they were told to watch and keep awake for seven nights, just as young men now fast and keep awake when they pray to their medicine. They tried to do this, and nearly all were awake through the first night, but the next night several dropped off to sleep, and the third night others were asleep, and then others, until, on the seventh night, of all the animals only the owl, the [cougar], and one or two more were still awake. To these were given the power to see and to go about in the dark, and to make prey of the birds and animals which must sleep at night. Of the trees only the cedar, the pine, the spruce, the holly, and the laurel were awake to the end, and to them it was given to be always green and to be greatest for medicine, but to the others it was said: "Because you have not endured to the end you shall lose your hair every winter."

Men came after the animals and plants. At first there were only a brother and sister until he struck her with a fish and told her to multiply, and so it was. In seven days a child was born to her, and thereafter every seven days another, and they increased very fast until there was danger that the world would not keep them. Then it was made that a woman should have only one child in a year, and it has been so ever since.[23]

Regrettably none of the European participants in initial encounters between Native Americans and Europeans were trained ethnologists and, as a consequence, most of their available written accounts lack the depth and richness of the materials collected by Mooney and his fellows in the second half of the last century. Enough was captured, however, in many initial encounters to provide tantalyzing glimpses of the richness of Indian world views and geographical understanding.

More typical of encounter accounts of Native American world views would be the one recorded by Fr. Chrestien Le Clercq based on his experiences with the Micmac Indians of eastern Canada's islands and peninsulas. When Le Clercq was residing with this tribe in the 1670s there was no generally accepted theory to explain the origin of New World populations. "It seems," he wrote, "as if this secret must be reserved solely to the Indians, and that from them alone one ought to learn all the truth about it."[24] Fortunately Le Clercq shared what he was able to learn:

They have . . . some dim and fabulous notion of the creation of the world, and of the deluge. They say that when the sun, which they have always recognised and worshipped as their God, created all this great universe, he divided the earth immediately into several parts, wholly separated one from the other by great lakes: that in each part he caused to be born one man and one woman, and they multiplied and lived a very long time: but that having become wicked along with their children, who killed one another, the sun wept with grief thereat, and the rain fell from the heaven in such great abundance that the waters mounted even to the summit of the rocks, and of the highest and most lofty mountains. This flood, which, say they, was general over all the earth, compelled them to set sail in their bark canoes, in order to save themselves from the raging depths of this general deluge. But it was in vain, for they all perished miserably through a violent wind which overturned them, and overwhelmed them in this horrible abyss, with the exception of certain old men and of certain women who had been the most virtuous and the best of all Indians. God came then to console them for the death of their relatives and their friends, after which he let them live upon the earth in a great and happy tranquility, granting them therewith all the skill and inginuity necessary for capturing beavers and moose in as great number as were needed for their substance.[25]

If this has a "sanitized" ring to it the reason is easily found. In Fr. Le Clercq's words, he omitted "certain other wholly ridiculous circumstances" of the Indian's creation story "because they do not bear at all upon a secret which is unknown to men, and reserved to God alone." Priest that he was, Le Clercq felt compelled to strip the metaphorical and supernatural trappings from the Indians' mythology and left only its skeleton postured in a crudely Catholic form. In this, Le Clercq's account is typical rather than exceptional.

As in the cases of the Aztecs and Incas, discussed above, the Indians of North America constructed towns and structures as metaphors of their views of the world and cosmos. Space limitations restrict us to a single example selected from the study of the Delaware Indian Big House Ceremony published by anthropologist Frank G. Speck. At the core of the ceremony was the metaphorical message embodied in the lodge structure within which the twelve-day ceremony took place. Speck wrote:

The Big House stands for the Universe; its floor, the earth; its four walls, the four quarters; its vault, the sky dome, atop which resides the Creator in his indefinable supremacy. To use Delaware expressions, the Big House being the universe, the center post is the staff of the Great Spirit with its foot upon the earth, its pinnacle reaching to the hand of the Supreme Deity. The floor of the Big House is the flatness of the earth upon which sit the three grouped divisions of mankind, the human social groupings in their appropriate places; the eastern door is the point of sunrise where day begins and at the same time the symbol of the beginnings of things, the western door the point of sunset and symbol of termination; the north and south walls assume the meaning of respective horizons; the roof of the temple is the visible sky vault. The ground beneath the Big House is the realm of the underworld while above the roof lie the extended planes or levels, twelve in number, stretched upward to the abode of the "Great Spirit, even the Creator," as Delaware form puts it. Here we might speak of the carved face images, . . . the representations of the center pole being the visible symbols of the Supreme Power, those on the upright posts, three on the north wall and three on the south wall, the manitu of these respective zones; those on the eastern and western door posts, those of the east and west. . . . But the most engrossing allegory of all stands forth in the concept of the White Path, the symbol of the transit of life, which is met with in the oval, hard-troden dancing path outlined on the floor of the Big House, from the east door passing to the right down the north side past the second fire to the

west door and doubling back on the south side of the edifice around the eastern fire to its beginning. This is the path of life down which man wends his way to the western door where all ends. Its correspondent exists, I assume, in the Milky Way, where the passage of the soul after death continues in the spirit realm. As the dancers in the Big House ceremony wend their stately passage following the course of the White Path they "push something along," meaning existence, with their rhythmic tread. Not only the passage of life, but the journey of the soul after death is symbolically figured in the ceremony.[26]

Of all the Contact encounters between Europeans and Native Americans one of the most revealing took place in 1607, between Capt. John Smith and Powhatan's Indians of eastern Virginia. While foraging for food the nearly starved Smith was taken captive and brought to "Opechankanough, King of Pamaunkee." To gain the chief's favor Smith gave him "a round Ivory double compass Dyal." The Indians "marvailed at the playing of the Fly and Needle, which they could see so plainely, and yet not touch . . . because of the glasse that covered them."[27]

Anxious to keep his captors' minds off torture or other unpleasant occupations, Smith began instructing the Indians on "the roundnesse of the earth, and skies, the spheare of the Sunne, Moone, and Starres, and how the Sunne did chase the night round about the world continually; the greatnesse of the Land and Sea, the diversitie of Nations, varietie of complexions and how we were to them *Antipodes*, and many other such like matters . . ."[28]

In Smith's judgement, at the end of his discourse, the Indians "all stood as amazed with admiration." But, in view of what followed, this judgement should be challenged. As Smith's account continued, "notwithstanding, within an houre after they tyed him to a tree, and as many as could stand about him prepared to shoot him" with their bows and arrows. Rather than "amazed with admiration" the Indians were ready to dispatch Smith as an outsider whose

Theodor de Bry's engraving showing Pocahontas saving Capt. John Smith from his sentence to death by head bashing. Never one to waste space in his copper plate engravings, de Bry shows a sequence of the adventures Smith experiences as Powhatan's captive in 1607. In the background a throng of Indians, many with war clubs raised, are shown marching Smith to his death. On the left, the Indian with the death-dealing club is stopped in midswing to avoid hitting Pocahontas who has thrown herself across Smith to protect him from the blow. In the close-up vignette, de Bry has attempted to illustrate Smith's description of the Indian ceremonial discourse explaining their trencherlike world view. Notice the circles of grain and corn around the fire and the cloaked Indian laying sticks in the circles. Although Smith wrote of "a bunch of small stickes prepared for that purpose," de Bry chose to show a bundle of faggot-sized sticks. The Indian with outstretched arms may represent Powhatan "strayning his armes and hands with such violence that he sweat, and his veynes swelled" (Theodor de Bry, America, Part XIII (1634), Rare Book and Special Collections Division).

world view was unintelligible and potentially offensive with respect to their own. At the last moment, however, the Chief, "holding up the Compass in his hand," gave the order to keep Smith alive. He was marched to their "Towne" where "all the women and children staring" beheld him.

Smith was then made to witness a symbolic three-dance ritual which he described in detail as follows:

the souldiers first all in fyle performed the forme of a *Bissone* so well as could be; and on each flanke, officers as Serieants to see them keepe their orders. A good time they continued this exercise, and then cast themselves in a ring, dauncing in such severall Postures, and singing and yelling out such hellish notes and screeches; being strangely painted, every one his quiver of Arrowes, and at his back a club; on his arme a Fox or an Otters skinne, or some such matter for his vambrace; their heads and shoulders painted red, with Oyle and *Pocones* mingled together, which Scarlet-like colour made an exceeding handsome shew; his

Bow in his hand, and the skinne of a Bird with her wings abroad dryed, tyed on his head, a peece of copper, a white shell, a long feather, with a small rattle growing at the tayles of their snakes tyed to it, or some such like toy.[29]

After three similar dances the Indians departed and Smith was led away to a longhouse "where thirtie or fortie tall fellowes did guard him."

Smith was then taken on a long journey to Powhatan's other Indian towns along the Rapahannock and Potomac rivers before being returned to the principal seat "Pamaunkee." Here the Indians "entertained him with most strange and fearfull coniurations [conjurations]; *As if neare led to hell, Amongst the Devils to dwell.*" What Smith was about to receive from his captors was his final lesson on the true nature of the cosmos. His journey through the many flourishing Indian towns of Virginia was doubtlessly to acquaint him with their world and power in the here and now. The ceremonies he described in the following extract provided him a view of their Upper and Lower Worlds:

early in a morning a great fire was made in a long house, and a mat spread on the one side, as on the other; on the one they caused him [Smith] to sit, and all the guards went out of the house, and presently came skipping in a great grim fellow, all painted over with coale, mingled with oyle; and many Snakes and Wesels skins stuffed with mosse, and all their tayles tyed together, so as they met on the crown of his head in a tassell; and round about the tassell was as a Coronet of feathers, the skins hanging round about his head, backe, and shoulders, and in a manner covered his face; with a hellish voyce, and a rattle in his hand. With most strange gestures and passions he began his invocation, and environed the fire with a circle of meale; which done, three more such like devils came rushing in with the like antique tricks, painted halfe blacke, halfe red; but all their eyes were painted white, and some red stroakes like Mutchato's [mustachios], along their cheekes: round about him those fiends daunced a pretty while, and then came in three more as ugly as the rest: with red eyes and white stroakes over their blacke faces; at last they all sat downe right against him;

three of them on the one hand of the chiefe Priest, and three on the other. Then all with their rattles began a song, which ended, the chiefe Priest layed down five wheat cornes: then strayning his armes and hands with such violence that he sweat, and his veynes swelled, he began a short Oration: at the conclusion they all gave a short groane; and then layd downe three grains more. After that, began their song againe and then another Oration, ever laying downe so many cornes as before, till they had twice encircled the fire; that done they took a bunch of little stickes prepared for that purpose, continuing still their devotion, and at the end of every song and Oration, they layd downe a stick betwixt the divisions of Corne. Till night, neither he [Smith] nor they did either eate or drinke; and then they feasted merrily, with the best provisions they could make. Three days they used this Ceremony; the meaning whereof they told him, was to know if he intended them well or no. The circle of meale signified their Country, the circles of corne the bounds of the Sea, and the stickes his [Smith's] Country. *They imagined the world to be flat and round, like a trencher; and they in the middest.*[30]

It is clear that the Indians regarded Smith as someone of high status and worthy of such an extended ritual discourse. It is to be regretted that no one was on hand to provide him with a full translation of the remarkable ceremony he was fortunate enough to witness.

Were such a full account available it might assist in unraveling the mystery of the artifact known as "Powhatan's Mantle," a treasure of Oxford University's Ashmolean Museum. Powhatan's Mantle is a cloak fashioned of four tanned deerhides and decorated with thirty-seven figures made of small shell beads sewn onto the garment. It may have been the "gowne" Powhatan gave to Christopher Newport on May 23, 1607, to seal the military alliance they had agreed to. Anthropologist E. Randolph Turner III has suggested that the thirty-four small shell roundlets sewn on the mantle represent the districts under Powhatan's control.[31] It might be added that Capt. John Smith probably visited many if not all of those districts during his enforced walkabout organized by Opechankanough, Powhatan's half-brother and chief of Pamaunkee, who orchestrated his uncomprehended ceremonial introduction to the Indian world view.

When Smith and the original Virginians arrived to found Jamestown, Powhatan was making strenuous efforts to gain firm control over his subject tribes and fight off incursions by his enemies from afar. Rather than treating the Englishmen like gods or exotics, Powhatan attempted a strategy of incorporating them as useful elements in his geopolitical scheme for control over eastern Virginia. Even the famous head bashing from which heroine Pocahontas "saved" John Smith was, in all probability, the penultimate ceremony through which Smith was to become initiated into the kin-oriented society over which her father Powhatan held sway. The final ceremony took place two days after the Pocahontas "rescue" when a fearsome Powhatan "more like a devill than a man with some two hundred more as blacke as himselfe, came unto him [Smith] and told him now they were friends . . ." When Capt. John Smith's accounts of Virginia's first years are purged of their romantic hyperbole, heavy ethnocentric bias, and egocentric exaggeration, they reveal Powhatan to have been following a perfectly rational and intelligent strategy for dealing with a group of poorly organized but militarily threatening intruders who had strayed onto the stage of the socioterritorial drama formed by his efforts of chiefdom expansion.

Testimony concerning the geographical knowledge and cartographic ability of Powhatan's people abounds in the rich encounter literature that grew out of the Jamestown enterprise. In the tract titled "A relation of the Discovery of our River, from James Forte into the Maine: made by Captaine Christofer Newport: and sincerely writen and observed by a gent: of ye Colony," the adventures of an exploration party trying "to finde ye head of this

Ryver, the Lake mentyoned by others heretofore, the Sea againe, the Mountaynes Apalatsi, or some issue" are summarized. What Newport and his fellows were most hoping to find was an easy route to the ocean we now call the Pacific. Part of the motivation directing first Sir Walter Raleigh's colonists and then the Jamestown adventurers to the Carolina-Virginia coastal area was the lingering hope that the continent narrowed sufficiently in these latitudes to make a crossing to the Pacific feasible. Ever since Verrazano, in 1524, had reported the Carolina Outer Banks to be "an isthmus a mile in width and about two hundred long" separating the Atlantic from the "oriental sea . . . which goes about the extremity of India, China and Cathay," European maps either showed or hinted at the presence of a great gulf of the Pacific called Verrazano's Sea in these latitudes. Here is a clear case of a geographical misconception being as important in decision making as any true geographical fact.

As knowledge of the American Great Lakes began to permeate Europe the concept of Verrazano's Sea weakened so the Jamestown explorers had been charged with penetrating the backcountry to find whatever was there be it sea, lake, or mountains called "Apalatse." The famous map of Virginia which Capt. John Smith published in 1612 is one of several available in facsimile through the publication program of the Library of Congress. For its date, it is an astoundingly complete and accurate portrayal of the Chesapeake Bay tidewater region. When it is examined closely an extensive area in the upper right hand corner of the map from about 35°50' to 40°40' can be seen to be shaded to represent water—either the oriental sea or some great lake. Powhatan's enemies the "Massawomeks" are indicated as living in the vicinity of the unnamed water body.[32]

Gabriel Archer, who was the "gentleman" who wrote the "relaytion" of Newport's exploration party, told of how they proceeded upstream for about thirty-four miles above Jamestown when they encountered eight Indians, or as he called them "salvages," in a canoe. Through friendly words and gestures the explorers communicated their mission to the Indians and sought their assistance. Archer wrote that "one seemed to understand our intenyon, and offered with his foote to Describe the river to us."[33] Wishing to have a more permanent map than a toe tracing in the sand Archer "gave him a pen and paper (shewing first ye use) and he layd out the whole River from the *Chesseian* [Chesapeake] bay to the end of it so farr as passadge was for boats." In elaboration of what the Indian cartographer had drawn "he tolde us of two Islets in the Ryver we should passe by . . . and then come to an overfall of water, beyond that of two kyngdomes which the Ryver Runes by, and a grate Distance off, the Mountains Quiranh as he named them: beyond which by his relation is that which we expected."[34] This last being a veiled reference to the much sought but elusive western sea the Englishmen expected to find.

The exploration party, thus forewarned of what to expect, proceeded up the river soon coming to where "the shoare began to be full of greate Cobble stones, and higher land" at the inner margin of the Coastal Plain. Following the now narrowed river for another two miles they came to "the Ilet mentyoned which I call Turkey Ile." It is interesting to note that Turkey Island is still shown on maps as lying some miles downstream from Richmond.

Continuing upstream, Archer and the other explorers reached the town of "Arahatec," one of the chiefs owing allegiance to Powhatan. While being entertained by Arahatec they received news of Powhatan's pending arrival. When the great chief arrived all present save Arahatec and the Englishmen stood. "gyftes of dyvers sortes, as penny knyves, sheres, belles, beades, glasse toys &c." were showered on Powhatan. The great chief responded by appointing five Indians to guide the English up the river and sending messengers ahead to order that they be provided with food en route.

Before leaving Arahatec's town, Archer had the Indian cartographer with the dextrous foot draw the map of the river again, before "kyng Arahatec" for his evaluation. Archer and the others were doubtlessly overjoyed when Arahatec "in every thing consented to his Draught and it agreed with his first relatyon." Passing his test with flying colors the Indian was "found a faythfull fellow," and "appointed guyde for us."

Just below the low falls and rapids where Richmond, Virginia's capital, is now located the English explorers reached Powhatan's seat which Archer named "Pawatahs Towre [Towne]." It was situated on a high hill overlooking a cultivated floodplain near the river where "wheate, beane, peaze, tobacco, pompions, gourdes, Hempe, flaxe etc." were growing. When they were ushered into Powhatan's presence, Chief Arahatec extended a "friendly wellcome" and fed and entertained the Englishmen before settling down to more serious matters.

In the conference that followed Powhatan outlined his chiefdom in terms of all the Indian groups that "were frendes with him, and (to use his owne words) Cheisc, which is all one with him or under him." Under the heading *Chessipan* was the enemy and those towns subject to him. On hearing this Archer and the English "tooke occasion to signifye our Displeasure with them also." In effect they were taking Powhatan's cause as their own. Powhatan, described as "very well understanding by the words and signes we made," proceeded "of his own accord" to enter into a formal league of friendship with the English. At the conclusion of Powhatan's oration, Captain Newport "kyndly embraced" the alliance, and, "for concluding therof," Powhatan "gave him [Newport] his gowne, put it on his back himselfe, and laying his hand on his breast saying *Wingapoh Chemuze* (the most kynde words of salutatyon that may be) he satt Downe."[35] Powhatan had good cause to be pleased with his alliance, for Newport also promised to defeat his enemies the *Wiroans* and *Monanacha* and make him "king" of their country by bringing 500 English soldiers to his aid in the coming autumn!

Continuing up the river the explorers were not long in reaching the falls of the James River "in which fall it maketh Divers little Iletts, on which might be placed 100 water milnes [mills] for any uses." Since the boats would no longer be of use they returned to Powhatan's seat and in the evening enjoyed an informal meal with the chief and his people. After the dinner during which Powhatan ate "very freshly of our meat, Dranck of our beere, Aquavite, and Sack" the Englishmen quizzed him about the river. They wanted to know how far it was to the headsprings "where they gat their Copper, and their Iron." Not deigning to answer their questions at that point, Powhatan promised to meet them at the falls the next day.

At the falls the English, in company with their friendly Indian cartographer, awaited Powhatan's arrival. When he made his appearance the Indian mapmaker-guide coached them in the proper shouts of welcome that Powhatan's station demanded. Sitting on the bank overlooking the falling waters of the James River, Powhatan launched into a discourse plainly aimed at discouraging any further penetration of the interior by the English. Not convinced of their reliability, the cautious Indian did not want to chance their meeting his enemies. As Archer wrote, "he began to tell us of the tedyous travell we should have if wee proceeded any further, that it was a Daye and a halfe Jorney to *Monanacah*, and if we went to *Quiranck*, we should get no vittailes and by tyred, and sought by all meanes to Disswade our Captayne from going any further: Also he tolde us that the *Monanacah*

was his Enmye, and that he came Downe at the fall of the leafe and invaded his Countrye."[36]

Realizing how important Powhatan's goodwill was to their survival, Captain Newport reluctantly cut short the exploration and ordered the party back to their boats. Before departing the neighborhood that would one day become Richmond, however, he selected an islet "at the mouth of the falls" and "set up a Crosse with this inscription *Jacobus Rex.* 1607. and his owne name below." To the disappointment of the Englishmen, Powhatan and his followers departed before the erection of the cross and so missed the ceremony and cheers that followed a prayer of dedication. In an effort to transmit word of the nature and significance of the ceremony to Powhatan in terms designed to flatter him, Newport fabricated the following prevarication concerning the cross which he told to the Indian guide named Nauiraus, who was known to be the brother-in-law of Chief Arahatec: "Our Captayne told him that the two Armes of the Crosse signifyed king *Powatah* and himselfe, the fastening of it in the myddest was their united Leaug, and the shoute the reverence he Dyd to *Pawatah*, which cheered Nauiraus not a little."

Above its falls the river gave the appearance of flowing through very rocky and hilly terrain. Before leaving the fall zone of the James River Archer quizzed the Indian guide-cartographer concerning the river's course on the Piedmont. The map drawing "kynde Consort," as Archer called him, told them "that after a Dayes jorney or more, this River Devydes it selfe into two branches which both come from the mountaynes *Wuirank*." "Here," the reliable Indian informant, "whispered with me that theer *caquassan* [copper] was gott in the bites of Rockes and betweene Cliffes in certayne vaynes."

The Indians that John Smith and the Jamestown pioneers encountered were at an intermediate position on our hypothetical scale of social and material development. It is clear from the accounts that their high degree of social stratification was made possible by their productive agricultural system. The Jamestown accounts also make plain the fact that it was the agricultural surpluses of Powhatan's tribesmen that made the colony's early survival possible. Near the opposite end of such a hypothetical scale of Indian societal evolution would be found tribal groups like the Micmacs of Canada's Gaspé region.

The Micmacs followed a largely hunting-fishing-gathering way of life. Their homes were wigwams covered with sewn birchbark sheets that Father Le Clercq described as "so light and portable, that our Indians roll them up like a piece of paper, and carry them thus upon their backs wheresoever it pleases them."[37] Such portability was necessary for their seasonal movements—near the seacoast in summer and in the forests in winter.

Little if any sociopolitical stratification existed in a society where "it is the business of the head of the family, exclusively over all others, to give orders that camp be made where he pleases, and that it be broken when he wishes."[38] Leaders, although referred to as chiefs, had little or no coercive power over other members of the group. According to Fr. Chrestien Le Clercq, who lived among the Micmacs in the 1670s, there were only two or three individual Indians who had any sort of authority, and that was feeble at best. The "chief" he appeared to be most familiar with oversaw the assignment of hunting territories, held the band's collective fur harvest, and disbursed their material goods according to need, more in the role of a respected elder than someone with true coercive power.

In spite of these facts, the Micmacs appear to have been the equals of Aztecs or Powhatans when it came to their ability to draw excellent maps. Le Clercq wrote: "They have much ingenuity in drawing upon bark a kind of map which marks exactly all the rivers and streams

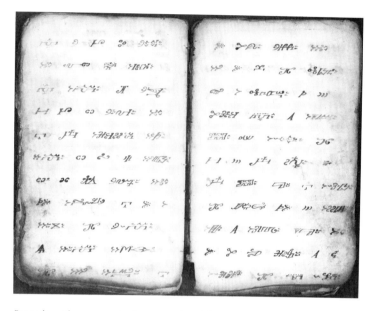

Pages from the manuscript known as the "Micmac Prayer Book." Although the provenance of this document is difficult to determine, it appears to be written in a system of symbols or "hieroglyphic" characters invented by Fr. Chrestien Le Clercq when he ministered to the tribe in the 1670s. Le Clercq found the language spoken by his congregation to be "beautiful and very rich in its expressions" and their "speeches . . . always very elegant." As he began teaching the children their prayers Le Clercq noticed that some of them "made marks with charcoal upon birch bark, and counted these off as they repeated each word of the prayers." Building on this foundation Le Clercq proceeded to formalize a scheme in which, "each arbitrary letter signifies a particular word and sometimes two together" (Micmac Prayer Book, Manuscript Division).

of a country of which they wish to make a representation. They mark all the places thereon exactly and so well that they make use of them successfully, and an Indian who possesses one makes long voyages without going astray."[39]

Although he does not discuss the Micmac maps in detail it seems probable that they were, like most Native American maps, based on a topologic rather than a Euclydian geometry. This conclusion can be supported by what Father Le

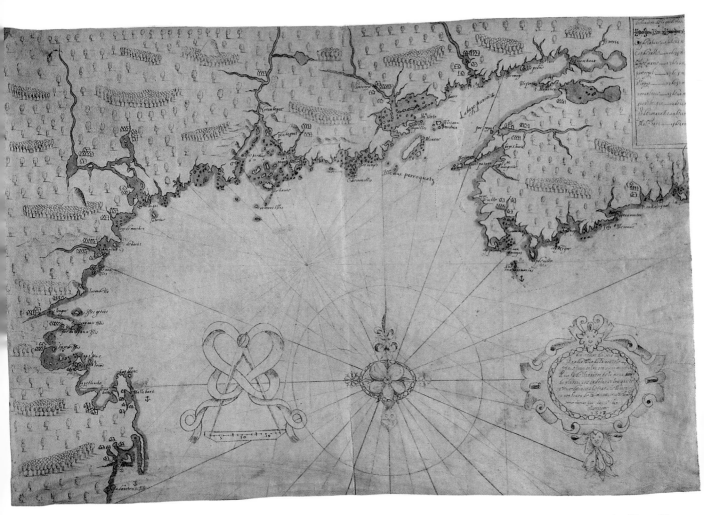

Samuel de Champlain, founder of New France, personally prepared this elegant chart of the Gulf of Maine for presentation to King Henry IV. Rarely can one study original maps drawn by explorers of Champlain's stature. Most of the great maps from the Age of Discovery were drawn by professional cartographers, working from notes and sketches, and engraved by professional engravers for printing in multiple copies. Beyond its rarity, this chart is of particular interest because Champlain incorporated Indian cartography and geographical information along with his own direct observations in its compilation. The chart includes the area of the Massachusetts coast where Champlain had local Indians draw a map with charcoal he provided them. One of the great cartographic treasures in North America, this unique vellum chart came to the Library of Congress as part of the bequest from Henry Harrisse, the distinguished lawyer, bibliographer, and historian of discovery and exploration (Harrisse Collection, Geography and Map Division).

Clercq wrote with respect to distance as it was reckoned by his Indian companions: "They reckon distances only by the points and capes which are found along the rivers or coasts. They count and measure them also by the length of time which they take in their voyages, and by the number of nights which they are obliged to sleep on the way, not counting either the day of their departure or that of their arrival."[40]

Most readers have had experience with maps like these; i.e., maps depicting places in terms of travel time rather than some absolute distance, like miles or kilometers. Many city subway or bus route maps sacrifice true directions and distances for ease of rider comprehension. In a word, they too are topologic maps.

To date one of the least explored topics in the literature of the Age of Discovery is the role played by Native Americans as guides and cartographers for the Europeans bent on exploring their home territories. It is abundantly clear from the narratives and journals of scores of those European explorers, from Columbus on-ward, that Native American cartographers and guides in every region of the New World con-tributed immeasurably to outlining and filling in the detail of the New World map. Even be-fore they landed, Europeans like Bartholomew Gosnold took Indians aboard their ships where they chalked accurate sketch maps of the ap-proaching coast and inlets on hatch covers or decks.

Samuel de Champlain, "founder of New France," wrote of how comprehensive and help-ful Indian geographical intelligence and map-ping was as he pushed his exploration up the St. Lawrence River valley:

I had much conversation with them regarding the source of the great river and regarding their [the Huron] country, about which they told me many things, both of the rivers, falls, lakes, and lands, and of the tribes living there, and whatever is found in those parts. Four of them assured me that they had seen a sea, far from their country, but that the way to it was difficult, both on account of enemies, and of the wild stretches to be crossed in order to reach it. They told me also that during the preceding winter some Indians had come from the direction of Florida, beyond the country of the Iroquois, who were familiar with our ocean, and friendly with these latter Indians. In short they spoke to me of these things in great detail, show-ing me by drawings all the places they had visited, taking pleasure in telling me about them. And as for myself, I was not weary of listening to them, because some things were cleared up about which I had been in doubt until they enlightened me about them.[41]

Even earlier, in 1605, while surveying the coasts of the Gulf of Maine for the vellum chart reproduced here, Champlain gained important information from Indians near Cape Ann in present day Massachusetts. Approaching the cape from the north Champlain wrote of how his party "caught sight of a canoe in which were five or six Indians."[42] The Indians approached the French pinnace for a closer look and then landed on the cape and began to dance. Cham-

plain went ashore and gave each of them a knife and some biscuit which, in his words, "caused them to dance better than ever."

After the Indians finished their dance, Cham-plain "made them understand as well as I could, that they should show me how the coast trended." To make his request clear to the In-dians Champlain used charcoal and drew the local bay and cape for them. The Indians, un-derstanding his need, took the charcoal and, as Champlain wrote, "they pictured me . . . another bay which they represented as very large."[43] This large bay is now known as Massa-chusetts Bay. Within their charcoal map outline of Massachusetts Bay the Indians "placed six pebbles at equal intervals," as Champlain wrote, "giving me thereby to understand that each one of these marks represented that number of chiefs and tribes." Much to the French explorer's satis-faction "they represented within the [map] a river which we had passed [the Merrimac], which is very long and has shoals."[44]

The flow of geographical intelligence from these New England Indians did not stop with their artfully crafted map. They went on to tell the French "that all those who lived in this re-gion cultivated the land and sowed seeds like the others we had previously seen." As the en-counter drew to a close the Indians departed to inform their fellows of the arrival of exotic white-skinned visitors from the north. "Having indicated to us the direction of their home," Champlain wrote, "they made signal-smokes to show us the site of their settlement."

As Champlain continued the reconnaissance of the Massachusetts coast and islands he found that he "recognized in this bay everything that the Indians at Island Cape [Cape Ann] had drawn for me."[45] It is hard to imagine a more favorable judgement of Native American geo-graphic and cartographic capability than this from the pen of Samuel de Champlain, explorer extraordinaire and founder of New France.

CHAPTER FOUR

CHRISTOPHER COLUMBUS FINDS THE WAY

First Encounters on the Islands in the Ocean Sea

First of all, the discovery of America, or of the Americans, is certainly the most astonishing encounter of our history.
*The Conquest of America,*Tzvetan Todorov

COLUMBUS'S RÉSUMÉ

Christopher Columbus was one of several Genoese navigators of his day familiar with the Atlantic facade of Europe and Northern Africa. His son claimed, and most experts believe, that he had voyaged aboard ships bound as far as Iceland, an important source of salted fish for Europe's Roman Catholics. If that claim is true, Columbus may well have gained some knowledge of the lore concerning the early Norse voyages to Greenland and beyond. Even if he had been aware of their early voyages, however, it probably would have done little or nothing to change his basic plan since, on the Behaim globe and presumably in Columbus's mind, Vinland would have lain comfortably near the northeasternmost corner of Asia. A good candidate for Vinland on the Behaim globe is a large island near the North Pole where according to the caption, "white falcons" were caught. As discussed in Chapter 2, most experts agree that the Behaim world map is close or identical to the map in Columbus's mind when he set out on his 1492 voyage.

Based on an analysis of Columbus's own statements, it can be concluded that he had sailed the full extent of the Mediterranean Sea from west to east, along the Atlantic coast of Africa as far as present day Ghana and probably north to England. He lived for a period in the Madeira Islands and was familiar with the Cape Verde and Canary groups. While it does not appear that he had sailed to the Azores Islands, Columbus was doubtlessly well acquainted with them through Portuguese informants. For his day, Columbus compiled an excellent résumé of navigational experience and accomplishments.

If there is one Columbus attribute on which all experts have come to an agreement, it is that he was an excellent navigator and ship handler.

HENRY THE NAVIGATOR

In his ambition to sail west to reach the wealth of the Indies, Columbus was walking in the footprints of Portugal's Prince Enrique—Henry the Navigator. Early in his own career Henry had set out to find "whether islands or a continent were to be found outside the world described by Ptolemy." Islands he had found, but no contact was made with any land of continental dimension except Africa by the time he died. Moorish control of the strait of Gibraltar had been broken by the conquest of Ceuta, but the eastern Mediterranean Sea lanes and commercial links overland to the Far East remained firmly under Moslem control.

Prince Henry, like so many Age of Discovery figures, is the subject of continuing controversy. Some experts see him as one of the first European leaders to realize that geographical knowledge gained by exploration could contribute to a country's betterment through expanded trade and commerce. Others paint him as a medieval-minded, second-rate leader who was unshaken in his belief in the legendary Prester John. In the twelfth century Prester John had emerged as the supposed author of a letter to either the Pope or Holy Roman Emperor in which he boasted of his superior wealth and power. His realm was so vast that in one direction his territory reached out four months' journey. In the other direction it was greater than anyone could tell. "Only if you could count the stars of the heaven and the sands of the sea would you be able to form an estimate of our dominion and our power," was one of the many fantastic claims attributed to the mysterious Prester John.[1]

Incredibly the legend of Prester John lived

A portrait of Christopher Columbus based on a painting by Laurens Lotto dated 1512, six years after the Admiral of the Ocean Sea died. Because it was painted while family members and friends who knew Columbus were on hand to criticize, many experts feel that this is a good likeness. No drawing or painting of Columbus from life is known to exist. In the biography attributed to Columbus's son Ferdinand, the Admiral is described as, "a well-built man of more than average stature, the face long, the cheeks somewhat high, his body neither fat nor lean. He had an aquiline nose and light-colored eyes: his complexion too was light and tending to bright red. In youth his hair was blonde, but when he reached the age of thirty, it all turned white" (Prints and Photographs Division).

on long after Henry's demise and Portugal's rounding of Africa. The fabled priest-king whom Henry supposedly hunted in Africa did not completely disappear from the European world view until the eighteenth century when an English traveler-explorer, James Bruce, journeyed to and reported on Abyssinia, as Ethiopia was then called.

THE TOSCANELLI MAP

The critics of Henry argue that Portugal's discoveries along Africa's west coast grew as accidents from his impractical schemes aimed at forming an alliance with the Christian King Prester John and leading another Crusade to free the Holy Land. They would have the reader believe it was not until long after Prince Henry died that the Portuguese, under King Alfonso V, set out deliberately to sponsor voyages around Africa to reach India by sea.

It was also at this time that the famous and controversial Florentine physician, Paolo del Pozzo Toscanelli, entered the Columbus story. Although many highly regarded scholars believe the episode to be a hoax and post facto invention, Columbus's son and biographer wrote "Master Paolo, physician . . . a Florentine and a contemporary of the Admiral's also played a large part in encouraging him to undertake his voyage."[2]

According to Ferdinand Columbus, Toscanelli sent his father a copy of a "Sea-chart" showing a route from Portugal to "the Indies where the spices grow" which he had prepared for the king of that country in 1474. The map was described by Toscanelli as showing the Atlantic coast "from Ireland on the north to the end of Guinea." "Directly west beyond those familiar coasts and the islands which lie on that route" was shown "the beginning of the Indies, with the islands and places at which you are

bound to arrive."[3] The King of Portugal and Columbus, in his turn, were advised not to "marvel at my calling 'west' the regions where the spices grow, although they are commonly called 'east'; because whoever sails westward will always find those lands in the west, while one who goes overland to the east will always find the same lands in the east." In a later letter Toscanelli was supposed to have written directly to Columbus, the Florentine physician pointed out that the route he was recommending would "appear still more plainly upon a sphere" than on the charts he had sent.

COLUMBUS IN PORTUGAL

Although there was a break in the schedule of voyages following Henry's death, by about 1470 the King of Portugal resumed sending out expeditions to make definite discoveries ever farther south along the African coast. By 1475 Cape Catherine, 2 degrees south of the equator, had been reached and in 1488 Bartholomew Dias reached and named the Cape of Good Hope. As Ferdinand Columbus makes amply clear, his father, having taken up residence in Lisbon in 1479, was intimately aware of these activities. Indeed the evidence indicates that Christopher, his father, and Bartholemew, his uncle, were in the business of preparing and selling marine charts in that busy Atlantic port.

When Columbus approached the King of Portugal to seek backing for his scheme to sail due west to the Indies, rather than south along the tropical African coasts, he was rebuffed and, according to Ferdinand, "grew angry" with the monarch. According to Columbus, the king secretly sent a caravel on the route "whither the Admiral had proposed to go" in order to avoid paying "the great rewards he demanded."[4] The surreptitious expedition, lacking people with Columbus's "knowledge, steadfastness, and ability," failed in its goal—a predictable outcome in the opinion of those sceptics who doubt that it took place. Not only did the king's explorers fail but, according to the Admiral, they returned to Lisbon "making fun of [his] enterprise and declaring that no land could be found in those waters."[5] Whether or not this episode was apocryphal, as some experts believe, it is reasonably certain that any Portuguese expedition to find lands in the west would have sailed from Lisbon to the Azores for final provisioning and fitting out. An attempt to sail west from the Azores was guaranteed to fail since the islands are squarely in the belt of prevailing westerly winds. Assuming it to have taken place, the westerlies doubtlessly beat back the king's secret expedition as it would any explorer sailing west in those latitudes.

COLUMBUS MOVES TO SPAIN

Never one to take an insult calmly Columbus decided to quit Lisbon and seek some other royal patron for his enterprise. His brother Bartholomew was dispatched to England where, after falling into the hands of pirates and many years of hardship, he is supposed to have "gained some renown through his maps" and had interviews with King Henry VII. If Ferdinand can be believed, the King of England was impressed by a world map Bartholomew Columbus presented to him in 1498. Indeed, it was claimed that the English king was moved to accept gladly the Admiral's terms and summoned him to his court. "But God had reserved that prize for Castile," Ferdinand wrote, "for by that time the Admiral had successfully completed his enterprise."[6]

In 1484, Christopher Columbus secretly departed Portugal, "fearing the King might seek to detain him." His destination was the rival kingdom of Castile "to try his fortune there." After very nearly persuading a wealthy Spanish count

to back his enterprise, Columbus came to the attention of Queen Isabela. It took a year of waiting until the would-be explorer of a new route to India gained an audience with the queen.

At the time of Columbus's arrival, the country now known as Spain did not exist. Rather, it was still in the process of unifying and consolidating in the aftermath of centuries spent pushing Moslem invaders back to Africa. In 711 A.D. a Moslem army crossed the narrow strait separating Western Europe from Africa and in the next several decades Moslem control was extended over almost the whole of the Iberian Peninsula. For the next seven centuries the dominant theme in Iberian history was the Christian *reconquista* (reconquest) of the peninsula. By the end of the thirteenth century only the Kingdom of Granada on the Mediterranean coast of Southern Spain remained in Moslem hands.

Along with the reconquest proceeded political consolidation. One of the most significant steps in the political unification of Spain was the marriage, in 1469, of Isabela, heiress to the crown of Castile, and Ferdinand, heir to the crown of Aragon. In practical terms this union left only two small Iberian areas plus Portugal not under their control. The area now known as the Basque region in the northern Pyrenees formed the small Kingdom of Navarre, and on the south coast was the last Moorish holdout the Kingdom of Granada. Navarre straddled the Pyrenees Mountains and was safely under the control of the Christian King of France, but Granada remained a challenge to the most Christian monarchs dedicated to the restoration of Christianity over the whole of Iberia.

The new sovereigns quickly began programs aimed at establishing their authority over the many provinces making up their now unified realm. Part of this process involved the reduction of the power of the great nobles and diverting taxes from their provincial treasuries to the royal coffers. As Ferdinand and Isabela worked to get a firm grip on political and fiscal control so they strove to gain a similarly firm hold on religious affairs. In the area of ecclesiastic appointments, for example, they blocked any papal attempts to appoint nonsubjects to high church offices in Spain. The church was thus made to serve as a strong support of their government. Ferdinand is reported to have said that, "what blood is to the human body religion is to the state."

In due course Granada became a major concern. Granada was a rich prize Ferdinand and Isabela wished to add to their increasingly centralized and powerful kingdom. The spirit and fervor of the *reconquista* was easy to reignite in a war against Muslim Granada. Finally, after a decade of fighting, in 1492, Granada the last Moorish stronghold surrendered to end the seven-century-long presence of Moslem control on the Iberian Peninsula. By the terms of the peace treaty Muslim citizens of Granada were allowed to continue to follow their religion. The intolerance and religious zeal that characterized the age, however, soon resulted in growing pressure to compel their conversion to Christianity. In 1502 a royal decree commanded all Moslems residing in Castile to embrace Christianity or leave the country. Many chose to abandon their property and migrate to North Africa, but the majority remained and made an outward show of accepting the new faith of their conquerors.

Jews in Spain had earlier been forced to adopt Christianity. Because many of the Jewish *conversos* (converts) were deemed lax in their Christian beliefs, courts of Inquisition had been instituted in 1478. It was the mission of the Inquisition to cleanse Spanish society of nonbelievers and backsliding *conversos*. Ironically, the day Columbus set sail, August 3, 1492, was the deadline for all Jews to leave Spain.

TRYING TO SELL THE ENTERPRISE

In view of these momentous preoccupations it is not surprising to find that Columbus was kept waiting in the backwater of Ferdinand and Isabela's court. From Columbus's perspective, however, it was a period of frustration and aggravation that seemed endless. As Ferdinand Columbus revealed, part of the frustration and delay was brought on by Columbus himself. Still smarting from the duplicity of Portugal's king, Columbus was more secretive than ever concerning his plan "fearing lest it be stolen from him in Castile as it had been in Portugal."[7] As a result the council of geographers Queen Isabela established to evaluate his enterprise had a difficult time in forming a judgement of it. The reports the monarchs received from the geographers "were as varied as their grasp of the subject and their opinions," wrote son Ferdinand.

Some of the geographers correctly argued that the world was much larger than Columbus was estimating. They felt that it might take as long as three years to sail across the ocean and others doubted that it could ever be navigated. If Columbus is to be believed, some of the queen's savants even argued that "one who left the hemisphere known to Ptolemy would be going downhill and so could not return"![8] The more Columbus explained the less they seemed to understand—they sound like good bureaucrats with orders to stall. In the end they "condemned the enterprise as vain and impossible and advised the Sovereigns that it did not conform with the dignity of such great princes to support a project resting on such weak foundations."[9]

Rather than refusing their support outright, the Spanish monarchs told Columbus that the war against Granada and other pressing matters would have to reach their conclusion before they could decide on his offer. Vexed and frustrated, Columbus considered leaving Spain to seek support from the French king. In the end, however, he took the advice of the head of the monastery at La Rabida and remained in Spain and "rejected the offers that other princes had made him." In company with his friar-counselor, Columbus traveled to the Spanish camp where the Sovereigns were overseeing the final stages of the seige of Granada. Columbus's extravagant demands of reward rather than the merits of his enterprise appear to have caused Queen Isabela to refuse his request for royal support and, as his son wrote, "the negotiation went up in smoke" on the eve of Granada's surrender.

What Columbus was demanding as a reward for successfully finding a sea route to India was summarized by his son Ferdinand as follows:

That he should be Admiral of the Ocean Sea, with the title, prerogatives, and pre-eminencies enjoyed by the Admirals of Castile in their jurisdictions, and that he should be viceroy and governor over all the islands and mainland, with the authority and jurisdiction possessed by the Admirals of Castile and León; that he should have absolute power to appoint and remove all the officers of administation and justice in all the said islands at his will and pleasure; that all government posts and municipal councilorships should be given to one of a list of three persons nominated by him for each position; and that he should appoint justices to sit in every port of Spain that trafficked and traded with the Indies, these justices to decide all matters relating to trade. In addition to the salaries and customs duties appertaining to the said offices of admiral, viceroy, and governor, he demanded a tenth of all that should be bought, bartered, found, or produced within the limits of his admirality: thus, if 1,000 ducats were found on a certain island, 100 would be his. And because his enemies were saying that he risked nothing of his own, being only captain of the fleet for the duration of the voyage, he demanded one eighth of all that he brought home himself paying an eighth part of the total expense of the expedition.[10]

It is not hard to see why a monarch like Isabela would have second thoughts and hesitate to enter into such a contract.

COLUMBUS RECEIVES CAPITULATIONS

Fortunately for Columbus one of the queen's advisers, Luis de Santangel, intervened on his behalf and persuaded Isabela to accept the terms of his offer. All that the harassed queen requested was that the details of the arrangement "be put off until she had a breathing space after the exertions of the War of Granada." According to Ferdinand's account of his father's life, Queen Isabela "was even ready to pledge her jewels for the cost of the expedition."[11] The gallant courtier Santangel, grateful to the queen for accepting his advice, spared her that bother by lending her the necessary funds himself. The peevish Columbus was sent for and *capitulations* containing exactly what he had demanded were signed and sealed. The years of waiting in the smothering atmosphere of court intrigue had finally paid off for the persistent Genoese navigator who passionately wished to discover a sea route to the Indies. If his enterprise were to succeed, his victorious Spanish monarchs could steal the march on neighboring Portugal and corner the spice trade.

THE VOYAGE TO THE INDIES BEGINS

With his treasured *capitulations* in hand, Columbus left Granada for the small port Palos on May 12, 1492. There he raised and equipped his three-ship flotilla for the voyage to the Indies. The *Santa Maria*, owned by a Juan de la Cosa, was designated his flagship. The smaller *Niña*

Columbus lived in an uncertain and notably litigious society, one that placed great weight on documents of many sorts. Shown here is a vellum page from the collection of documents known as Columbus's Book of Privileges. According to Columbus expert and biographer, Samuel Eliot Morison, the Admiral spent much time and effort completing and making copies of the Book of Privileges that he began compiling sometime before his third voyage. The document shown here is the second Bull of Pope Alexander VI, extending to Spain the same privileges, in respect to the lands discovered by Columbus, as had been granted to Portugal in respect to their African discoveries (Manuscript Division).

and *Pinta*, captained by brothers named Pinzon, rounded out the fleet. Perhaps the most important thing to know about the first leg of Columbus's momentous first voyage is that on leaving Palos, on Spain's southern Atlantic coast, his course was set to the south not to the west. As Ferdinand wrote "on August 3rd he set sail for the Canaries, having ninety men aboard the fleet." Unlike the Azores which lie almost directly west from Lisbon, the Canary Islands lie off the southern coast of Morocco at approximately 28 degrees north latitude. The almost 8 degrees of latitude that separate the Azores and Canary Island groups may not seem terribly important at first glance, however, in terms of the wind patterns of the Atlantic, those 8 degrees were of the greatest significance. By sailing to the Canaries on his "SW by south" heading Columbus was leaving behind the antagonistic belt of prevailing westerly winds and approaching the belt of winds that would later be known as the trade winds. Blowing from the northeast and east toward the west in the northern hemisphere "the trades on the oceans are the steadiest winds of the earth."[12]

Many experts who have written about Columbus feel that he had profited through his sailing experiences by gaining an appreciation of the Atlantic's wind systems. In their arguments this becomes the key factor in his choice of a due west course from the Canary Islands to the Indies. On the other hand there are those who argue that he chose this course and latitude because he felt that the island he called Cipangu lay directly west of the Canary Islands at a distance of about 2,400 nautical miles. Whatever the reason, he could hardly have made a better choice.

In his log of the voyage, Columbus may give evidence of his appreciation of the trade winds in his decision to change the *Niña*'s Portuguese lateen rig for square sails which are more efficient when sailing before the wind. On the other hand he may have decided to alter the *Niña* simply to have all three of his ships carrying the same rig and thus be more likely to keep in convoy.

COLUMBUS'S *DIARIO DE A BORDO*

True to his promise to his monarchs, Columbus kept a daily log or *Diario de a bordo* of his voyage. Unfortunately, however, no complete copy of the *Diario* is known to have survived. What has been preserved is a handwritten abstract of a copy of the original log that Columbus presented to Queen Isabela. The abstract was prepared by Fray Bartolomé de Las Casas, who is best known as the author of *Historia de las Indias* and defender of the rights of the native peoples of New Spain. Las Casas, in his youth, had witnessed Columbus's triumphant return to Seville after his first voyage, and his father and an uncle took part in the Admiral's second voyage. Las Casas titled his abstract *El Libro de la primera navegacion* (Book of the First Navigation) but it is more often referred to as the *Diario de Colón* or simply Columbus's Journal.[13] Certain portions of the Journal abstract were written in the first person or as Las Casas put it "in the formal words of the Admiral." Until an authentic copy of the full *Diario* is discovered, Las Casas's abstract will remain the closest and best source of what Columbus did, thought, and saw on his first voyage to the islands he believed were the Indies. In the judgement of Robert H. Fuson, a highly regarded Columbus expert and translator of a recently published version of the log, nothing in the document Las Casas left us "suggests anything less than a completely truthful account of the voyage, from beginning to end."[14] In his translation of the *Diario* Fuson drew on other writings of Las Casas and Ferdinand Columbus's biography of his father to fill gaps

present in Las Casas's abstract. The result is a highly readable account of history's most momentous ocean voyage.

Rather than attempting a review of that voyage here we will keep a focus on those elements and passages that bear on the Admiral's encounters with the Native Americans he met and interacted with. On Sunday, September 16th, his entry helps to confirm the generally held view that Columbus shared the image of an island cluttered approach to Asia that Martin Be-

Engraved in the late sixteenth century, this print showing Columbus bidding farewell to the monarchs Isabela and Ferdinand at Palos, his port of departure, in 1492, is romanticized fiction. It does, however, provide some impression of the activities associated with the readying of an overseas expedition as well as the costumes, ships, and architecture of postmedieval Europe (Girolamo Benzoni, America pars quarta historia Occidental India, *Part IV,* Historia Sive, *Rare Book and Special Collections Division).*

When Columbus returned from his voyage in 1493 he sent Ferdinand and Isabela a letter reporting his discoveries. Unfortunately that letter has not survived. With it, however, was a second letter addressed to no one in particular and intended to serve as a public announcement of Columbus's discovery. A copy of that letter, bearing an endorsement naming the Royal Treasurer, Raphael Sanchez, was quickly sent to Rome where it was translated into Latin and published on April 29, 1493. This first page of that letter that begins "Epistola Christofori Colom" is made from an original in the Library of Congress Incunabula Collection. This is the edition that spread his news throughout Europe (Rare Book and Special Collections Division).

haim showed on his globe. On that day several tufts of very green seaweed that appeared to be freshly "torn from the earth" caused all hands to judge that an island was near. The Admiral agreed that they might be near an island but went on to opine that it was not the mainland "for the mainland I take to be further on." Clearly he anticipated finding the waters off eastern Asia crowded with achipelagos and the large bulk of Cipangu. Birds in flight, whales, and clouds on the horizon were other false clues raising the hopes of island landfalls in the apprehensive voyagers.

THE FIRST ENCOUNTER

The first encounter between Columbus's expedition and the natives of the Bahamas took place on the morning of Friday, October 12, 1492, on the island the natives called *Guanahani*. As Columbus took formal possession of their home in the name of his sovereigns, Ferdinand and Isabela, the uncomprehending islanders gathered to look on. In his first letter reporting his achievement, Columbus wrote:

I reached the Indian sea, where I discovered many islands, thickly peopled, of which I took possession without resistance in the name of our most illustrious Monarch, by public proclamation and with unfurled banners. To the first of these islands, which is called by the name of the blessed Saviour (San Salvador), relying upon whose protection I had reached this as well as the other islands; to each of these I also gave a name, ordering that one should be called Santa Maria de la Concepcion, another Fernandina, the third Isabela, the fourth Juana, and so with all the rest respectively.[15]

THE SEARCH FOR GUANAHANI

The moment this material is read the question of the location and modern identity of *Guanahani*-San Salvador springs to mind. It is a question that has spawned as much scholarly debate in recent years as the question of the genuineness of Yale's Vinland Map did a decade and more before. Like the Vinland Map controversy, the debate concerning the identity of Columbus's first landfall in the New World has not ended.[16]

Published statements bearing on the location and identity of *Guanahani* can be traced to the work of the early eighteenth-century English naturalist Mark Catesby who traveled to the Bahamas in 1731 to draw and record fish. Citing no source for his assignment, Catesby stated that the island "formerly called Salvador, or Guanahani" was Cat Island. Although the historical record reveals some difference of opinion on the identity of the first landfall island, anything resembling a scholarly debate had to wait until 1825 when Martin Fernandez de Navarrete published Columbus's *Diario*. A number of Columbus scholars, all utilizing the descriptions contained in the log as their point of departure, subsequently attempted to recreate the Admiral's course to and through the Bahamas in October 1492. In their published reports a large number of islands from Turks on the south to Eleuthra on the northern end of the eastern Bahama Islands group were named as candidates for *Guanahani*, the first landfall. Readers not familiar with the Bahamas should realize that Turks Island lies almost four hundred miles to the southeast of the northern end of Eleuthera.

Emerging as the preeminent Columbus scholar publishing in English, the Harvard-based historian of discovery, Samuel Eliot Morison, seemed to have closed the debate when he accepted Watlings Island as *Guanahani* in his Pulitzer Prize-winning book, *Admiral of the Ocean Sea: A Life of Christopher Columbus*, and subsequent publications. One of a small number of Columbus students who challenged Morison, Pieter H. G. Verhoog published a modest book titled *Guanahani Again* in the Netherlands in

num copia falubritate admixta hominũ : quæ nifi quis viderit:credulitatem fuperat . Huius arbores pafcua & fructus / multũ ab illis Iohanę differũt . Hæc præterea Hifpana diuerfo aromatis genere / auro metallifcʒ abundat.cuius quidem & omnium aliarum quas ego vidi : & quarum cognitionem ʒaheo incolę vtriufcʒ fexus ;nudi femp incedunt :

None of the maps Columbus prepared to show the islands he discovered on his voyages has survived. This fanciful woodcut illustration was published in Basel, in 1494, and has some maplike attributes. Behind the ship and a totally imaginary castle are shown several islands with the names Columbus applied to the first islands he encountered in the Bahamas. "Salvatorie" on the right represents the landfall island Guanahani. Although a matter of lively debate, many experts associate Guanahani with the island now named San Salvador in the Bahamas (Thacher Collection, Rare Book and Special Collections Division).

1947. Verhoog gained a hearing for his *Guanahani* thesis in the United States through the *Proceedings of the U.S. Naval Institute* (vol. 80) where he published an essay titled "Columbus Landed on Caicos," in 1954. Verhoog carried the authority of a navigator with a long and distinguished career with the Holland-American Line in his criticism of Morison's Watlings Island (now named San Salvador) landfall argument.

As he neared the end of his life, Captain Verhoog requested by correspondence that the membership of the Society for the History of Discoveries consider his arguments for a Caicos landing by Columbus. In the ensuing discussion at the Society's annual meeting held in Columbus, Ohio, in the autumn of 1980, a number of scholars were inspired to make fresh appraisals of the first landfall and route through the Bahamas question. At the 1981 meeting of the Society for the History of Discoveries held in Athens, Georgia, two sessions were devoted to scholarly papers delivered by members elucidating the identity of the island where Columbus first set foot in the New World and his route from there to Cuba. Revised versions of these papers were subsequently published in the Society's journal, *Terrae Incognitae* (vol. 15). The reception of that volume encouraged the Wayne State University press to publish the essays along with a restatement of Commodore Verhoog's (regrettably by then deceased) thesis under the title *In the Wake of Columbus: Islands and Controversy*, in 1985.

No single route or island was agreed upon by all of the scholar-authors, nor did the membership of the Society for the History of Discoveries subscribe to any preference. As in all serious scholarship the search was for truth. In this case truth in the historical record of one of humankind's most momentous events. The member-researchers and their audience were dedicated to the ideal that no single hypothesis is rendered sacrosanct merely by the stature of its author, however glowing the luster of his or her scholarly credentials. In the minds of some at least, Adm. Samuel Eliot Morison's vigorous pronouncements in favor of the Watlings Island as *Guanahani* identity had tended almost to place further research on the question outside the pale of scholarly respectability.

In the 1980s the circle of scholars working on the Columbus landfall and route through the Bahamas problem widened and many new research methods were brought to bear. The spirit of congeniality and cooperativeness that characterized the debate was, however, somewhat dampened when Joseph Judge, senior associate editor of the *National Geographic Magazine*, published an article titled "Where Columbus Found the New World" in the November 1986 issue. Using the National Geographic Society's enormous resources and prestige Judge had, somewhat secretly, undertaken his own research effort aimed at determining Columbus's route and first landfall in the Bahamas. Judge concluded that "Christopher Columbus first came to the New World at reef-girt, low and leafy Samana Cay, a small outrider to the sea lying in haunting isolation in the far eastern Bahamas, at latitude 23°05' North, longitude 73°45' West."[17] There was nothing new about the selection of Samana Cay as *Guanahani*. It had been nominated a hundred years before by Gustavas V. Fox, a U.S. Navy captain and assistant secretary of the Navy during the Civil War. The aspect of Judge's sophisticated research effort that troubled some of the landfall debate circle was his shift from scientific hypothesis to what smacked of dogmatic pronouncement when he penned his final paragraph:

Thus six separate lines of evidence converge on the sands of Samana. Perhaps infallible proof will come only with discovery of the original Columbus log and chart. But until that day comes, we must conclude that it is impossible to explain the facts at our disposal in any other way. The solution to the [landfall] mystery is Samana Cay.[18]

In spite of Judge's pronouncement the debate goes on.

Whether the first recorded encounter between men of Europe and people of the Americas to occur since the days of the Norse voyages took place on San Salvador, Samana Cay, or any one of the other half dozen island candidates is not a matter that need concern us here. The important fact is that the encounter was described in colorful detail by Christopher Columbus in the log of his first voyage across the Atlantic.

THE ENCOUNTER DESCRIBED

It was two hours past midnight when land was sighted and sails were lowered to leave only enough canvas for "jogging" or tacking back and forth until daylight. As the island of *Guanahani* came into clear sight, naked people were seen on the beach. Columbus broke out the royal banner and the Pinzon brothers from the *Niña* and *Pinta* brought two flags, each with a green cross and letters F and Y surrmounted with crowns on either side of the cross. With the expedition's armed launch colorfully dressed in the flags and banners they came ashore with zeal.

The "very green trees and many ponds and fruits of various kinds" they saw must have been indescribably welcome after such a voyage. The Admiral, ever mindful of his royal duty, quickly gathered the landing party to witness formal declarations of possession in the name of their most Catholic majesties Ferdinand and Isabela. The natives of *Guanahani* lost no time in gathering to investigate the colorful and unexpected happening on their sunlit strand. For what followed, Las Casas quoted Columbus's own narrative:

I . . . in order that they would be friendly to us—because I recognized they were people who would be better freed (from error) and converted to our Holy Faith by love than by force—to some of them

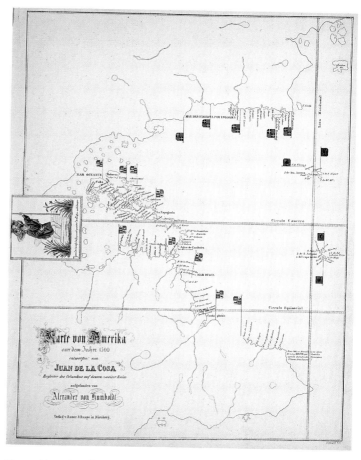

Pictured here is a facsimile of the western portion of a world map drawn by Juan de la Cosa in 1500. It was prepared by the internationally renowned naturalist-explorer, Alexander von Humboldt, and published in 1853. At the time the original map was drawn, Cosa was one of the most well-informed of Spain's Caribbean pilots. He had sailed first to the Indies with Columbus's second expedition in 1493–1494. Many experts in the history of discovery credit the Cosa map with being the earliest extant map showing Columbus's island discoveries. The island "La Hispaniola," for example, is clearly outlined and named. The placement of the painted figure representing Saint Christopher carrying the Christ Child may indicate that Cosa was unsure about whether the land area shown to the north was connected to the area in the south. In preparing his facsimile Humboldt chose to omit many of Cosa's original features such as wind heads, elaborate compass roses, and rhumb lines, for the sake of clarity. The flags along the coasts relate to the royal houses that had sponsored explorations and made claims to the areas flagged (F. W. Ghillany, Geschichte des Seefahrens Ritter Martin Behaim . . . (Nuremberg: 1853), Geography and Map Division).

I gave red caps, and glass beads which they put on their chests, and many other things of small value, in which they took so much pleasure and became so much our friends that it was a marvel. Later they came swimming to the ships launches where we were and brought us parrots and cotton thread in balls and javelins and many other things, and they traded them to us for other things which we gave them such as small glass beads and bells. In sum, they took everything and gave of what they had very willingly. But it seemed to me that they were a people very poor in everything. All of them go around as naked as their mothers bore them; and the women also, although I did not see more than one quite young girl. All those that I saw were young people, for none did I see of more than 30 years of age.[19]

It is interesting to note the nature of the trade goods given—red caps, glass beads, and other things of small value—with which Columbus was supplied. Samuel Eliot Morison, Columbus biographer and expert, pointed out that the Admiral's trade goods "were exactly what the Portuguese had found to be in most demand among the Negroes" they encountered in Africa.[20] Could it be possible that Columbus knew more than he had revealed when it came to the inhabitants of the Indies? Or was he simply a prudent planner who surmised that what was in demand in Africa beyond the world known to Ptolemy would be equally prized in the Indies?

As Columbus described the physical appearance of the native Bahamians he did not draw any direct comparisons to the African Blacks the Portuguese found on the Guinea Coast. Morison felt, however, that his description reflects such a comparison, albeit unstated. In Columbus's words the Native Americans were:

very well formed, with handsome bodies and good faces. Their hair [is] coarse—almost like the tail of a horse—and short. They wear their hair down over their eyebrows except for a little in the back which they wear very long and never cut. Some of them paint themselves with black, and they are the color of the Canarians, neither black nor white; and some of them paint themselves with white,

and some of them with red, and some of them with whatever they find. And some of them paint their faces, and some of them the whole body, and some of them only the eyes, and some of them only the nose. They do not carry arms nor are they acquainted with them, because I showed them swords and they took them by the edge and through ignorance cut themselves. They have no iron. Their javelins are shafts without iron and some of them have at the end a fish tooth and others of other things. All of them alike are of good-sized stature and carry themselves well. I saw some who had marks of wounds on their bodies and I made signs to them asking what they were; and they showed me how people from other islands nearby came there and tried to take them, and how they defended themselves; and I believed and believe that they come here from tierra firme to take them captive. They should be good and intelligent servants, for I see that they say very quickly everything that is said to them; and I believe that they would become Christians very easily, for it seemed to me that they had no religion. Our Lord pleasing, at the time of my departure I will take six of them from here to Your Highnesses in order that they may learn to speak. No animal of any kind did I see on this island except parrots. All are the Admiral's words.[21]

The true motive behind Columbus's casually mentioned forceful kidnap of the gentle and hospitable *Guanahani* natives is made clear in his famous "First Letter" reporting the great discovery. The letter was translated into Latin for dispatch to Rome and publication within weeks of his return in the spring of 1493 (shown earlier in this chapter). Discussing the native people he found and called Indians, Columbus wrote:

Nor are they slow or unskilled but of excellent and acute understanding; and the men who have navigated that sea give an account of everything in an admirable manner; but they never saw people clothed, nor these kinds of ships. As soon as I reached that sea, I seized by force several Indians on the first island, in order that they might learn from us, and in like manner tell us about those things in these lands of which they themselves had knowledge; and the plan succeeded, for in a short time we understood them and they us, sometimes by gestures and signs, sometimes by words; and it was a great advantage to us.[22]

Thus Columbus became the first in a long line of New World explorers to rely on the geographical knowledge and cartographic abilities of the native people they encountered. Unfortunately his claim of mutual understanding was more a boast than a report of the true state of their ability to converse one with another.

CARTOGRAPHERS FROM *GUANAHANI*

On Columbus's homeward voyage his Indian guides had an unusual opportunity to demonstrate both their detailed geographical knowledge and cartographic abilities before a royal inquisitor. A vicious late winter storm put Columbus (now aboard the *Niña*, the *Santa Maria* having been lost on the north coast of Haiti) "in great peril" near the coast of Portugal north of Lisbon. On the 4th of March, 1493, the Admiral, safe in Lisbon harbor, wrote that "all mariners here say that never has there been so bad a winter or so many losses of ships." A few days later the King of Portugal, Don João, invited Columbus to visit him at a monastery about thirty miles outside Lisbon. The Admiral brought some of the kidnapped Indians with him, doubtlessly to convince the king concerning his discovery.

During their interviews Columbus assured the Portuguese king, as he shortly would the Spanish monarchs, of the intelligence and understanding of his Indian captives. As a test of their capability and Columbus's truthfulness, Don João ordered a bowl of dried beans brought into the room. He then scattered them on a table and ordered an Indian to arrange them in the form of a rough map of his homeland. The Indian deftly complied by grouping clusters of beans to represent Hispaniola and Cuba and single beans to represent the smaller islands of the Bahamas and Lesser Antilles. "The king," Las Casas wrote, "observing this geographical

game with a gloomy countenance, as if by inadvertence disarranged what the man had set forth, and commanded another Indian to play map maker with the scrambled beans."[23] The second Indian reassembled the bean chart of the Antilles "and added many more islands and lands, giving us an explanation of all that he had depicted and indicated in his own tongue, although nobody understood it."

According to the account by Las Casas, the king had first believed that Columbus's discoveries lay in Portugal's sphere of influence as confirmed by the Treaty of Alcaçovas and the 1481 papal bull *Aeterni Regis*. When he saw the maps fashioned by Columbus's Indians Don João realized that lands and islands quite outside any legitimate claim that Portugal could make had been described. According to Las Casas, the king could no longer hide his great chagrin and "in a wave of passion smote his breast and cried in a loud voice, 'O man of little comprehension!' and 'Why did I let slip an enterprise of so great importance?'—these or similar words."[24] King João was, of course, deeply regretting his failure to back Columbus in his enterprise when he had the opportunity in 1484. When he regained his composure he rewarded the Bahamian cartographers with "some scarlet-clothes."

COLUMBUS AND THE LUCAYAN NATIVE PEOPLE

According to Columbus, his Indian guides believed that he "was descended from heaven, although they have been living with us for a long time, and are living with us to-day." That the Indians might have accounted for his exotic invasion as having come from the underworld of their cosmos would never have been considered by the ever egotistical Admiral. He continued his letter describing the versatile watercraft in which his Indian guides and their fellows navigated their island-studded sea:

On every island there are many canoes of a single piece of wood; and though narrow, yet in length and shape similar to our row-boats, but swifter in movement. They steer only by oars. Some of these boats are large, some small, some of medium size. Yet they row many of the larger row-boats with eighteen cross-benches, with which they cross to all those islands, which are innumerable, and with these boats they perform their trading, and carry on commerce among them. I saw some of these row-boats or canoes which were carrying seventy and eighty rowers.[25]

In view of what Columbus wrote concerning the watercraft and navigational and cartographic capabilities of his Indian captives, it would appear more than likely that his route through the Bahama and Lucayan Islands from *Guanahani* to Cuba followed generally the routes used by large dugout canoes. If this was the case, researchers attempting to recreate Columbus's route to determine the identity of the islands he described should consider the dugout routes preferred by Indian navigators among the factors being employed to test their several hypotheses.

GOLD AND COLUMBUS

Columbus's log entry for his second day in the New World, October 13, 1492, contains the first mention of a substance that remained a major obsession until he died—gold. He told of the *Guanahanian's* eagerness to trade their "balls of spun cotton and parrots and javelins and other little things that it would be tiresom to write down." No ethnographer, Columbus reveals his lack of interest in the Indians' material possessions and handiwork. He was, however, "attentive and labored to find out if there was any gold." Some of the Indians "wore a little piece hung in a hole they have in their noses."[26] Thus

his appetite was whet for what Indians sometimes called the sweat or excrement of the sun.

Some Columbus scholars have arrived at the conclusion that the Admiral's career is to be understood in terms of his greed for the gleaming metal. Others have argued that this line of reasoning is an oversimplification and that Columbus knowingly employed the lure value of gold in manipulating his crews as well as his Spanish monarchs and their advisers. Tzvetan Todorov espouses this argument and cites as evidence statements made by Ferdinand Columbus as well as his father. Ferdinand wrote about the apprehensions of the homesick crew after leaving the familiar waters of the Canary Islands:

This day they completely lost sight of land, and many sighed and wept for fear they would not see it again for a long time. The Admiral comforted them with great promises of land and riches.[27]

Again, in his log entry preceding the account of the sighting of land in the Bahamas, Columbus told of how "the men could no longer stand it" and "complained of the long voyage." The Admiral did his best to quiet their fears by "giving them good hope of the benefits that they would be able to secure" when they returned rich and glorified from discovering the Indies.[28]

Todorov argued that despite his apparent preoccupation with gold "greed is not Columbus's true motive: if wealth matters to him, it is because wealth signifies the acknowledgement of his role as discoverer; but he himself would prefer the rough garment of a monk." In Todorov's view "gold is too human a value to interest Columbus to any real degree, and we must believe him when he writes, in the journal of the third voyage: 'Our Lord knows well that I do not bear these, sufferings to enrich myself, for, certainly I know that everything in this age is vain except what is done for the honor and service of God.'"[29]

Whether for greed or as a means to assure his glory, the quest for gold directed Columbus at almost every turn as he navigated from the Bahamas to Cuba and Hispaniola and through the Caribbean Sea. Much in Columbus's past experience and research supported the ancient theory that gold was the product of heat and consequently was to be found in tropical regions. He had been to the Portuguese trading posts on what came to be known as the African Gold Coast. The legendary Golden Cheronese he read of was what we now know as the Malay Peninsula projecting south from eastern Asia deep into equatorial climes. On each of his four voyages Columbus chose increasingly more southerly tracks in his continuing search for gold which began on the beach of *Guanahani*, his first landfall.

Significantly the most analytical observations of native languages recorded in Columbus's log of the first voyage dealt with the words meaning gold. As the Admiral was coasting Hispaniola on his return to Spain, a landing was made to pick up yams for food on the homeward voyage. While on the beach the victualing party encountered an Indian the Admiral surmised to be a Carib, a people known for their ferocity and cannibalism. In their exchange the Indian told Columbus that nearby to the east there was "a great deal of gold." Columbus described how as he said this the Indian pointed "to the poop of the caravel, which was quite large, meaning that there were pieces that big."[30] Predictably the Admiral did not consider the probability that the Indian was trying, through sign language, to indicate that the mountains of Hispaniola were the sources of the gold. The suspected Carib "called gold *tuob* and did not understand *caona,* as they call it in the first part of the island, nor *nocay* as they called it in San Salvador and in the other islands." The Admiral continued his impromptu vocabulary lesson by pointing out that "in Hispaniola they call *alam-bre* a base gold, *tuob.*" The differences between the vocabularies, the Admiral concluded, resulted from the great distances between the lands the Indians inhabited.

When Columbus spied the first small gold nose rings on the beach at *Guanahani* he asked where the metal was obtained. "And by signs I was able to understand that, going to the south or rounding the island to the south, there was a king who had large vessels of it and had very much gold . . . and so I will go to the southwest to seek gold and precious stones." Before leaving *Guanahani* Columbus provided a description which is a frequently cited piece of evidence in the first landfall debates mentioned above. According to the Admiral as quoted by Las Casas:

This island is quite big and very flat and with very green trees and much water and a very large lake in the middle and without any mountains; and all of it so green that it is a pleasure to look at it.[31]

On the next day Columbus, with a party in the ship's boat and launches from the caravels, followed the island's off-shore reef northeast "to see what there was in the other part, which was the eastern part" of San Salvador. The party was afraid to accept the natives' shouted invitations to come ashore "seeing a big stone reef that encircled that island all around." Between the reef and shore they observed "depth and harbor for as many ships as there are in the whole of Christendom" with a very narrow entrance.[32] Within the reef, which Columbus terms a "belt of stone," there were some shallows "but the sea is no more disturbed than inside a well." Columbus also saw "a piece of land formed like an island, although it was not one, on which there were six houses." "This piece of land might in two days be cut off to make an island, although I do not see this to be necessary since these people are very naive about weapons," he added.[33]

As he set sail from San Salvador Columbus

wrote that he "saw so many islands that I did not know how to decide which one I would go to first." The kidnapped Indian guides "told me by signs that they were so very many that they were numberless." From memory the Indians could give the names of more than a hundred islands. Surely this must be the island strewn sea within which the Admiral confidently expected to find Cipangu!

THE ABORIGINAL INDIES DESCRIBED

Columbus's Log of the 1492–93 voyage southwest through the Bahamas and along the northeastern coast of Cuba, northern Haiti, and the Dominican Republic, contains the earliest European observations of the aboriginal landscape of the New World. Although he completed three more voyages into the Caribbean world and made landfalls in Central and South America none of Columbus's other writings save his First Letter which echoes the Log, adds much of substance to these observations. His account of the second voyage in 1493 might have augmented the first Log, had it survived. From then on, however, he became absorbed in other matters which could be broadly described as political and it is doubtful the he prepared any additional insightful descriptive reports or logs.

With Columbus and following in his wake, however, were several Spanish observers of the Native American scene whose written accounts have survived. Dr. Chanca, a man of medicine, for example, accompanied Columbus on the second voyage. Chanca's published letter is one of the best-known accounts of that enterprise. Some others were what today would be recognized as well-to-do tourists along for the adventure. One of these was an Aragonese gentleman named Coma and another was a Genoese named Michele Cuneo; both wrote letters which were subsequently published. Ferdinand Columbus

included in his biography of Columbus the "Relation of Fray Ramón concerning the Antiquities of the Indians," "which He, Knowing Their Language, Carefully Compiled by Order of the Admiral." Fr. Ramón Pane was assigned by the Admiral to prepare an account of native beliefs. Unfortunately Fray Ramón was of limited ability and his potentially valuable report suffers from a lack of insight that a more intellectually gifted investigator might have brought to the assignment.

It is to the writings of three truly remarkable chroniclers that the reader interested in learning about the Indians and aboriginal conditions the earliest Europeans encountered in the Caribbean must turn. These are Peter Martyr, Bartolomé de Las Casas, and Fernández de Oviedo. Peter Martyr d'Anghiera was an Italian cleric with excellent connections. He was a confidant of pope and high clergy, and lived at the Spanish court as tutor and mentor to the royal princes. Martyr wrote long chatty letters concerning the discoveries of new lands and their strange inhabitants which he learned of by interviewing those who returned from overseas adventures. The letters were collected into what he termed *Decades*, which comprise a famous running account of the discoveries from 1493 until almost the time of his death in 1526. Although he never came to America himself Martyr composed a rich and valuable panorama of its nature and natives.

Fernández de Oviedo y Valdés was a late arrival to the Indies who went as an official with the party of Pedrarias Dávila. He published *Sumario de la Natural Historia de las Indias* in 1526. It included mainly his observations made on the western Caribbean mainland or *tierra firme* with only slight mention of conditions on the island of Hispaniola. He moved to the island and lived in Santo Domingo for most of the period from 1532 to 1546, during which he undertook his magnum opus, *Historia General y Natural de las*

Indias. Going from the western rim of the Carib-bean world to Hispaniola took him from an area where native life was still relatively unchanged to one where it was in an advanced state of de-cline. By interviewing the island's earliest set-tlers and through observation Oviedo was able to reconstruct the original conditions of Hispan-iola. As the titles of his works reveal he had a strong interest in natural history. He described the region's native plants and animals and the uses made of them by the natives. Oviedo met Las Casas at court in Spain where their opinions were sought in developing Indian policy for the new and expanding overseas empire. Their backgrounds, temperaments, and New World experiences led them to clash in court disputes concerning Spain's evolving Indian policy.

Bartolomé de Las Casas is better known as a polemicist than as a historian and geographer of the Indies. No one, however, was more inti-mately experienced or better informed about the Caribbean world and its natives than this priest who rose to become bishop of the New World diocese of Chiapa in southern Mexico.[34] His interest and acquaintance with the Indies doubtlessly began when his father and uncle joined Columbus's second expedition in 1493. His father returned to Spain in 1498 accompa-nied by an Arawak Indian slave who became the first Indian acquaintance and informant of young Bartolomé. In 1502 Las Casas sailed to the New World with Nicolás de Ovando. In Hispaniola Las Casas took part in campaigns against the Indians and was awarded the labor of Indians to produce food and wash gold in the center of the island. After a ten-year residence in Hispaniola Las Casas took part in the occupa-tion of Cuba and became one of the island's *en-comenderos* or trustees of a native community, responsible for collecting their tribute. Later in his life Las Casas joined the Dominican Order and took up his pen to begin writing his monu-mental *Historia de las Indias,* a labor of love that continued to occupy him almost until his death at the age of ninety-two. As we noted in the dis-cussion of his transcription of Columbus's *Dia-rio,* he was careful to reveal whether he was para-phrasing, condensing, or quoting his sources, a discipline not widely shared in his era. He spent about forty years writing the history of the His-panic discoveries from Columbus's first encoun-ters to 1520, a year which is still accepted as ter-minating its formative first stage. Thanks to his first-hand knowledge of the persons and places involved he was able to introduce many other-wise unrecorded facts that help illuminate and flesh out our understanding of the encounters taking place during those important first years. Las Casas can be read with the certain knowl-edge that no other European was as interested in or knew so well the Indian participants in those dramatic encounters.

COLUMBUS LAYS PLANS TO RETURN

Even before his first voyage was completed Co-lumbus was laying plans for his return. The sinking of the *Santa Maria* on Christmas Day in 1492 had made it necessary to leave thirty-nine crewmen behind in a fortified post the Admiral named Navidad. Ever the optimist, Columbus wrote in his Log that "he trusts in God that on his return, which he intended to make from Castile, he would find a barrel of gold, which those whom he had left there should have ob-tained by barter."[35] With this and the other great wealth he expected to bring his sovereigns within three years they could undertake a new crusade and conquer the Holy Places. On the day before he departed his last anchorage on Hispaniola, he wrote in his Log that fifty cara-vels each year could be loaded with "chili which is their [the Indians] pepper, of a kind more valuable than [black] pepper."[36]

Firm planning for a return waited, however, until he reached Barcelona where he met with Ferdinand and Isabela. The advance news of his discoveries Columbus sent them had "caused them great joy" and they ordered that a "solemn reception be held for him as befitted one who had rendered them so great a service." In his *Life of the Admiral*, Ferdinand Columbus wrote of how:

All the Court and the city came out to meet him; and the Catholic Sovereigns received him in public, seated with all majesty and grandeur on rich thrones under a canopy of cloth of gold. When he came forward to kiss their hands, they rose from their thrones as if he were a great lord, and would not let him kiss their hands but made him sit down beside them.[37]

Surely this was the crowning moment in Christopher Columbus's long and often troubled life.

COLUMBUS COLONIZES THE INDIES

When Columbus returned with his second expedition in 1493 it was vastly larger in scale than his first. As many as 1,200 would-be colonists were eager to board the seventeen-ship flotilla and sail west to seek their share of the riches waiting on the islands so colorfully described by the Admiral. The islands of the West Indies were no strangers to waves of invaders—archaeological evidence indicates that they were swept by at least three earlier Native American culture waves before the Europeans arrived. The first of these was the primitive hunting, fishing, and gathering culture known as Ciboney. From whence the Ciboney came and when they arrived remain unknown. They were followed by the Arawak and Carib cultures both of which originated in South America and island-hopped into the Antilles.

By the time of the European encounter and conquest the Arawaks were occupying the Greater Antilles, the Bahamas, and southern Trinidad. They had eliminated the Ciboney peoples everywhere except for a few isolated refuge areas in westernmost Haiti and Cuba. The Caribs had followed the Arawaks and displaced them in the Lesser Antilles and on northern Trinidad. The Caribs were in the act of further expansion into Puerto Rico when they were checked by the Spanish.

Ciboney Indians practiced no cultivation and subsisted primarily on fish, manatees, turtles, and other sea creatures. Their villages were small, and they lived in crude rock shelters and caves. Their chief material possessions were the dugout canoes so vital in their food gathering. The Arawaks and Caribs were noticeably more advanced in terms of their material cultures. Both cultures included important agricultural components although the Arawaks had better-developed farming practices. Tubers rich in starch, such as the manioc used to produce cassava, yams, and arrowroot, as well as peanuts and some maize were cultivated by the island Indians. In addition to their food crops, the Arawaks grew tree cotton for their netting and hammocks and tobacco for use as a drug. All of the Caribbean Indians included hunting and fishing as important parts of their communal lives. Most experts theorize that the Arawaks and Caribs brought their plants and practices with them from South America. Only their notable lack of any form of alcoholic beverage is difficult to account for in such a theoretical model. The use of such beverages was widespread on the mainland coasts.

The productivity of Arawak agriculture allowed a highly stratified, aristocratic, native society to flourish. On December 16, 1492, Columbus described his surprise at encountering a solitary native canoeist far at sea off the coast of Haiti who had glass beads, hawks' bells, and brass rings aboard. The Indian was clearly bring-

An early woodblock engraving of an Indian dugout canoe used to illustrate Gonzalo Fernández de Oviedo's book La Historia General y Natural de las Indias . . . (1535). Oviedo lived much of his life on the islands and shores of the Caribbean and wrote extensively on the native life he found there. He described dugouts that were so large "they will carry one hundred to one hundred and thirty men." On his first voyage Columbus saw "canoes which were carrying seventy and eighty rowers" (Rare Book and Special Collections Division).

RIGHT: An early attempt to picture a manatee (Trichechus manatus), an herbivorous sea mammal that played an important part in the diets of the Caribbean Indians. Oviedo provided some unintended humor when he wrote, "I think that it is one of the tastiest of all fish, and one that tastes most like meat." Some of the manatees the Spaniards killed were so large that it took two teams of oxen to pull the cart carrying them to market (Oviedo, La Historia General . . . (1535), Rare Book and Special Collections Division).

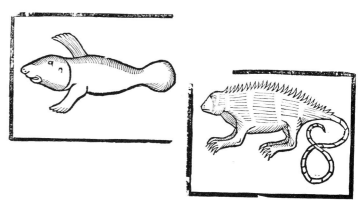

FAR RIGHT: Oviedo described the iguana as "a kind of serpent that is very fierce and fearful to look upon but is entirely harmless." The Indians used them for food but "very few men [Spanish] who have seen it alive . . . dare eat it." For some reason Oviedo believed that eating iguana meat was harmful to anyone who had suffered from syphilis "even though they have been cured for a long time" (Oviedo, La Historia General . . . (1535), Rare Book and Special Collections Division).

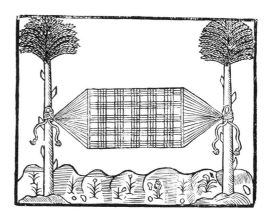

"The beds in which they sleep are called hamacas [hammocks], which are pieces of well-woven cotton cloth and of good and pretty tapestry," wrote Oviedo. He found the hammocks the Indians slept in very clean and quite comfortable (Oviedo, La Historia General . . . (1535), Rare Book and Special Collections Division).

Most New World Indians were accomplished farmers at the time of the first encounters. In this woodcut the European engraver has tried to illustrate some of their practices. The Arawaks, pictured here, heaped earth into beds of low mounds. The mounded beds provided excellent growing conditions for the cultivation of root crops and other food plants, upright and climbing. The mix of plants provided ground cover and cut down on erosion. In this scene the Indians are carrying bowls of water from a stream to irrigate their crops (Oviedo, La Historia General . . . (1535), Rare Book and Special Collections Division).

ing samples of the Admiral's exotic trinkets to a regional ruler or, as Columbus called him, "king." The canoe and Indian courier were taken aboard and carried to a coastal village where the ship anchored. When the "king" arrived on the beach Columbus "sent him a present, which he received with much ceremony." The "king" was described as about twenty-one years of age and was accompanied by "an old governor and other counsellors, who advised him and answered for him, and he himself said very few words."[38] The next day Columbus used the term *cacique* which he had learned was the Indian word "for the governor of that province."

Great caciques were hereditary rulers at the top of the Arawak sociopolitical system. Lesser caciques, nobles, commoners, and unfree people called *naborias* formed a society which seemed reminiscent of Spain's feudal past. It was a social system that was quickly adapted by the Spaniards as they spread their control over the islands. Perhaps, however, the most noteworthy aspects of the Caribbean and other American Indian cultures at the time of their conquest by the Europeans were their omissions.

For one thing the Indians had not developed any concept of the private ownership of land. Land and sea existed as communal fields of enterprise wherein the necessities of life were satisfied. Land, like sea, was never bought, sold, traded, or used for commercial gain in ways familiar to the Europeans of the fifteenth century. The other cultural omission which was to have a disastrous impact on the Indians was their lack of any beasts of burden, wheeled vehicles, or other sophisticated labor-saving tools and devices. Human muscle power comprised their chief energy source for accomplishing work on land or sea.

This is not to imply that the islanders led lives of drudgery. They used fire as an effective tool for clearing fields and hollowing logs for dugout canoes. Farm plots were dug with a primitive wooden spade used to heap the earth into low mounds. Called *montones* by the Spanish, these mounded beds varied in size and height depending on soil quality. They provided growing beds of loose well-aerated soils excellent for the cultivation of root crops along with other food plants, upright and climbing. The mix of plants provided an excellent ground cover against soil erosion. Clusters of these mounded beds further checked sheet erosion on sloping land. The system was beautifully adapted to the environmental conditions and remains virtually unchanged in those areas of the Antilles still devoted to subsistence agriculture.

While they required a large initial labor expenditure, once established the *montones* were fairly easy to maintain. As a result patterns of shifting agriculture, often thought to be a common trait of tropical native agriculture, are not revealed in Caribbean encounter literature. In those areas where it was needed, irrigation was commonplace. The Spanish acknowledged the Arawak system by demanding crop tributes from caciques based on the number of *montones* their tribesmen cultivated.

Columbus and other early arrivals wrote at length concerning the importance of the sea in native Caribbean life. Indian dugout canoes ranged in size from tiny one- or two-passenger craft to those large enough to accommodate fifty or more paddlers. Columbus reported one that he saw on Cuba that he thought could hold 150 Indians. Such large canoes, he felt, were evidence of large centers of population and long-distance trading to the mainland of Asia. To the Spanish the artistically carved paddles the Indians used to propel their craft resembled the flat wooden shovels used by bakers in Spain to remove bread from ovens.

Fishing with hooks and nets was supplemented in some cases by the use of remora or sucker fish on lines. The remora attached themselves to large fish or manatees which were then brought to the surface and taken by the Indians. Until they were decimated by the Spanish, manatees and large sea turtles were an important island food source. Land animals such as coneys and large hares were sometimes hunted with fire drives. Birds, including many waterfowl, pigeons, doves, and parrots, added to the available game stores the Indians subsisted on.

THE COLUMBIAN EXCHANGE

With the coming of the Spanish and the introduction of their animals, such as dogs and hogs that often went feral, the native fauna of the Caribbean islands and rimlands suffered dramatic impacts and irreversible change. In his groundbreaking book titled *The Columbian Exchange,* historian Alfred W. Crosby wrote of how:

The European immediately set about to transform as much of the New World as possible into the Old World. So successful was he that he accomplished what was probably the greatest biological revolution in the Americas since the end of the Pleistocene era.[39]

The most doleful chapter in the story of that biological revolution deals with the Native Americans an ill-informed Columbus chose to call Indians. Although the picture may have been somewhat overdrawn and exaggerated by the observers and authors of the historical record, the Caribbean Indian societies appear to have been enjoying a more or less harmonious balance between their numbers and the carrying capacities of their island homes. The tropical idyll Columbus and others described was largely true. Carib cannibals did on occasion sweep down on their more pacific Arawak neighbors

but, when contrasted with the devastation the Spanish soon wrought, these internecine attacks pale to insignificance.

Reliable information on how many Indians were living in the Caribbean islands, or anyplace else in the Americas at the time of the first encounters is difficult to establish. It is clear, however, that in the first decades of the Conquest the loss of Indian lives was nothing short of catastrophic. Las Casas was outspoken in his criticisms of a colonial system that saw, according to his claim, six out of every seven Indians die. They fell in droves to infectious diseases commonplace in the Old World, but against which they lacked resistance. The Spanish treated the Indians as an expendable source of labor in spite of legislation passed to protect them. Most of the Lucayan Arawak Indians Columbus found in the Bahamas and described so glowingly to his monarchs were probably captured by slavers during the period from 1509–1512 when the price of Indian slaves soared from 5 to 150 gold pesos per head. Their level Bahama Island homelands lacked hills or mountains in which they could elude the Spanish slaving parties and their dogs. The fact that Florida was "discovered" by a Spanish slaving expedition led by Juan Poncé de Leon looking for rumored still populous outlying Bahama islands is one of the many unsung ironies of American history. The Bahamas were the first but by no means the last islands to be depopulated in the first generation following Columbus's discovery in 1492. In that single generation the Indian population of the idyllic world the Admiral extolled in such glowing terms was reduced from a number estimated to be in the millions to a few remnant handfuls. This certainly was "the most astonishing encounter of our history."

CHAPTER FIVE

IN THE WAKE OF COLUMBUS

Conquest and Empire

But the Lord wished to punish the Indians, and so visited them with such shortage of food and such a variety of plagues that he reduced their number by two thirds, that it might be made clear that such wonderful conquests proceeded from His supreme hand and not from our strength or intelligence or the cowardice of the Indians; for even admitting the superiority of our men, it is obvious that the numerical preponderance of the Indians would have nullified this advantage.

The Life of the Admiral Christopher Columbus,
By His Son Ferdinand

COLUMBUS AS COLONY BUILDER

Columbus had made the discovery he promised and the terms of his *capitulations* with Ferdinand and Isabela went into effect. He and his heirs would have control of what he had found for perpetuity with an obligation to share the proceeds with the monarchs. It was an incredible arrangement. There were none of the provisions usually deemed essential to the founding of a colony such as procedures for settlers to obtain and own land or form self-governing communities or engage in any form of private economic activity. Nor were there any provisions for dealing with the Indians. All authority was vested in Columbus with virtually no limits of any sort on his powers. In essence it was a royal monopoly in the hands of Columbus.

In spite of this formula for potential disaster, people flocked to join the return expedition. Now at peace, Spain had no lack of idle hands anxious for a chance to gather the gold and other treasures Columbus claimed to have found in the Indies. With little or no selection process, eleven or twelve hundred volunteers were quickly signed up and, on September 23, 1493, a fleet of seventeen ships set sail from Cadiz. Only women and children were lacking to make the expedition a true microcosm of Spanish society with all the strengths and weaknesses that would imply. Livestock, stores of garden seeds and cuttings, seed wheat, and grape vines would assure that a Spanish lifestyle would soon be enjoyed by all—or so it seemed.

The Admiral led the convoy on a good crossing. Following a more southerly route than his first expedition, they reached Dominica, in the central Lesser Antilles, on November 3, 1493. Sailing north for Hispaniola, Columbus reconnoitered the Antilles, Virgin Islands, and Puerto Rico before reaching Navidad on November 28.

The party left at Navidad less than a year before was nowhere to be seen. According to the local Indians "soon after the Admiral's departure those men began to quarrel among themselves, each taking as many women and as much gold as he could."[1] One faction of ten Spaniards and their women had gone inland to mine or barter for gold in the land of a cacique named Caonabó (Caunaboa) who had killed them and then attacked and killed those remaining at Navidad. What unfolded at Navidad was a classic tale of greed, lust, and abuse of the Indians. It was, however, nothing more than a preface to the historical opus of conflict recorded in the decades that followed.

Named for Spain's queen, Isabela was the first European town founded in the New World. It was built on the north coast of Hispaniola farther to the east than the destroyed Navidad, at what Columbus incorrectly felt was an excellent site. Isabela, like the other early settlements the Spanish founded on Hispaniola, relied almost entirely on gold and Indian food and labor. Like Isabela, most of these pioneer towns faded as the gold deposits played out and the Indians rebelled or died. In 1496 a truly permanent settlement was started at Santo Domingo on the south coast to serve the nearby Jaina gold workings. Thanks to its excellent harbor the town quickly grew and became the base for further exploration as well as an administrative and military center. For a time called Ciudad Trujillo, but once more Santo Domingo, the capital

of today's Dominican Republic enjoys the position of being the oldest European city in the Americas. So dominant did Santo Domingo become in the early years that its name was often used to designate the entire island of Hispaniola.

COLUMBUS RETURNS TO DISCOVERY

Columbus began the Europeanization of the Caribbean world but he never relished the role of colony builder and administrator. As soon

The island of Hispaniola, seat of Spain's first Caribbean colony, is reasonably well outlined on this sixteenth-century map from a popular "Ptolemy" or book of maps and geographical descriptions that was published in Venice. Today the countries of Haiti and the Dominican Republic share this mountainous 29,000-square-mile island. Columbus first learned of it in 1492 from the Indians he took captive in the Bahamas. The Indian name for the island was Bohío. As Columbus sailed toward Hispaniola he wrote, "the Indians with me continued to show great fear . . . and kept insisting that the people of Bohío had only one eye and the face of a dog, and they fear being eaten. I do not believe any of this. I feel that the Indians they fear belong to the domain of the Great Khan" (Ptolemaeus, C. Geografia. 1599. Geography and Map Division).

as he had gotten the building of Isabela well underway and established a fortified post at the interior gold-producing area, he resumed his chosen role of discoverer. The Admiral's brother, Bartholomew, had been sent for and was expected to take over the running of operations on Hispaniola. On April 24, 1495, Columbus led a three-caravel expedition out of Isabela to find what lay to the west. His object was to explore the south coast of Cuba and locate the island of Jamaica which the Indians had told him about. Remaining convinced that Cuba was a part of the Asian mainland, in Peter Martyr's words, "he expected to arrive in the part of the world underneath us just near the Golden Cheronese, which is situated to the east of Persia."[2] Before turning back toward Hispaniola Columbus required everyone in the expedition to sign a formal deposition certifying that they had reached the mainland of the Orient.

During the five months he was away conditions at Isabela had deteriorated badly. Food was in short supply and a spirit of discontent was general throughout Hispaniola. Columbus's draconian measures aimed at an improvement of the situation worsened things and led to rebellion. A rift between Columbus and officers responsible to the crown opened and further worsened his position. Worst of all, relations with the Indians, never truly good, had broken down thanks to the excessive brutality of an officer assigned to lead reinforcements to the gold field outpost. Such a breakdown seemed almost inevitable to Peter Martyr who wrote:

It is a fact that the people who accompanied the Admiral in his second voyage were for the most part undisciplined, unscrupulous vagabonds, who only employed their ingenuity in gratifying their appetites. Incapable of moderation in their acts of injustice, they carried off the women of the islanders under the very eyes of their brothers and husbands; given over to violence and thieving, they had profoundly vexed the natives.[3]

INDIAN SLAVERY AND REVOLT

That a general Indian uprising broke out should come as no surprise. Punitive raids against the Indians, who now fought to expel the increasingly unwelcome Spanish invaders, soon turned to slaving raids. Up to this point the ships coming out from Spain with provisions and supplies were sent home empty. The unruly horde Columbus had brought from Spain would engage in no activities other than gold hunting, so nothing of bulk was produced. In early 1495 four ships sailed for Spain loaded with 550 Indian slaves. Aside from small amounts of gold, the first wealth of the Indies to reach Spain was in the form of slaves to be sold in Castile.

Michele Cuneo returned to Spain with this fleet. His account of preparations for sailing is a dismal story:

When our caravels . . . were to leave for Spain we gathered in our settlement one thousand six hundred male and female persons of these Indians, and of these we embarked in our caravels on February 17, 1495, five hundred and fifty souls among the healthiest males and females. For those who remained, we let it be known in the vicinity that anyone who wanted to take some of them could do so, to the amount desired; which was done. And when each man was thus provided with slaves, there still remained about four hundred, to whom permission was granted to go where they wished. Among them were many women with children still at suck. Since they were afraid that we might return to capture them once again, and in order to escape us the better, they left their children anywhere on the ground and began to flee like desperate creatures; and some fled so far that they found themselves at seven or eight days' distance from our community at Isabela, beyond the mountains and across enormous rivers; consequently they will henceforth be captured only with great difficulty. Among the captives was also one of their kings with two lieutenants whom it had been decided to kill the next day and they were confined for that reason but during the night they chewed through their ropes and escaped . . . But when we reached the waters near Spain two hundred of these Indians died, I believe because of the unaccustomed air which is colder than theirs. We

This fanciful woodcut was printed as an illustration for the edition of Columbus's first letter that was published in Basel in 1494. The Mediterranean-style rowing galley is placed incongruously off the shore of Hispaniola, here named "insula hyspana." It is obvious that the artist had no idea of the type of ships Columbus used in his voyage. The people on the island, some of whom are about to flee from the two Europeans in the boat, appear to be based on Columbus's description included in the letter. Columbus wrote: "The inhabitants of both sexes in this island . . . go always naked as they were born, with the exception of some of the women, who use the covering of a leaf, or small bough, or an apron which they prepare for that purpose." He went on to say that they were "naturally timid and fearful" in Contact encounters, but when reassured and at ease they were "very simple and honest, and exceedingly liberal with all they have." In spite of these commendable virtues Columbus and his fellows were so unabashedly Europocentric that they evidenced little if any guilt or remorse as they proceeded to enslave the Caribbean natives in the years that followed (Thacher Collection, Rare Book and Special Collections Division).

cast them into the sea. We landed the slaves at Cadiz and half of them were sick. They are not a people suited to hard work, they suffer from the cold and have a short life.[4]

COLUMBUS RETURNS TO SPAIN

Complaints against Columbus began to flow back to court in a growing tide. Realizing he would need to use all of his persuasive powers to buy more time from the monarchs the Admiral sailed for Spain early in March 1496. Rather than choosing the quick northern return route of his first voyage he followed his urge to go south and bucked trade wind and current to the Carib island Guadelupe. More time was lost while the Indian slaves on board were put to work making cassava bread from tubers stolen from Carib fields.

Back in Spain Columbus was well received by his monarchs. A great deal of time was required to hold what seemed to the Admiral like endless conferences to work out policies for the future of the colony. During this period refugees from Hispaniola were filtering back into Spanish society and their tales were far less favorable than the optimistic reports Columbus had been broadcasting at court. As a consequence there was no rush of volunteers to sign on for his modest six-ship third voyage which departed for Hispaniola at the end of May 1498.

COLUMBUS'S THIRD VOYAGE TO THE INDIES

Although nothing had been mentioned concerning any further exploration, Columbus divided the fleet sending three ships directly to Hispaniola while he took the remaining caravels on an unscheduled voyage of discovery to the south of where he had penetrated on his last voyage. According to his son Ferdinand, the

Admiral intended "to sail in search of the mainland."[5] He followed a course that took him far to the south of the Cape Verde Islands and almost to the latitude of Sierra Leone before turning to the west to finally approach Trinidad from the south. Coasting the southern flank of Trinidad, Columbus passed the freshwater outflow of the mighty Orinoco River delta and sailed through the Gulf of Paria to his first landing on the mainland of South America "never suspecting that the land of Paria, which he named Isla de Gracia, was a continent."[6]

Arriving at Santo Domingo on the south coast of Hispaniola at the end of August 1498, Columbus found a colony in chaos rather than the haven he needed after a hard voyage that had left him half blind. As his son wrote, "he found all at sixes and sevens, for all the families of the island were infected with a rebellious spirit. Part of the people he had left were dead, and of the survivors more than one hundred and sixty were sick with the French sickness [syphilis]."[7] To make matters even worse the three ships Columbus had sent ahead with relief supplies had not arrived. Further draconian measures only delayed the inevitable end of Columbus's attempt to administer the first European colony in the Indies. According to the chroniclers, Queen Isabela's support of the Admiral was withdrawn when she became upset by reports of his giving a slave to each colonist malcontent deciding to return to Spain. According to Las Casas she "became very angry, saying, 'What right does My Admiral have to give away My vassals to anyone?' and other such things."[8] Las Casas found it strange that the queen would show such anger about the 300 Indian slaves the Admiral gave to the repatriates and say nothing about the many others that the Admiral and his brother as governor had previously sent for sale in Spain. He was too politic a subject to suggest that the reason might have been that the crown had profited from the earlier shipments.

COLUMBUS RETURNS IN DISGRACE BUT SAILS ONE MORE TIME

A distinguished courtier named Francisco de Bobadilla was chosen to proceed to Hispaniola and investigate the state of affairs there. Fearing that drastic actions might be called for, Bobadilla was authorized to remove Columbus from his position as governor and replace him should that be required. The story of Columbus's arrest and return in chains with his brothers to Spain is widely known and so will not be repeated here.

Deprived of his civil authority, Columbus remained Admiral of the Ocean Sea and discoverer of the Indies. Using all of his wiles with the queen and playing on her sympathy, the Admiral gained her support for another voyage of exploration in the western seas and islands. With four ships provided by the crown Columbus, accompanied by his son Ferdinand, sailed from Cadiz on May 11, 1502, for his fourth and last voyage to the New World.

COLUMBUS'S HIGH VOYAGE

Following a track that took him close to the equator, a landfall was made on June 15, 1502, at Martinique, the next large island south of his last landfall at Dominica. After a few days of refreshment and rest, the fleet began what the Admiral referred to as his "High Voyage." Finding one of his ships to be "a crank and a dull sailor" that came close to shipping water whenever the sails were loaded, Columbus tried to put into port at Santo Domingo to trade her for a more seaworthy vessel. Not wishing to risk any attempt at a coup d'état, the governor refused entry to the Admiral and his fleet.

After riding out some heavy weather on the south coast of Hispaniola, the fleet headed "south toward the continent" according to

Ferdinand's account. On the Honduran coast they encountered an Indian dugout Ferdinand described as "a canoe long as a galley . . . freighted with merchandise" and with "a palm-leaf awning like that which the Venetian gondolas carry." Sheltered under the awning were "the children and women and all the baggage and merchandise" that the twenty-five paddlers were transporting.[9] The oldest crewmember, named Yumbé, was taken aboard the flagship to inform Columbus "about the secrets of that land and to persuade the others to talk to the Christians." Yumbé served as a pilot even to the point of drawing "a sort of chart of the coast" for Columbus.[10] When the limit of the area where his language was spoken was reached he was given presents and allowed to go free. Experts are divided as to the identity and origin of Yumbé and the seaborne Indian merchant traders. Certainly the fact that their cargo included such items as copper bells and axes, tools and weapons edged with obsidian, and artistic ceramics and that cacao beans were being used as currency, argues strongly for a Mayan connection. If this is the case, Yumbé deserves a place in the Mayan pantheon of heroes for leading Columbus to the east and away from the core-land of his people.

The Admiral, now often kept to his bunk by ill health, turned east to sail laboriously along the northern Honduras coast and then south to Panama. The abundance of gold there induced Columbus to establish an abortive settlement named Santa Maria near the mouth of the Rio Belén on Panama's Mosquito Gulf. A breakdown in relations with the local Indians soon forced the settlement's abandonment and Columbus and his expedition departed never knowing that they had been within an easy march of the Pacific Ocean. The ships were badly riddled by worms and rot and came near to sinking before they were beached on the southern coast of Jamaica.

After being shipwrecked on Jamaica for a year and five days, during which a bloody mutiny broke out and starvation threatened, Columbus and his surviving party of about one hundred were rescued. The Admiral finally arrived in Spain in November 1504 after an absence of two-and-a-half years. The hardest blow of all for the now sick and infirm Columbus was the cold indifference of his monarchs. Absolutely no notice was taken of his return and he was not summoned to court to make any sort of report. When Queen Isabela was on her death bed in late November 1504, Columbus was spurned and his last hope for what he deemed a just reward for his efforts and sufferings died with her. Columbus, surrounded by his family and a few loyal shipmates, crossed over the bar himself on May 20, 1506.

CONQUEST OF THE INDIES

By the time of Columbus's death, Hispaniola was a reasonably stable and comparatively well-run colony under the administration of Fray Nicolás de Ovando. Under Ovando, the military resistance and political structure of the Indians were broken by liquidating the major caciques. Surviving minor caciques were effectively made the overseers of the remaining Indians, who were forced to labor in the mines or fields. The governor controlled the allotment of Indians to Spanish entrepreneurs who employed them for economic gain. Unfortunately it was a system that included no provisions for the conservation of the labor force on which it rested. The native population was subjected to unbelievably inhuman treatment under what is known as the *encomienda* system. The catastrophic decline of the Indian population that resulted from these abuses and alien diseases was discussed in the preceding chapter.

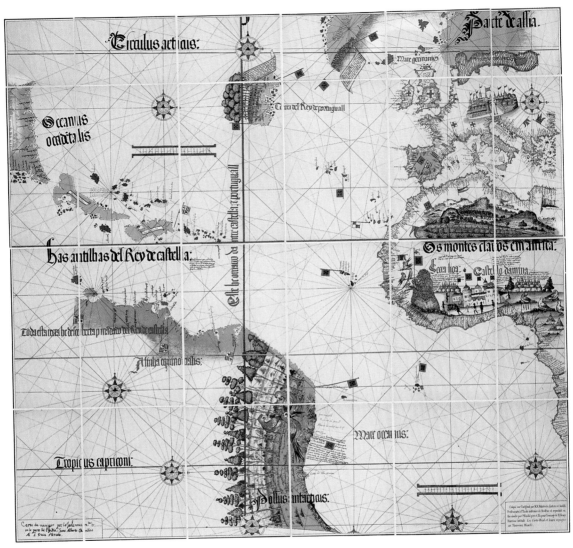

Western portion of the Cantino world map of 1502. Because some experts question the 1500 date usually given for the Juan de la Cosa map, the Cantino map may be the earliest to show the European discoveries in the Western Hemisphere. Alberto Cantino paid an anonymous Lisbon cartographer "12 golden ducats" to prepare secretly this copy of the official Portuguese map showing the discoveries of Columbus, John Cabot, and the Corte Real brothers in the western seas. Cantino forwarded the completed map to his patron in Italy, the Duke of Ferrara, sometime between October 1501 and November 1502. Notice the Line of Demarcation which divided the spheres of Spain and Portugal. Brazil and Newfoundland are both shown on the Portuguese side while the Caribbean islands, northern coast of South America, and a coast west of Cuba are on the Spanish side of the Line of Demarcation. The large landmass at the western edge of the map is a matter of debate, with many scholars identifying it with Florida or some other part of North America. Another school of thought identifies it with a "Horn" or projection of Asia as shown on the globe of Martin Behaim (illustrated in Chapter 2) or other Ptolemaic maps. This photograph was made from a beautifully colored facsimile of the original prepared by Henry Harrisse (Geography and Map Division).

The inevitable shortage of labor on Hispaniola helped trigger interest in the other islands. It was, however, the lure of gold that was the primary impulse for the spread of Spanish settlement from the Hispaniola core to other West Indian islands. Islands yielding gold were sought out and settled, whereas islands lacking gold were often bypassed or shown little interest by colonists.

JUAN PONCÉ DE LEON

Juan Poncé de Leon, who gained his greatest fame by discovering and naming Florida, was responsible for the initial settlement of Puerto Rico. In 1508 he led a party across the Mona Passage that lay between the eastern end of Hispaniola and Puerto Rico. The Indians they encountered were very friendly and led them to mountain streams where gold was found. San Juan, with an excellent harbor and close to the best gold-bearing streams, ultimately became the center from which Puerto Rico was developed. In a repetition of the events on Hispaniola the Indians were forced to grow food for the Spaniards, work in the mining activities, and act as carriers and general laborers. Like their fellows across the Mona Passage they rose in a desperate revolt and were defeated as their numbers dwindled through catastrophic death rates.

In a very short time Poncé de Leon became one of the richest men in the Indies. Through no fault of his own, he was replaced as governor of Puerto Rico when the king entered into a settlement with the heirs of Columbus. In 1512 the wealthy exgovernor received a royal *Capitulation* or patent permitting him to discover and settle the "Islands of Beniny" [Bemini] at his own expense. In March 1513, Poncé de Leon led three armed vessels on a voyage he claimed was for discovery, but many experts feel was really

This map of the Spanish discoveries in and around the Caribbean was printed from a woodcut in the 1511 edition of Peter Martyr's Oceani Decas, which was printed in Seville. Appropriately at the center of the map is the island of Hispaniola, shown as "Isla Española," with "Santjua" (Puerto Rico) to the east, "Jamaica" and "Isla de Cuba" to the west, and "los Incaíos" (the Bahamas) to the north. Beyond the Bahamas is a large coastline marked "Isla de Beimeni parte" which appears to have been Poncé de Leon's goal when he "discovered" Florida two years later. Another feature on this map that has stirred debate is the peninsula to the west of Cuba, named "Baya D'Lagartos" but often identified with the Yucatan Peninsula. Since the first documented expedition to sight Yucatan did not sail until 1517, this map was used by some as evidence of an earlier unrecorded voyage. In 1989, however, David W. Tilton laid that hypothesis to rest through a careful analysis of other maps from the first half of the sixteenth century. Tilton convincingly links "Baya D'Lagartos" with a stretch of the Honduran coastline that was well known by 1510 (Rare Book and Special Collections Division).

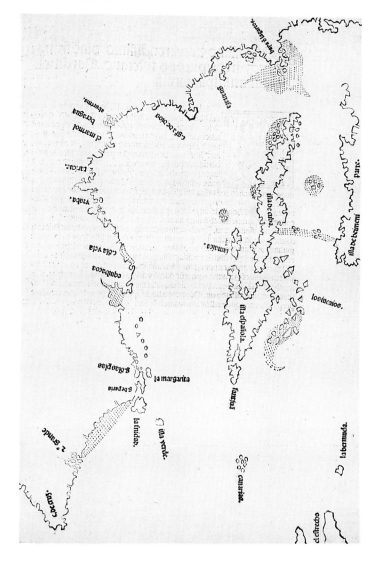

intended to capture Indian slaves on the Bahama Islands.

Present day scholars do not agree as to the details of the route Ponçé de Leon sailed, but according to the official historian of the Indies, Antonio de Herrera, the fleet called at *Guanahani*, the first island Columbus landed on two decades earlier. Sailing northwest from *Guanahani*, they reached a land they believed was an island on the day of the Feast of the Resurrection which was commonly called the Feast of Flowers, so they called it "La Florida."

When Ponçé landed after being hailed by Indians on the shore, a fight broke out. The Indians, armed with bows and arrows and spears tipped with "sharpened bones and fish spines," wounded two Spaniards with little hurt to themselves.[11] In another clash with Indians, four women were captured who were able to act as guides. The Spanish persisted in believing La Florida was an island in spite of the Indians' telling them it was a mainland and naming its "provinces" or chiefdoms. According to the Indians the land we now call Florida was named "Cautio" because the people "covered certain parts of their body with palm leaves woven in the form of a plait." Historian Herrera claimed that it was not for some years after Ponçé de Leon's explorations that the Spanish realized that Florida was a peninsula of a continent and not an island.

By far the most important discovery made by Ponçé de Leon and his pilot Anton de Alaminos had nothing to do with land, whether islands or main. When they crossed the Bahama Channel, as the waters between the east coast of Florida and the Bahama Islands came to be known, the ships sailed into the mighty flow now named the Gulf Stream. Within sight of the Florida coast sailing toward the south, "they saw such a current that, although they had a strong wind, they could not go forward, but rather backward . . . the current was so great that it was more powerful than the wind."[12] At a later date Alaminos would use his knowledge of the Gulf Stream's swift northern flow to pioneer the sea route that became the seaborne highway for ships and galleons carrying the wealth of the Americas home to Spain.

Although his landings on the stoutly defended beaches of Florida had failed to produce gold or anything else of exceptional value, Ponçé de Leon decided to attempt founding a colony there in 1521. His timing for such an adventure suggests that reports of Cortes's discovery of the Aztec's gold may have inspired Ponçé de Leon to try for a similar rich find in Florida. Using his great wealth he equipped a party of about two hundred colonists with fifty horses and sailed for the southwest tip of the peninsula. Shortly after their initial landing a devastating Indian attack forced the Spanish to beat a hasty retreat and delivered the expedition's leader, Ponçé de Leon, a mortal arrow wound. The wealthy discoverer-slave hunter and would-be colonizer of Florida died in Cuba shortly after the expedition's survivors landed there.

The exploration of Cuba had begun on the eastern end of the island closest to Hispaniola. When discovered, the gold deposits proved to be even richer than those of Puerto Rico. Havana was founded in 1519 but grew slowly until the center of Spanish interests shifted from Hispaniola to Mexico and the mainland. Then the excellence of its harbor and proximity to the Gulf Stream flowing through the Straits of Florida guaranteed Havana's importance to the empire. Cuba's internal development was interrupted and slowed by the loss of many colonists who were lured off the island to Mexico and other more promising colonies as they opened on the mainland.

Of all the islands of the Greater Antilles, Jamaica yielded the least gold and was the least attractive to the Spanish. Agriculture and livestock ranching proved to be the only sources of wealth the island could provide. As a consequence, very few Spanish colonists were attracted to Jamaica following its opening in 1512. By 1655, when the English conquered the island, fewer than fifteen-hundred Spaniards were living on the farms and ranches spread along Jamaica's coasts.

CONQUEST OF TIERRE FIRME BEGINS

The coast of Yucatan was first contacted in 1517 by adventurers sailing from Cuba across the Yucatan Channel "to make a descent on certain islands between Cuba and Honduras . . . to seize a number of the inhabitants and make slaves of them."[13] In spite of the fact that the Indians, who escorted them to shore in dugout canoes capable of carrying up to fifty men, led them into a nasty ambush, the Spaniards were very complimentary of their culture. In his account of that first encounter Bernal Diaz wrote of their "buildings of lime and stone wherein were idols of clay with diabolical countenances, and in strange unnatural postures, . . . three diadems, and some imitations of birds and fishes in alloyed gold."[14] In his enthusiasm Diaz revealed that the Indians' masonry buildings and gold gave the Spanish "a high idea of the Country we had discovered."

In the following year a second expedition added to what had been learned about the cotton-clad, maize-growing Mayan Indians of the Yucatan Peninsula. This in turn led to the dispatch of an expedition under the command of Hernan Cortés which landed on the coast of Mexico on April 22, 1519. Once he learned of the existence of a great Indian ruler high in the mountainous interior whose control extended over the coastal Indians, Cortés began to formulate a program designed to make him accept the suzerainty of the monarchs of Spain.

HERNAN CORTÉS ENCOUNTERS THE AZTECS

Cortés was quick to assess the political situation that then existed among the Indians of Mexico. What he discovered was an enormous Indian population that, as he wrote Emperor Charles V, "had been subdued by force not long previously." Rather than loyal and loving subjects of the distant Indian emperor who "took their children to sacrifice to his idols," Cortés was dealing with people who were eager to throw off an onerous Aztec yoke.[15] While their horses, sharp-edged steel weapons, armor, and primitive fire arms were important military advantages, the Spaniards could never have conquered the Aztec army and seized Mexico City without their tens of thousands of Indian allies.

To these allies, Cortés and his small force of audacious Spaniards must have seemed a far lesser evil than the mighty Montezuma whose agents exacted such heavy tribute from them. The gold that seemed to be the main objective of the Spanish was already being taken up as taxes to support the Aztec nobility's opulent life-style in the valley of Mexico.

In his second letter to the emperor, reporting his advance on the Aztec capital, Cortés told how he encountered "a great barrier built of dry stone and as much as nine feet high, which ran right across the valley from one mountain range to the other."[16] When he inquired as to the reason for the wall he was told that he was at the frontier of the province of Tlascalteca "whose inhabitants were Mutezuma's enemies and were always at war with him."[17] Montezuma's agents were eager for Cortés to follow a route that would avoid passing through Tlascalteca. Members of the coastal tribe who had allied with him earlier and whose advice he chose to follow assured Cortés that the Aztecs recommended the detour only "to prevent me from forming an alliance with that province."[18]

The story of Cortés's undertaking the conquest of the mighty empire of Montezuma with a force of five hundred men, fifteen horses and six primitive cannon is a frequently told tale that cannot be repeated here. It is, however, often told in a manner that omits or severely underestimates the role of Cortés's Indian allies in the Conflict encounter with Montezuma and the Aztec armies supporting his empire. The conquest of Mexico was in truth the result of Cortés's ability to weld the Indian enemies of the Aztecs into a force that could be led and directed by a relative handful of well-armed seasoned European military specialists. What the Spaniards taught their Indian allies was a new type of warfare, one in which the killing of enemies was the chief objective. Unlike the Europeans, the Mexican Indians fought primarily to take captives.

With the treasure-rich Aztecs brought to their knees by Cortés and his fellows, other Spaniards with similar ambitions cast their eyes toward the lands forming a great arc north of the Gulf of Mexico. Alonzo Alvarez de Pineda sailed from Florida to Mexico in 1519, proving that the Gulf of Mexico coastline formed the continuous facade of a large northern land area that came to be shown on maps as La Florida. His expedition had been financed by wealthy Governor of Jamaica Francisco de Garay.

This colorful coat of arms was awarded by Spain's Charles I to "the Most Illustrious Lord Don Hernando Cortés, Marqués del Valle," in recognition of his "pacification and colonization of . . . New Spain and its provinces." The patent delivering the arms included a lengthy and detailed narrative of Cortés's conquest of Mexico. The lower right-hand quadrant of the shield contains a representation of "the city of Tenochtitlan fortified on the water, in memory of the fact that by force of arms you conquered it and subjected it to our dominion." The seven faces in the yellow border around the shield symbolize "the seven captains and lords of the seven provinces . . . around the lake, who rebelled against us . . . to be shown as prisoners bound with a chain . . ." (Harkness Collection, Manuscript Division).

LUCAS VASQUES DE AYLLON SAILS NORTH TO CHICORA

Another wealthy civil servant and judge on Hispaniola, Lucas Vasques de Ayllon, also received royal permission to search out new lands to the north. The expedition Ayllon sponsored spent little effort in exploring and, contrary to his orders, captured over one hundred and fifty Indians to sell as slaves on the islands. One of the Indians learned Spanish and was baptized a

A drawing illustrating the codex titled "Relación . . . de la provincia de Michoacán" which is captioned "How the Cazonci and other lords tried to drown themselves." The Cazonci was the human representative of the God Curicaveri who was charged with conquering the entire earth in the cosmology of the Tarascan people. At the time of Cortés's conquest of Mexico, the Cazonci was named Tangaxoan and he held the position of master or governor and captain general in war. In this scene the Cazonci and his advisors were on the verge of suicide by drowning through fear and despair at the approach of the Spanish conquerors (Peter Force Collection, Manuscript Division).

By the time Gabriel Tatton, the London-based chartmaker, engraved this beautiful map in 1600, the main focus of New World interest had shifted from Hispaniola west to Mexico, Nova Granada, and California and north to Florida. Notice that mountain symbols, indicating a drainage divide, extend from the Atlantic to the west across the northern part of Florida leaving no place from the drainage system of the Mississippi River. This is a misconception that was not finally corrected until 1700. Much of the detail shown in the Florida portion of the map is apparently derived from the exploration headed by Hernando de Soto in 1540–1543. Similarly the discoveries of several other explorers are incorporated by Tatton in this map (Geography and Map Division).

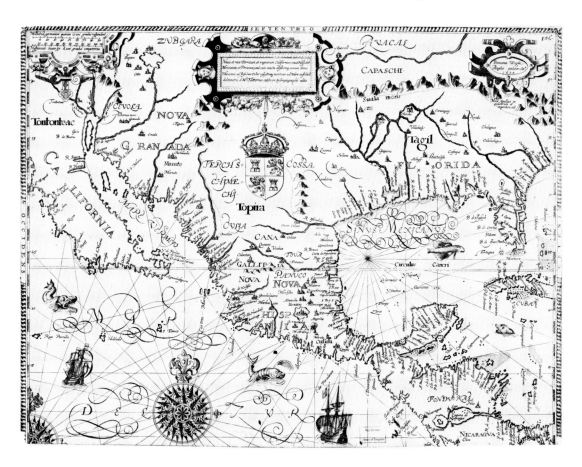

Catholic with the name Francisco de Chicora or Chicorama. His home province on the Carolina coast was named Chicora. Francisco accompanied Ayllon back to Spain and became famous as an informant about his people and native land for Peter Martyr, the historian author of *De Orbe Novo*.[19]

Ayllon maintained his interest in the lands to the north and, in 1525, recruited an expedition of 600 who were loaded onboard three large vessels. Because his object was founding a colony along the Atlantic coast of La Florida, Ayllon included a number of wives and children as well as African slaves in his company. The Indians of the area were quickly informed as to what lay in store for them by Francisco de Chicora who jumped ship at the first opportunity to rejoin his own people.

Recent research indicates that Ayllon may have chosen a spot near the mouth of the Altamaha River in Georgia to build his town.[20] According to the account published by the official Spanish chronicler Oviedo and based on reports of the expedition survivors, the area they settled was called "Gualdape." Oviedo described the site: "the land was level and very marshy but the river very powerful . . . at the entrance of it was a bay which ships could enter only at high tide."[21] The Indians of the area were said to be few in number and "living in great communal houses far from each other, constructed of very tall and beautiful pines, leaving a crown of leaves on top . . . with a space between the two sides of from fifteen to twenty feet, the length of the walls being three hundred or more feet . . . covered all with matting interwoven between the logs where there may be hollows or open places. Furthermore they cross these beams with other pines placed lengthwise on the inside, increasing the thickness of their walls . . . Their temples have walls of stone or mortar (which mortar they make of Oyster shells)."

The mention that the Indians were "few in number" may indicate that the native people around Ayllon's town, San Miguel de Gualdape, had been impacted by the epidemic of smallpox that experts feel must have swept across much of North America in the period 1520–1524. Disease and malnutrition soon began to take their toll of the colonists, with Ayllon himself dying of fever. The slaves revolted and Indians killed off many unwary colonists who strayed away from the encampment. Faced with nothing but failure and death the colonists withdrew for Hispaniola in the winter of 1527. Death continued to take its toll, however, with 150 of the survivors dying of exposure on the homeward voyage.

No cartographer was better qualified to produce a map summarizing the state of New World exploration at the end of almost three decades of effort by the Europeans than Diego Ribero. A Portuguese by birth, Ribero spent his most productive period working in the service of Spain as an expert cosmographer-cartographer. He was on close personal terms with most of the notable pilots and explorers of his period. As Spain's Cosmographer Royal, Ribero was responsible for keeping the "padron real," or official world map, revised and up-to-date as reports of new discoveries were received at court. Pictured here is the analytical facsimile of Ribero's original map that was prepared by the German student of the discovery and exploration of North America, Johann Georg Kohl. Kohl's large collection of map facsimiles were produced a century-and-a-half ago and before photocopying was available. They were deemed important reference material by the U.S. Department of State where they were held before coming to the Library of Congress (Kohl Collection, Geography and Map Division).

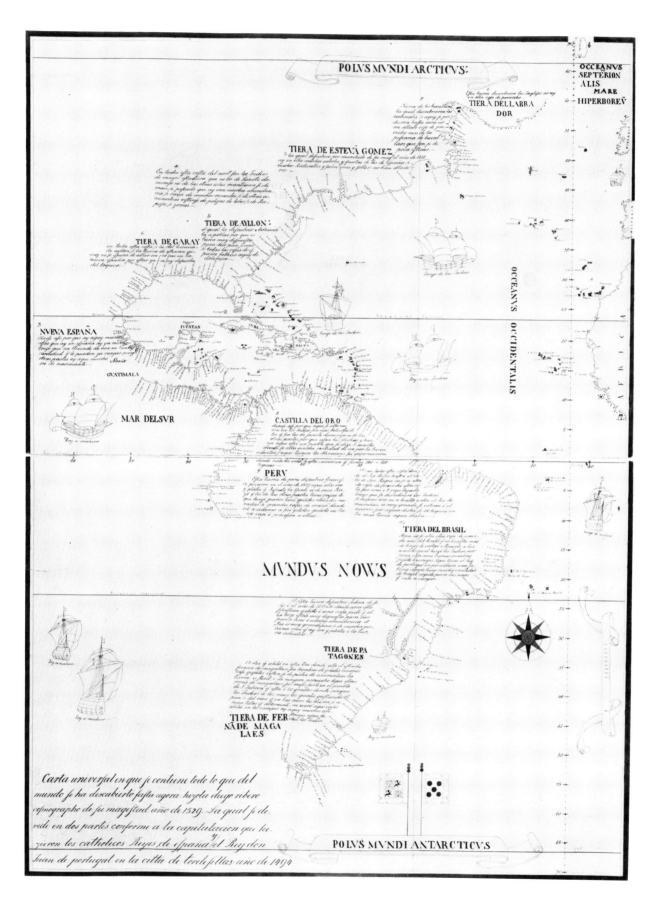

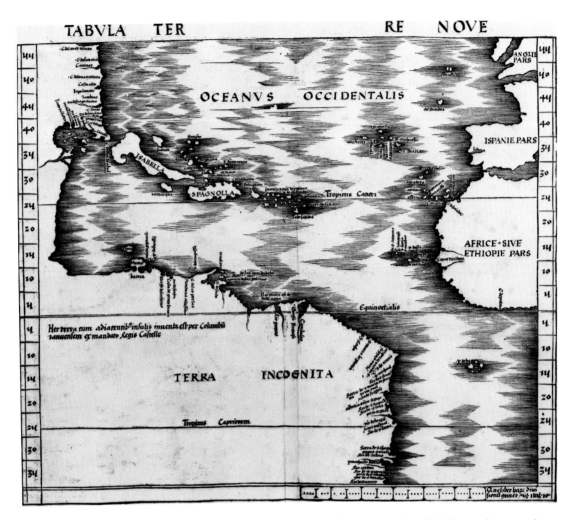

This map by Martin Waldseemüller was published in the edition of Ptolemy's Geography, titled Geographie opus, that appeared in Strassburg in 1513. By this time Waldseemüller appears to have reconsidered the wisdom of his rush to name the New World (Tabula Terre Nove) in honor of Amerigo Vespucci on his 1507 map. Notice that Columbus is given credit for his discoveries in the name of the crown of Spain. Notice also that Cuba is correctly shown as an island and is named Isabella. The land shown to the west of Cuba is terminated by the edge of the map so the viewer can only speculate as to its nature and whether it is part of an island or mainland. This was the first map solely devoted to the coasts and islands of the New World to be included in a Ptolemy. Although Waldseemüller was no longer naming the New World "America" after Vespucci, the genie was out of the bottle and other cartographers quickly adopted the name (Geography and Map Division).

PANFILO DE NARVAEZ AND
THE ISLAND OF FLORDIA

While Ayllon and his would-be colonists were losing their struggle to survive on the Atlantic Coast north of Florida, the Cuban conqueror who had been outmaneuvered earlier by Cortés, Panfilo de Narvaez, received a detailed set of *Capitulations* from the King of Spain allowing him to "explore, discover and settle the lands that lie between Rio de las Palmas and the island of Florida." With his commission as Governor and Captain General of the colony, Narvaez was required to accept a long list of restrictions. It is worth quoting a short section of the *Capitulations* because they make clear the fact that the king and his advisors were well aware of the many abuses that earlier conquistadors and colonists had inflicted on the native people of the Caribbean islands and Mexico:

Whereas we have been informed and are aware that the unrestrained greed of some of our subjects who went to Our Islands and the Mainland of the Ocean Sea, and the bad way they treated the native Indians of these Indies, Islands and Mainland, in the great and excessive work that they gave them, keeping them in the Mines to extract gold, and in the pearl fisheries . . . and the farms, making them work excessively . . . not giving them clothing and food . . . treating them with cruelty and callowness worse than if they had been slaves, that these have been the cause of the death of a large number of these Indians: so much so that many of the islands and part of the mainland were left barren and unpopulated . . . which has also a great impediment to the conversion of these Indians to Our Holy Catholic Faith . . . which has been and is a great disservice to the Lord Our God.[22]

Passing regulations outlawing the abusive treatment was a relatively simple matter for the king. Their enforcement, however, proved to be almost impossible on the distant frontiers of a young and rapidly growing empire.

Narvaez quickly set about organizing a large expedition to sail from Spain to his new colonial enterprise. Although the overwhelming majority of the party of 600 were soldiers, Narvaez did include a few women and a number of African slaves along with a group of friars to look after the conversion of the Indians. After a difficult crossing from Spain and long delays in Santo Domingo and Cuba the expedition, now about half its original size, sailed into the Gulf of Mexico in the spring of 1528. Making a landfall somewhere near Tampa Bay, Narvaez decided to move overland up the Florida peninsula to the Indian settlement at the site of modern Tallahassee.

He lost no time in putting aside the king's admonitions for kindness toward the natives and took captive the first four Indians encountered. Discovering "traces of gold" in the Indians' charnel house caused considerable excitement and the predictable demands to know where it had been obtained. "Having by signs asked the Indians whence these things came, they motioned to us that very far from there, was a province called Apalachen, where was much gold, and so the same abundance in Palachen of everything that we at all cared for."[23] Here we glimpse an example of an Indian strategy that was employed in countless stress-filled encounters with impatient, single-minded, gold-seeking Europeans. It was a strategy of "tell them what they want to hear and what will get them to leave as soon as possible." Invariably it took the form of assurances that some distant group had gold and foodstuffs in abundance. In many instances the Indians were probably telling about their trading partners from whom they did in fact receive commodities and articles not produced in their immediate localities.

Struggling overland the Narvaez party was soon in a bad way. As one member complained:

We were going without being able to communicate with the Indians by use of speech and without an interpreter and we could but poorly understand ourselves with them, or learn what we desired to know of the land; that we were . . . entering, a country of which we had no account, and had no knowledge of its character, of what there was in it, or by what people inhabited, neither did we know in what part of it we were; and besides all this, we had not food to sustain us in wandering we knew not whither; that with regard to the stores in the ships, rations could not be given to each man for such a journey, more than a pound of biscuit and another of bacon.[24]

The author of this critique of Narvaez's ill-founded plan to march overland "in quest of a port and land that should be better," was one of history's greatest survivors, Alvar Nuñez Cabeza de Vaca. Cabeza de Vaca was vigorous but unsuccessful in arguing that the whole expedition should reembark and "seek a harbor and a soil better than this to occupy, since what we had seen of it was desert and poor, such as had never before been discovered in those parts."

Narvaez was unmoved in his decision to send the ships on up the coast to search for a harbor that his pilots assured him "stretched up into the land a dozen leagues" and could not be missed by his party "marching ever by the shore" toward Panuco in Mexico. On the first day of May 1528 Narvaez with a party of 300 including three clergymen and forty mounted cavalry, took leave of the ships to begin their ill-fated trek to Apalachen and the cruel deaths that would ultimately claim all but four of their number.

For the first two arduous weeks they "saw not an Indian, and found neither village nor house." When finally they encountered a party of "two-hundred natives, more or less" on the opposite bank of a swift river, "they so insulted us with their gestures that we were forced to break with them." Managing to take captive five or six of the Indians the Spaniards were guided to their village and found "a large quantity of maize in a fit state to be gathered." "Besides the weariness in which we came, we were exhausted from hunger," wrote Cabeza de Vaca.[25]

CONFLICT TURNS TO DISASTER

When they finally realized that the large harbor the pilots promised they would find did not exist, Narvaez decided to head directly for Apalachen with the Indian captives serving as guides. After further Conflict encounters with Indians, in which additional captives were taken, the party "suffering great hunger" and "great fatigue," and many with "galled shoulders from carrying armor on the back," the conquerors attacked and seized Apalachen. "The town consisted of forty small houses, made low, and set up in sheltered places because of frequent storms. The material was thatch," wrote Cabeza de Vaca, who with nine other cavalry and fifty infantry had taken the place. In the town they found only women and children. The men soon returned to find the invaders off guard. "They began discharging arrows at us . . . killed the horse of the assessor and at last taking to flight, they left us," Cabeza de Vaca recalled. Little more than supplies of maize and deerskins plus some "Mantelets of thread, small and poor with which the women partially cover their persons" were found at Apalachen.[26]

The Indian warriors attacked again "with such promptness and alacrity that they succeeded in setting fire to the houses in which we were." The Spanish troops sallied against their attackers but found that because of the terrain and cover they could "do them no injury, save in the single instance of one Indian, whom we killed." After remaining as unwelcome guests for twenty-five days and exploring the region around Apalachen, the Spanish departed in quest of the sea and a town called Aute.

Attacks by the Indians of the region, however, did not cease. Often they would attack the Spanish column at difficult water crossings or where fallen trees made the cavalry ineffective. Of one such encounter Cabeza de Vaca wrote:

Some of our men were wounded in this conflict, for whom the good armor they wore did not avail. There were those this day who swore that they had seen two red oaks, each the thickness of the lower part of the leg, pierced through from side to side by arrows, considering the power and skill which the Indians are able to project them. I myself saw an arrow that had entered the butt of an elm to the depth of a span.[27]

Cabeza de Vaca came to respect his warrior adversaries:

The Indians we had so far seen in Florida are all archers. They go naked, are large of body, and appear at a distance like giants. They are of admirable proportions, very spare and of great activity and strength. The bows they use are as thick as the arm, of eleven or twelve palms in length, which they will discharge at two hundred paces with so great precision that they miss nothing.[28]

After nine days of almost constant attack the Spanish reached Aute only to find "all the inhabitants gone and the houses burned." Fortunately the gardens, "full of maize, beans and pumpkins were in great plenty, all beginning to be fit for gathering," had not been burned by the fleeing villagers. With Aute's crops to sustain them the Spanish sent out reconnaisssance parties to find a route to the coast. Needless to say the Indians continued their attacks and added to their score of horses and soldiers killed and wounded. Sickness overtook the embattled and exhausted Spanish and, as Cabeza de Vaca related, "there were not horses enough to carry the sick, who went on in increasing numbers day by day, and we knew no cure."

Arriving at the beach "we saw on our arrival how small were the means for advancing farther." Even more damning was the fact that in Cabeza's words, "there was not anywhere to go: and if there had been, the people werc unable to move forward, the greater part being ill." After discouraging an attempted defection by the cavalry the seriously ill governor of the expedition, Panfilo de Narvaez, accepted the consensus view that their only escape would come through building vessels and sailing along the coast to Mexico. At first hearing, this seemed an impossibility since the sick and battle-weary band of soldiers lacked the skills, tools, and materials needed for such an undertaking. Necessity, however, was the mother of invention and in answer to their prayers "one of the company [came] saying that he could make some pipes of wood, which with deer-skins might be made into bellows." As de Vaca wrote "we told him to set himself to work . . . making of nails, saws, axes, and other tools of which there was such need, from the stirrups, spurs, crossbows, and other things of iron there were."[29]

By killing a horse every third day the work force was fed and by dint of hard labor they built five boats of "twenty-two cubits" length in just over two weeks—a remarkable feat! Hair from the horses' manes and tails was used to make ropes, and shirts were used for sails. Caulking came from the "fibre of the palmito" and, thanks to the knowledge of a Greek named Don Theodoro, pitch was made from pine resin. Most difficult to find on the sandy coastal plain of Florida's Gulf Coast proved to be large stones to use as anchors and ballast.

ESCAPE BY SEA

The five boats were loaded and when forty-nine or fifty survivors piled in each with their provisions and clothes "not over a span of the gunwales remained above water." Water for drinking was stored in leathern bottles fashioned by taking the skin from the horses' legs whole. Needless to say, these ingenious water containers soon rotted to leave the survivors thirsty in their growing distress. It was a doleful embarkation Cabeza de Vaca described as the crude flotilla set to sea:

the boats were so crowded that we could not move: so much can necessity do, which drove us to hazard our lives in this manner, running into a turbulent sea, not a single one who went having a knowledge of navigation.[30]

The story of the voyage of Narvaez's ill-fated survivors as they coasted westward is even more dreadful than what had gone before. Predictably the jerry-built boats began to leak and, caught in the current off the Mississippi's mouth, they were swept far out of the sight of land and out of sight of one another. On November 6, 1528, with most of his companions near death,

Cabeza de Vaca's boat washed up on an island inhabited by Indians who proved to be friendly. In return for "beads and hawk-bells" the Indians brought the survivors "a large quantity of fish with certain roots, some a little larger than walnuts, others a trifle smaller, the greater part got from under the water with much labor."

BEFRIENDED BY INDIANS

When they attempted to continue their voyage their boat was capsized in the surf and the sur-

Johann Georg Kohl's "A Map Showing the Progress of the Discovery of the Gulf of Mexico." Kohl used colors and captions effectively in preparing maps to summarize the explorations of the three coasts of the United States. Here he shows the landing places and routes of de Ayllon, de Narvaez, Poncé de Leon, and several other explorers who came afterward. Kohl was an internationally recognized expert in the history of the discovery and exploration of North America active during the middle decades of the nineteenth century. His historical research was extensively employed by the U.S. Coast Survey (Kohl Collection, Geography and Map Division).

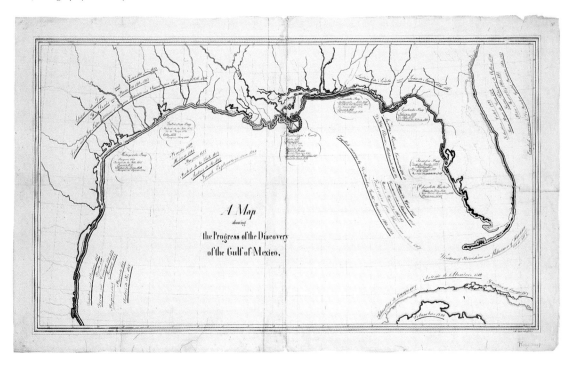

vivors "escaped naked as they were born, with the loss of all they had." Suffering cruelly in the harsh November storm winds, de Vaca described himself and his fellows as "nearer to death than to life." Even their friendly Indian benefactors "were alarmed and turned back" when they unexpectedly came upon the shivering, naked Spaniards on the beach. As Cabeza de Vaca recalled, "the Indians, at sight of what had befallen us, and our state of suffering and melancholy destitution, sat down among us, and from the sorrow and pity they felt, they all began to lament so earnestly that they might have been heard at a distance, and continued so doing more than half an hour."[31]

Thanks to the assistance of the Indians, who built several large fires at intervals between the castaways and their village, the Spaniards were able to struggle from fire to fire and reach shelter before they expired from exposure. Another of the boats had capsized only four miles from where de Vaca's had wrecked so the two crews were soon reunited. The late winter season was incredibly hard on the survivors as well as their Indian hosts. De Vaca wrote "the cold and tempestuous weather" was such that the Indians could no longer pull up roots and "the cane weirs in which they took fish no longer yielded anything." The Spaniards dispersed into small groups they called "messes" to better forage and survive. According to Cabeza de Vaca, a mess of five Spaniards quartered on the coast "came to such extremity that they ate their dead; the body of the last one only was found unconsumed." It is revealing to note that de Vaca reported the Indians to be very disturbed by this act of cannibalism among the Spanish survivors. According to de Vaca, if the Indians had known that the Spaniards were capable of such abominable acts they would have killed them at the outset. One wonders whether ritual cannibalism was also taboo to these coastal Texas Indians.

CABEZA DE VACA BEGINS AN EXODUS

Eventually de Vaca and his fellow survivors were absorbed into the Indian society as virtual slaves and traveled with them for several seasons digging roots and doing other menial work for their keep. When the Indians gathered for the prickly pear season in southeastern Texas, Cabeza de Vaca with two Spaniards and the black slave Estevan, "a Moor," joined in escaping from their Indian masters to make their way to the Spanish settlements far to the west. By posing as healers they were able to travel from one Indian group to another and move slowly across the wide northern part of Mexico toward the Pacific Ocean. On their route they encountered buffalo that Cabeza de Vaca likened in size to the cattle in Spain. He described their "small horns like the cows of Morocco" and hair that he termed "very long and flocky like the merino's." He liked the meat and told of how the Indians made blankets, shoes, and shields from the hides. When Cabeza, Estevan, and the other two survivors finally encountered the first fellow Christians they had been seeking through their years of hardship and survival, they were saddened and dismayed. Their first encounter was with a party of Spanish slave hunters who had been demoralizing the Indians of the northern Mexican frontier. At the time of this encounter the survivors were in company with a large number of friendly Indians who had been terrorized and dislocated by slaving parties. In all some six hundred of the uprooted Indians eventually gathered where Cabeza met with the mounted Spanish slave hunters. Out of their apparent affection for the wandering healers and in hope of persuading the slavers to spare them, the Indians presented them stores of corn and other foodstuffs as well as "a store of robes of cowhide [buffalo]." The slavers, however, were extremely jealous of the fact that Cabeza and his ragged and sun-blistered companions were held in such high esteem by the Indians while they were feared and despised. Their interpreter was ordered to tell the Indians that Cabeza and the other survivors were Spaniards like they who had been lost for a long time and that "they were the lords of the land who must be obeyed and served." As Cabeza de Vaca wrote later:

the Indians cared little or nothing for what was told them; and conversing among themselves said the Christians lied: that we had come whence the sun rises, and they whence it goes down; we healed the sick, they killed the healthy; that we had come naked and barefooted, while they had arrived in clothing and on horses with lances; that we were not covetous of anything, but all was given to us we directly turned to give, remaining with nothing; that the others had only purpose to rob whomsoever they found, bestowing nothing on anyone.[32]

"Even to the last," de Vaca wrote, "I could not convince the Indians that we were of the Christians."

Much has been written concerning the creation of the so-called "Noble Savage" as a philosophical or literary device designed to point up moral and social flaws in seventeenth- and eighteenth-century European society. If Cabeza de Vaca is to be believed, and there is no reason not to believe him, what he described here could be taken as an inventory of attributes representing the "Noble European" to the Indians of this reported encounter.

MEXICO AND TALES OF CIBOLA

When Cabeza de Vaca and his fellow survivors reached Mexico in 1536, they were sensations who brought stories that seemed to promise Indian cultures with great wealth living in the unexplored regions to the north. The Viceroy of Mexico began to lay plans for the exploration of the north to check out rumors of rich Indian

cities there. A Franciscan named Marcos de Niza was sent, with the Moor Estevan as his guide, as an advance party to check on the tales that Cabeza de Vaca, Estevan and the others had been telling. In his instructions, the Viceroy made it clear that Fray Marcos and the African Estevan were to carry out a careful geographical survey of the region north of the Spanish settlement frontier in Nueva Galicia.[33]

Fray Marcos and Estevan with "a large number of Indians from Petallán and from the town called Cuchillo distant some fifty leagues from the said town" set out on their reconnaissance on March 7, 1539. The account of the exploration in Fray Marcos's report is quite confusing, and the route followed is hard to reconstruct. It would appear that when they reached a point thought to be in southern Arizona the party broke up with Estevan and some Indians heading north "to see whether . . . information could be obtained of something important of what we were seeking."[34]

Some days later Estevan sent one of the Indians back to Fray Marcos who, in his official report, related the message he carried:

He [the Indian messenger] says and maintains that, in the first province, there are seven very large cities, all under one ruler, with large houses of stone and lime. . . . He says that the doorways to the best houses have many decorations of turquoises, of which there is a great abundance, and that the people in these cities are very well clothed. He told me many other details, both of these seven cities and of other provinces farther on, each one of which he claims to be much more important than these seven cities. In order to find out from him how he came to know this, we had a good many questions and answers, and I found him quite able to express himself. I rendered thanks to our Lord.[35]

The first of the fabulous Seven Cities, Cibola, lay thirty days of travel ahead the Indian told Fray Marcos. Messages from Estevan kept arriving and the air seemed full of reports of Cibola as the priest hurried forward to rendezvous with the Moor.

ESTEVAN DIES AT CIBOLA

Before reaching Cibola, Fray Marcos was met by Indians with the sad news of Estevan's death on the outskirts of Cibola. He was told of how the audacious Moor had sent messengers ahead "with his gourd, just as he was in the habit of doing so that they might know he was coming." Estevan's gourd rattle of welcome had "some strings of jingle bells and two feathers, one white and the other red." Rather than insuring his welcome into Cibola, Estevan's red feather and jingle bells inspired anger in the Zuni Indian leader who received it. He told the messengers to leave and tell Estevan "not to enter the city or he would kill them all." Estevan, counting on his bravado and black skin to win over this chief as they had so many others in the past, "told them that it was of no importance, that those who showed anger received him better."[36] Continuing on, Estevan was seized and robbed of his exotic possessions. When he tried to escape from his pueblo cell "people from the city pursued him and killed him and some of the Indians traveling with him." Fray Marcos claimed to have pushed on at great risk to his own life and got within sight of Cibola. His description of the city was probably a fabrication based on Indian reports. Even at their height none of the Zuni pueblos ever came even close to being the size of Mexico City as Fray Marcos claimed Cibola to be.[37]

The commander of Coronado's naval arm, Hernando de Alarcon, gained the details of Estevan's tragic deaths from the Indians in an unusual manner. Alarcon and a party in boats traveled up the Colorado River from its mouth and reported at length on the Indian groups they encountered. One of Alarcon's first queries to the Indians he met dealt with Cibola, its location and character. When he asked his usual questions of one group he was told that the "lord" of Cibola had a dog like Alarcon's own.

Later when the Indians observed the Spaniards eating from China plates they said that the chief at Cibola had some like them, "but that they were green, and no one had them except the Chieftain."

When he enquired as to how the chieftain acquired his rare plates and dog Alarcon was told the following:

The plates, four in all, he had obtained with the dog and other articles from a bearded negro. However, he did not know whence he had come. He had heard that the chieftain ordered him killed.[38]

At least one of the Indians who had accompanied Estevan survived and made his way back to Mexico City where he entertained Viceroy Mendoza with a flute he had been given and taught to play while a captive in Cibola.[39]

ESTEVAN REMEMBERED

Centuries later the story of the black slave Estevan's death at the hands of the Zuni was learned in a novel and revealing way by an anthropologist-pioneer of the research method known as "participant observation." He was Frank Hamilton Cushing whose work on the Zuni peoples of New Mexico caused Claude Levi-Strauss to place him with Lewis Henry Morgan "as one of the great forerunners of social structure studies."[40] Cushing's account is worthy of repetition here as one of the rare instances of an Indian version of an original encounter episode. Cushing was recalling an evening spent with the Zuni in their pueblo when he wrote:

One night as I sat reading an old work of travel by the firelight in the little room they had assigned me, one by one four old men came in, rolled their corn husk cigarettes, and fell to watching me. For a long time they smoked and nodded at one another. Finally one of them, acting as spokesman for the rest, punched my foot with his out-stretched fingers and exclaimed,

"Little Brother!"

"What?" I asked.

"Look here. What do the marks in that paper-fold say to you?"

"Old things," said I.

"How old?"

"Maybe three hundred years; maybe three hundred and fifty," I chanced to reply.

"Three hundred and fifty years," he repeated. "Three hundred and *fifty!* How long is that?"

"Why three hundred and fifty years."

"I know," said he. "I *know!* But three hundred and fifty sheep, that's easy! Three hundred and fifty *years—that* takes too *long*. Hold, little brother, lay out three hundred and fifty corngrains on the floor in a straight line, then we can tell how long three hundred and fifty years is."

The corn was brought in a twinkling and curious to see the result, I began placing it, kernel by kernel, in a straight line across the floor. Meanwhile, the old men bent eagerly over my back, wrinkling their foreheads, counting up their long-nailed fingers, conferring together, and sliding the corn grains here and there with little slivers. When I had nearly completed the number they began, wholly after their own fashion, to reckon.

"Now that's one father," said they, "and his son growing up; *one! two!*

So they went on until they reached nearly the end of the row, when suddenly the eldest jumped up, his face beaming with inner light, and exclaimed,

"Why *here*, brothers, ten men's ages, *eleven!* That must have been when our ancients killed the Black Mexican at Kiä-ki-me. Hold, little brother, does your old book tell anything about that?"

"No," said I to him most eagerly, "but you must."

"Why yes, of course," he replied, while the others settled back to their cigarettes. And he began:

"It is to be believed," said he, "that a long time ago, when roofs lay over the walls of Kiä-ki-me [Hawikuh in Spanish accounts], when smoke hung over the house-tops, and the ladder-rounds were still unbroken—It was then that the Black Mexicans came from their abodes in Everlasting Summerland. One day, unexpected, out of 'Hemlock Cañon,' they came, and descended to Kiä-ki-me. But when they said they would enter the covered way, it seems that our ancients looked not gently on them, but with these Black Mexicans came many Indians of Só-no-li, as they call it now, who carried war feathers and long bows and cane arrows like the Apaches, who were enemies of our ancients; therefore these our ancients, being always bad tempered and quick to anger, made fools of themselves after their fashion, rushed into their town and out of their town, shouting, skipping and shooting with sling-stones and arrows and war clubs. Then the Indians of Só-no-li set up a great howl, and then they and our ancients did much ill to one another. Then and thus, was killed by our ancients, right where the stone stands down by the arroyo of Kiä-ki-me, one of the Black Mexicans. . . . Then the rest ran away, chased by our grandfathers, and went back toward their country in the Land of Everlasting Summer. But after they steadied themselves and stopped talking, our ancients felt sorry; for they thought, 'Now we have made bad business, for after a while, these people being angered, will come again.' So they felt always in danger and went about watching the bushes. By and by they did come back, those Black Mexicans, and with them many men of Só-no-li. They wore coats of iron and even bonnets of metal and carried for weapons short canes that spit fire and made thunder. Thus it was in the days of Kiä-ki-me."

The reader of today cannot help but join Cushing's sense of wonder as he reflected on the Zuni's ability to recount their tribal memory of an event that transpired more than three centuries before. Cushing observed:

If we but call to mind the red feathers on Estevanico's mace, which to the Zuñi is a symbol of violence, and if we further reflect that Indians seeing the Negro for the first time must have thought there were others like him, and been filled with the idea, the parallels in the two relations evidence how far we may, within certain limitations, trust to the accuracy of at least *Zuñi* Indian tradition.[41]

Estevan's fellow explorer of the way to Cibola, Fray Marcos is accused of lying by many scholars who have studied his extravagant descriptions of the Indian pueblos of New Mexico. Still others feel that his earlier experiences in Peru led him to embroider on and exaggerate descriptions he gained from Indians of things and places he never actually saw for himself, although claiming to have. Whatever his motivations and sources may have been, one thing is certain and that is that Fray Marcos's glowing reports of Indians with high culture in the north confirmed the suspicions already in the mind of an energetic young Spanish officer with close ties to the Viceroy of Mexico, Francisco Vásquez de Coronado. Coronado met Fray Marcos on his return from the wilderness and escorted him to his interviews with the viceroy. With Viceroy Mendoza's full support Coronado undertook the organization of a major entrada into what is now the southwestern United States.

CORONADO'S ENTRADA

It has been suggested that there were political reasons for the viceroy's outspoken support for an expedition to Cibola and the fabulous Seven Cities. For one thing it would forestall any similar effort by Hernan Cortés to expand his power base by founding a new colony to the north. For another, it has been argued, the promise of riches in the north, being purposely so publicly spread abroad, would attract a growing element of idle and potentially unruly citizens and remove them as a problem for the viceroy's administration. Such an agenda, if it did exist, was easily carried forward by the genuine lure that riches and glory held for the idle Spanish hidalgos so numerous in Mexico at the time.

For whatever motives, Coronado organized an entrada that was termed by contemporaries "the most brilliant company ever assembled in the Indies to go in search of new lands." Viceroy Mendoza and a train of dignitaries journeyed for 500 difficult miles from the capital at Mexico City to bid them godspeed and review the 230 mounted and 62 foot soldiers, friars with their own escort, and the Indian guides and bearers who went unmentioned in the otherwise detailed official muster rolls. From other accounts and documents, including Coronado's later testimony, it is clear that the whole company engaged in the entrada was far larger than the army muster rolls reveal. In all there were

about one thousand horses and six hundred mules and donkeys plus as many as thirteen hundred Indians employed in the entrada led by Coronado. It was a formidable force aimed at discovery and conquest.

To cooperate with the land force, a sea expedition under Alarcon was also organized. In part this reflected the erroneous geographical beliefs the Spanish and other Europeans held at the time. It was thought that there was an embayment of the Pacific reaching deep into the continent north of Mexico and as a consequence the lands Coronado would be exploring would have a coastline. Food and supplies, it was reasoned, would be most easily delivered by ship to coastal supply depots from which Coronado and his force would draw what they needed. The fleet under the command of Hernando de Alarcon sailed up the Gulf of California and explored the lower reaches of the Colorado River. Needless to say no embayment of the Pacific reaching southern Arizona was found.

Coronado's expedition began its march on February 23, 1540, amidst the pomp and fanfare of the viceroy's farewell. Led by Indian guides and traveling on well-trod Indian trails, they headed north to find Cibola and the Seven Cities from the small Mexican frontier town, Compostela, in what is now the state of Nayarit. After an arduous trek Coronado and an advance party reached Cibola at the end of the first week in July. The Indians attacked the Spanish column before they reached the pueblo of Hawikuk which was their name for what Fray Marcos identified as Cibola. On the following day the Indians continued to resist Coronado's friendly overtures and the pueblo was stormed and occupied. In spite of his gilded helmet, which he termed a "very good headpiece," Coronado was seriously hurt by stones raining on his head as he tried to scale a ladder to reach an entrance to the pueblo, there being no doors on the ground floor.

Coronado did a good job of hiding what must have been an enormous disappointment when he reported what he found at the Zuni pueblo. First he candidly assured the viceroy that Fray Marcos had "not told the truth in a single thing that he said, but everything is the opposite of what he related, except the name of the cities and the large stone houses."[42] The people he found seemed to him to be "fairly large and intelligent." They had cotton obtained through trade because the climate was too cold for its local growth. Coronado felt certain that "they have a quantity of turquoises, which they had removed with the rest of their goods except the maize." He found a couple of "points of emerald and some little broken stones, rather poor" and some other stone crystals which his servant had since lost. All-in-all, the seven villages making up Cibola were interesting for their pueblo house styles but were far from being the gleaming centers of great wealth that were hoped for; nor were the other fabulous kingdoms Fray Marcos had reported as lying beyond Cibola. One, the kingdom of Totonec, Coronado learned was nothing more than "a hot lake, on the edge of which there are five or six houses." A far cry from the marvelous place of great riches where the good priest reported cloth was made.

OFF TO QUIVIRA

Disappointed but not defeated, Coronado resumed the exploration by sending out detachments to various quarters where Indian information seemed to promise cities or mines might be found. One Indian Coronado encountered was named the Turk because to the Spanish he looked like one. The Turk was apparently a member of a Plains tribe who had been taken captive and transported far from his home and people. He told Coronado about the endless herds of buffalo covering the plains where he lived. The Spanish curious to know more about these shaggy "cattle," sent a detachment with the Turk as guide to travel east and verify the reports. On the way "the Turk told so many and such great tales about the riches of gold and silver found in his land that the Spaniards did not care to look for the cattle, and as soon as they saw a few they turned back to report the rich news to the general."[43] Coronado was taken in by the Turk's tales and the search for the kingdom called Quivira was on!

Thanks to the Turk's convincing tales and the predictable Spanish lust for gold, Coronado carried his explorations into the land of present day Central Kansas. Once again, however, the intrepid leader of the gleaming entrada suffered deep disappointment when he reached his hard won goal. He found no golden city nor even pueblos like those of Cibola. He wrote of how "the guides . . . had described to me houses of stone with many stories: and not only they are not of stone, but of straw, but the people in them are as barbarous as all those I have seen and passed before this."[44] To add insult to injury, the Turk conspired with the Kansas Indians to bring about the destruction of the expedition. According to Coronado the wily Turk "told them not to give the general any maize, that if they did not provide it, the horses would soon die; that they should keep an eye on certain of the best horses in order to kill them, for once the horses were dead then they could kill the Christians."[45]

In 1542 Coronado and his troop returned to Mexico disappointed in having found the mundane reality rather than mythical promise of the Seven Cities of Cibola and the Kingdom of Quivira. It has been said that the march back through Mexico had about it the air of a retreat. Coronado and his men had been the first Europeans to gaze into the awesome depths of the Grand Canyon and ride across the vastness of the Great Plains thronged with its endless herds of

bison, but in their minds the entrada was a failure because stores of gold had not been found.
Quivira was not another Tenochtitlan, nor
was Cibola another Cuzco. Another sixty years
would elapse before Spanish eyes would once
again look across the plains of Central Kansas.

SOTO'S ENTRADA

The culmination of Spanish attempts to penetrate the interior of North America from the
southeast came at almost the same time as Coronado's entrada into the Southwest. The record
of Hernando de Soto's expedition has been jus-
tifiably heralded as one of the greatest sources
of information on the topography and Indian
cultures of the southeastern and south-central
parts of what is now the United States. The expedition had its inception in the royal *Capitulations* of April 20, 1537, through which the king
transferred the rights to Florida formerly held
by Narvaez and Ayllon, both now deceased, to
Captain Hernando de Soto.[46]

At the time Soto was one of the wealthiest
veteran conquerors who had been in Peru with
Pizzaro. Only someone with enormous wealth
could afford to mount an entrada on the scale of
Soto's. His had been the rags-to-riches story of
the Indies that inspired hidalgos by the thousands to come to the New World. Soto had arrived in Darien with Pedrarias in 1514 while still
a teenager owning nothing more than his sword
and shield. In Panama and Honduras he grew
rich by plundering the Indians and their temples
and tombs. He was in the vanguard of the conquest of Peru, preceding Pizarro across the
Andes to encounter the Inca Atahualpa at his
seat in Cajamarca. Although he escaped implication in the dastardly murder of Atahualpa,
Soto shared in the huge ransom that had been
paid for the Inca's release. After Cuzco was con-

quered he served as the city's lieutenant governor and continued to amass a fortune.

Still a young man when he returned to Spain,
Soto married well and was accepted by the
higher nobility. His energy and ambition un-
quenched, Soto petitioned for the right to lead
an entrada and establish a government to be
known as the Province of Florida. In the process
he was to have the right to "conquer, pacify,
and populate the lands that there are from the
Province of the Rio de las Palmas to Florida." It
is interesting to note how the king's *Capitulations* with Soto acknowledged the importance of
the Indian grave and tomb robbing that had
been so profitable in Peru and Panama. The *Capitulations* clearly specified the share the Crown
expected from Soto for:

all gold and silver, stones, pearls, and other things
that may be found and taken, as well in the graves,
sepulchers, *ocues,* or temples of the Indians, as in
other places where they are accustomed to offer
sacrifices to their idols, or in other concealed religious precincts, or buried in house, or patrimonial
soil, or in the ground, or in some other public
place, whether belonging to the community or an
individual . . .[47]

It would be correct to conclude that nothing, sacred or profane, was omitted from Soto's "license to steal" from the Indians he expected to
encounter in La Florida. As one scholar pointed
out, Soto's expedition is remarkable in the annals of colonialism for the shameless manner in
which it announced its objective as unlimited
plunder.

To assist in organizing and equipping his expedition Soto was appointed Governor of Cuba
by the king. After a careful process of selection,
some six hundred fighting men were chosen to
form Soto's expeditionary force. They sailed
from Spain for Cuba on April 7, 1538, aboard
seven ships Soto purchased and loaded with
supplies. Foodstuffs were collected on Cuba
while an advance party was sent to reconnoiter

a suitable landing place on the mainland and seize local Indians to act as guides.

With preparations completed, the expedition sailed from Havana on May 18, 1539. The landing was begun in the bay named Espiritu Santo, believed to be Tampa Bay, on May 30. Like many identifications of explorers' landing places and routes of travel, Soto's landing place and route through the United States' South is currently a matter of debate. For most of the past fifty years the findings of the U.S. De Soto Commission, chaired by the distinguished anthropologist John R. Swanton, were accepted as an accurate summary of where the Soto expedition landed and traveled. The De Soto Commission's final report was submitted in 1938 and published in 1939. In the early 1980s an anthropologist at the University of Georgia and some of his students began a careful review of the De Soto Commission's findings in light of relevant translated documents and archaeological findings that had not been available to Swanton and the other De Soto Commission members. As a result of this work, Charles Hudson and his coworkers began publishing papers in the mid-1980s that argued for significant changes in Soto's route from the one the De Soto Commission had mapped. For one thing the Hudson group's route places the Indian town Cofitachequi far to the east of the Savannah River where Swanton and his colleagues determined it to be. This is only one of several major departures in the route of Soto as plotted by the Swanton and Hudson groups. On the question of Tampa Bay as the Soto expedition's landing site, Swanton and Hudson are in agreement but other workers are less convinced. At least one line of argument would place the expedition's landing on the east coast of Florida near Cape Canaveral, and there may be still other candidates for the Soto landfall.

Wherever the landing place may have been on the Florida peninsula it saw a force of over seven hundred treasure seekers come ashore from the fleet of ten ships that carried the Soto expedition from Cuba. Of that number 600 were soldiers including 330 foot, with most of the remainder having mounts. A pack of large fighting dogs and their handlers formed a particularly frightening force to the Indians they intimidated and savaged. Among the other expedition members were four priests, four friars, and four women, who are known by name. Several artisans, skilled in bridge and boat construction, would assist in river crossing and, if need be, help avoid the disaster suffered by the poorly equipped and manned Narvaez expedition that had preceded Soto to these shores. Perhaps the most unsung passengers of all were the swineherds with a herd of hogs from Soto's home region of Extremadura, in Spain. On Cuba these animals had proven that they could range for themselves and multiply with little or no care and still be herded and driven when necessary. On the journey with Soto they multiplied prodigiously and provided a mobile source of emergency rations that saved the Spaniards' lives on more than one occasion.

Soto's differed from the expeditions that had gone to Florida before in that he had no interest in establishing a permanent coastal settlement of any sort. Rather he modeled his entrada after those of the conquistadors who had found great wealth among the high culture Indians of the interiors of Mexico and Peru. Basic to his plan was a reliance on Indian food supplies. The typical procedure Soto followed, as his army moved across the southern landscape, was to capture the chief or cacique of a local chieftainship and force his people to ransom him with stocks of maize and other food stuffs and a number of bearers to carry the baggage to the next major Indian center, where the process was repeated. As the trek wore on, numbers of Indian women were demanded as well as bearers and food.

In his wake, Soto appears to have left European contagious disease pathogens which had even more disastrous and long-term impacts. Thanks to the accounts of later Spanish explorers such as Tristan de Luna and Juan Pardo, who visited areas impacted by Soto twenty or more years later, some assessment of the devastation wrought by the Soto entrada is now being developed by scholars.[48] What is being written adds another grim chapter to the narrative titled *The Columbian Exchange* by historian Alfred W. Crosby that was discussed earlier.

In his rambling progress Soto led his army with its train of kidnapped Indians and hundreds of forest-ranging hogs across parts of Florida, Georgia, South and North Carolina, Tennessee, Alabama, Mississippi, Arkansas, Louisiana, Texas, and, if some researchers are accepted, Missouri. En route, the Appalachian Mountains and Mississippi River were successfully crossed and Plains Indians were encountered. From the Plains Indians Soto eagerly sought to learn the way to "the other sea" as he termed the Pacific Ocean. Over most of his circuitous route he traveled, like Coronado, on well-trod Indian trails from one productive chiefdom to another with Indians acting as guides and informants, albeit not always willingly.

Like Coronado at the hands of the Turk, Soto sometimes followed what could be termed "blind alleys" recommended by his Indian guides. One such incident took place in middle Georgia. On his way from Florida to Georgia Soto had taken an Indian youth to act as an interpreter and guide. When they got to an Indian town named Patofa in Central Georgia the youth, "began to foam at the mouth and throw himself to the ground as if possessed by the devil." The Spanish prayed over the stricken youth and the fit subsided. When he regained his composure the boy told Soto that "four days journey thence toward the rising sun was the province of which he spoke" when taken captive. When he had

been captured near Tallahassee in Florida, the youth had claimed to be from a land called Yupaha that was ruled by a woman. He claimed that she was a powerful chieftainess who collected tribute from many neighboring chiefs who gave her "clothing and others gold in abundance." His tale convinced Soto when "he told how it [gold] was taken from the mines, melted, and refined, just as if he had seen it done, or else the devil that taught him."[49]

OFF TO YUPAHA

When the Patofa Indians realized that Soto was preparing to march due east they vigorously advised against it. According to the account of the episode:

The Indians of Patofa said that they knew of no settlement in that direction, but that toward the northwest they knew a province called Coça, a well provisioned land and of very large villages. The cacique told the governor that if he wished to go thither, he would furnish him service of a guide and Indians to carry; and if in the direction indicated by the youth he would also give him all those he needed and with mutual words of affection and promises they said farewell to each other.[50]

The apparent cordiality between Soto and Patofa may surprise some readers in view of what has been said about the entrada's overall adverse impacts on the Indians. This encounter, it should be kept in mind, occurred early in the march when Soto and his men were still practicing some restraint in their demands on the Indians. Still more important is the fact that Patofa and other lesser caciques appear to have regarded Soto as an incredibly powerful paramount chief. The Indians of the chieftainships over much of the South at this time appear to have been accustomed to unannounced visits by paramount chiefs, their households, and large retinues, who expected to be well supplied from town stores and treated with deference similar to that which Europeans paid to their peripatetic royal courts of the day. To Patofa Soto came and behaved as a mighty paramount chief would and he was treated accordingly.

Predictably the lure of gold to the east won out over assurances of well-stocked corn cribs in the chieftainship now called Coosa that spread across northwestern Georgia and neighboring Alabama. Accepting his youthful guide's estimate of a four-day march Soto took only enough maize from Patofa to meet their needs for that length of time. Even so a prodigious quantity of grain was needed to sustain the army and its horses plus 700 Indian bearers. The fact that Soto's enormous entrada could travel so far and for such a long period by living off the Indians serves to highlight the productivity of the aboriginal agricultural economy that existed in the American South at the time of the first encounters.

After marching for two days beyond the anticipated four, Soto noticed that the Indian trail they had been following "gradually grew narrower until it was all lost." This was not what he expected to find as he approached the domain of the powerful chieftainess about whom the youth had told such glowing tales. After a particularly difficult crossing of a wide river with a powerful current (Savannah?) Soto, now very angry "threatened the youth and made as if he would throw him to the dogs because he had deceived him, saying that it was a march of four days, and for nine days he had marched making seven or eight leagues on each day and now the men and horses were become weak because of the great economy which had been practiced with regard to the maize."[51]

The Indian youth, thoroughly shaken and in reach of the jaws of Soto's snarling war dogs, admitted that he did not know where he was. Only the pleas for mercy by Juan Ortiz, who had himself been a prisoner of the Indians for many years and understood the youth, managed to save him from a horrible death. Later Indians who incurred Soto's anger were not so lucky as this youth.

The lack of Indians and stores of maize they had encountered in eastern Georgia kept the army from retracing its path. Only Soto's hogs, now multiplied to a herd of over three hundred, kept the army from starvation as they struggled eastward. Food supplies were so short that the Patofa Indian bearers were sent home. The expedition was saved by a scouting party that happened on a small Indian town some twelve or thirteen leagues farther on. The army struggled forward "each one according as he could march and his strength aided him." Fortunately the town was fully stocked with parched maize and some Indians were captured who assured Soto that the province of Cofitachequi was only two days farther.

Before too long, perhaps near the banks of the Congaree River in South Carolina, Soto was greeted by the "cacica" or Chieftainess of Cofitachequi who was carried to the river on a sort of litter by "certain principal Indians." She crossed the river, to where Soto was waiting, in an Indian "canoe with an awning at the stern and on the bottom of which was already spread a mat for her and above it two cushions one on top of the other on which she seated herself." The cacica of Cofitachequi addressed Soto in terms that suggest she, like the cacique of Patofa, regarded him as a powerful paramount chief to whom deference and generosity should be accorded. This was probably a very fortunate situation for Soto and his exhausted troop who might have had serious difficulty in defending themselves against a large-scale Indian attack.

To underscore her words of welcome and obeisance, the cacica presented Soto "a quantity of the clothing of the country . . . namely, blankets and skins." These bulky gifts probably impressed Soto far less than the "long string of pearl beads" she took from her own neck and threw around his. After an exchange of "many gracious words of affection and courtesy" she ordered the canoes to be used to ferry Soto and his men across the river.

Once lodged in the town Soto was presented with another gift "of many hens." When the cacica noticed the way that the Spaniards valued the pearls they were given she "told the governor that he might order certain graves . . . to be examined for he would find many." Soto had this done and "fourteen arrobas of pearls were found, babies and birds being made of them." This cache of pearl effigies taken from Indian graves in South Carolina was the nearest Soto came to finding the great wealth he sought among the Indians of the South.

Space restrictions will not allow us to follow Soto and his expedition further in this chapter. In 1542, three years after his landing in Florida and shortly before his death, Soto appeared to have realized the futility of his quest. Sick with fever and exhaustion, Hernando de Soto died and was committed to a watery grave in the Mississippi River where his body would be safe from Indian desecration. Amazingly about three hundred Spaniards survived what had been one of the most arduous entradas undertaken during the Age of Discovery. They struggled into the Gulf Coast town of Panuco, Mexico, in the autumn of 1543, sun-burned, dressed in patches of animal hides taken from Indians and empty-handed. It would be two decades before the Spanish would take another serious look at the mainland of La Florida. Only fear of the threat posed by an attempted French colony there proved to be a strong enough motivation to bring the Spanish to settle in the area now within the State of Florida.

CHAPTER SIX

COMPETITION

IN THE NORTH

Portugal, France, and England

For our ocean is more prolific than the Albanian sow, to which tradition assigned thirty pigs at a litter; and more liberal than a generous prince. Does it not each year disclose new lands, new nations, and vast wealth?

De Orbe Novo, Peter Martyr D'Angheras

Columbus was not the only late-fifteenth-century Genoese navigator actively probing the Atlantic to find a route to Asia. While Christopher Columbus was sailing for the monarchs of Spain, a wealthy, Genoa-born merchant named John Cabot convinced England's king to back him in a similar enterprise in the north. Some time after he gained Venetian citizenship and wealth as a merchant, John Cabot made his way to Bristol, England's second largest port.

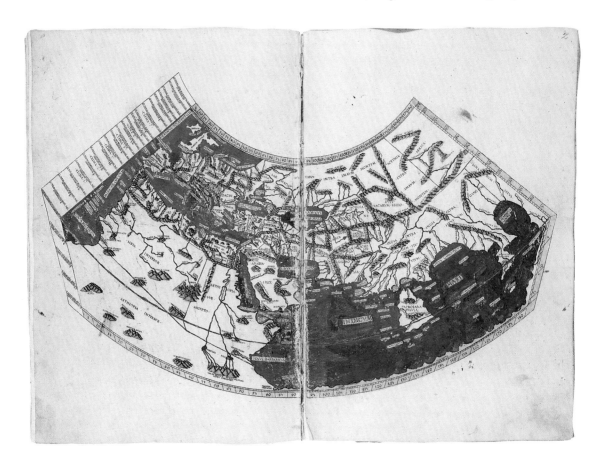

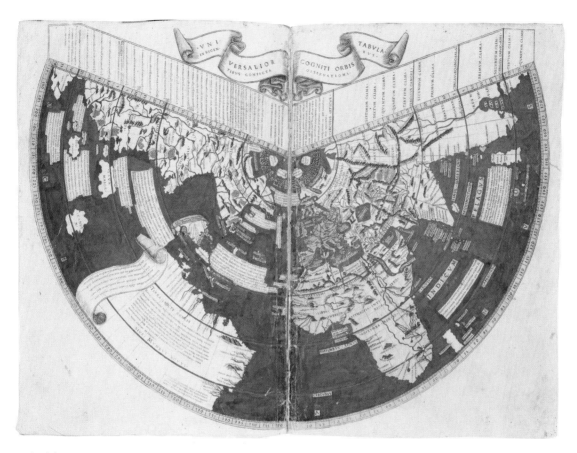

Both of these attractive maps appeared in the edition of Ptolemy's Geographia published in Rome in the year 1507. The first shows a world view which is only slightly different from the one included in the 1482 Ulm edition of Ptolemy in Chapter 2. Gone, however, are the traditional wind heads that decorated the edges of the 1482 version, and the landlocked nature of the Indian Ocean is less strongly stated on this 1507 map. There is nothing shown, however, that even suggests the wider world view that the discoveries of Christopher Columbus, John Cabot, Amerigo Vespucci, and the Corte Real brothers were suggesting in the minds of some European cosmographers. That wider world view was presented by way of the map titled "Universalior Cogniti Orbis Tabula" by a German cartographer named Johan Ruysch. Little is known about Ruysch's life, but there is evidence which suggests that he may have been with John Cabot on his famous voyage in 1497. Notice that Ruysch's map takes the form of an opened cone on which has been projected the earth's surface from the North Pole to almost 40 degrees south latitude. Ruysch's map is one of the earliest printed maps to show the discoveries made in the New World. Because of this it reached and influenced a wide audience of curious Europeans who were not privy to the earlier manuscript depictions like the Cantino Map in Chapter 5. Notice that Greenland (Gruenlant) and Newfoundland (Terra Nova) are both shown as peninsulas of northern Asia while Spain's Caribbean discoveries are shown as islands and the mass of northern South America is termed "Mundus Novus" or New World (Geography and Map Division).

CABOT AND THE BRISTOLMEN

By the 1480s Bristol merchants were sponsoring voyages to investigate reports of islands said to lie in the Atlantic to the west of Ireland. The Bristol navigators gained their knowledge of the North Atlantic as fishermen and in a fish-based trading network linking Iceland, the British Isles, and Northwestern Europe with the Iberian Peninsula and ultimately the Mediterranean Basin. It is likely that concern over shrinking fish stocks in the traditional grounds encouraged the Bristol magnates to make an occasional investment in voyages of exploration in quest of the legendary "Isle of Brasil," the northern equivalent of Columbus's "Antillia." According to one report, the Bristol merchants were in the habit of sending from two to four ships a year "in search of the island of Brazil and the Seven Cities."[1] While this report may have exaggerated the number, it is certain that voyages of exploration in the Atlantic west of Ireland were sailing from Bristol during the last decade of the fifteenth century.

The scheme of discovery that John Cabot proposed to England's king probably shared much with the enterprise Columbus gained support for in Spain. Cabot proposed sailing west to Asia by way of the island of Brasil on a shorter more poleward course than that followed by Columbus. While refusing to back Cabot's enterprise directly, King Henry VII of England did issue a patent allowing Cabot "to sail to all parts, regions and coasts of the eastern western and northern sea, under our banners, flags and ensigns."[2] In that vast watery compass Cabot was permitted to "conquer, occupy and possess whatsoever islands, countries, regions or provinces of heathens and infidels . . . which before this time were unknown to all Christians." By this device England avoided the appearance of being in direct competition with Spain and Portugal in the race for a sea route to Asia while still asserting a right to discover and occupy unknown islands or lands. Such an assertion meant little at the time but became a significant basis for argument when England did begin actively to challenge the Iberians in overseas trade and colony building. The right of prior discovery was to become a frequently cited principle in the early evolution of international law.

With the king's patent in his hands, Cabot was ready to test his thesis. A Bristol chronicler reported that Cabot sighted land in the west on June 24, 1497, after a swift voyage from Bristol aboard the ship *Mathew.*[3] According to Samuel Eliot Morison's reconstruction of Cabot's voyage, he made his first North American landing only a few miles from the L'Anse aux Meadows site on Newfoundland. This is the place mentioned in Chapter 2 as the location of Leif Ericson's Vinland Viking settlement. If Morison was correct, this is a truly rare coincidence! Upon his return from the voyage, Cabot rushed to London to inform the king. He appears to have been treated as a celebrity and King Henry rewarded him with a gift of ten pounds "to hym that found the new isle." Unfortunately there are no documents to provide a first-hand account or description of where Cabot explored and what he described to his backers and the king. Unlike Columbus, Cabot left us no log of his voyage so what is known must be gleaned and inferred from the letters and reports of others.

In February of 1498, Cabot received a second royal patent allowing him to organize an expedition to the "loande[land] and Isles of late found" by him. According to one contemporary report, Cabot planned to sail south along the coast he had found until he reached Cipangu [Japan] where he felt the jewels and spices of world trade originated. Once established there he intended to set up a trading factory to make London "a more important mart than Alexandria."[4]

Late in the spring of 1498, four ships were sighted sailing past Ireland on a westward course and were presumed to be Cabot's fleet. They were never seen or heard from again. We can only speculate on what befell Cabot's second voyage to the New World. There is no questioning the fact that he made contact with the New World at least once because a few years later Gaspar Corte Real found a broken Italian gilt sword and silver earrings in the possession of Beothuk Indians he kidnapped in Newfoundland and brought to Lisbon. There is no way of determining whether these artifacts were from Cabot's first or second voyage, however.

Probably the most intriguing evidence that seems to shed light on John Cabot's second voyage was found in a Paris antique shop in 1833. It was in the form of a copy of a world map believed to have been prepared in about 1500 by Juan de la Cosa (illustrated in Chapter 5). Cosa was a cartographer who had sailed to the New World with Columbus on his second voyage in 1493–1494. On this map, Hispaniola and Cuba, as well as the Bahama and other Antilles Islands, are identified and recognizable. To the north of these islands a mainland coast is diagramatically suggested and shown to curve to the east. Along that coast, roughly on the latitude of the Iberian Peninsula, a number of flags and coastal place names are explained as bordering the "Mar descubrierto por inglese," or sea discovered by the English. Although far from conclusive, several experts have argued that this is evidence of the survival of some of the ships with Cabot in 1498.[5] If the map by Juan de la Cosa is accepted as convincing evidence of the second Cabot voyage of exploration, he or his survivors must have followed the coast for a long distance. Some scholars have suggested that the coastline from Delaware north to Newfoundland is represented as having been discovered by Cabot on the Cosa map. Of course Cabot, Cosa, and their contemporaries were cer-

tain that these were the coasts of eastern Asia.

Whatever their extent, it is clear from the evidence that the English discoveries were being acknowledged in Spain at about the time the Cosa map was being drawn. In a patent granted to Alonso de Ojeda by Ferdinand and Isabela in early June 1501, for example, Ojeda was instructed to:

go and follow that coast which you have discovered, which runs east and west, as it appears, because it goes toward the region where it has been learned that the English were making discoveries; and that you go setting up marks with the arms of their Majesties, or with other signs that may be known, such as shall seem good to you, in order that it be known that you have discovered that land, so that you may stop the discovery of the English in the direction.[6]

As this passage from Ojeda's royal patent is read it is not hard to imagine that a map like the one attributed to Juan de la Cosa was in the author's mind if not his sight. Clearly the Spanish monarchs were interested in terminating any further opportunities for the English to stake a claim to these coasts by prior discovery. The English foot, however, was squarely in the door that would eventually open to reveal that these discoveries were not in Asia but on the coast of a new continent formed by the slowly emerging European realization that North and South America existed. These linked continents lay quietly like a veiled Colossus between the Atlantic and the still-to-be discovered and named Pacific Ocean. Two more decades of discovery would pass before Europeans finally expanded their world view to include the reality of the Americas.

In contemporary terms the most important discovery John Cabot made was found in the waters he sailed through on his approach to Newfoundland. His course took him over one of the planet's biological bonanzas, the level banks covered by shallow, fish-rich, ocean water extending from the island's eastern shores toward the coasts of Western Europe. In a letter to the Duke of Milan written in December 1497, Raimondo de Soncino told of the King of England's luck in having "gained a part of Asia, without a stroke of the sword." While Soncino did not seem to have much confidence in Cabot himself, he did believe the reports of the Bristol sailors with him who asserted "that the sea there is swarming with fish, which can be taken not only with the net, but in baskets let down with a stone, so that it sinks in the water."[7] These same knowledgeable Bristolmen stressed how "they could bring so many fish that this kingdom would have no further need of Iceland." Within only a few years fishermen from the ports of western England, France, Spain, and Portugal were visiting the fishing grounds that came to be named the Grand Banks of Newfoundland. Unlike the soon exhausted gold of the Caribbean Islands, the cod fish of the Grand Banks were a marvelously rich and renewable resource which yielded a generous, health-assuring wealth of dried and fresh protein to countless humans over half the globe. Capt. John Smith knew whereof he spoke when he argued "the sea is better than the richest mine knowne" in his *Description of New England*. It is to be regretted profoundly that even the breeding stocks of these historic Atlantic fishing banks are currently being severely stressed through continued overfishing in an age that sometimes boasts of being enlightened.

PORTUGUESE EYES TURN TO THE NORTH

News of Cabot's discoveries attracted the attention of leaders in Portugal as well as Spain. Portuguese navigators based in the Azores, like their English counterparts in Bristol, regularly heard tales of islands being seen to the west

and, as a consequence, reports of Cabot's sightings fell on ready ears. In the past both Portugal and Spain had obtained papal endorsements in the form of letters and decrees which amounted to papal grants of exclusive control over offshore territorial acquisitions or discoveries (illustrated in Chapter 4). In 1455 and 1456, for example, Portugal received the exclusive right to trade and acquire territory in the region south of Africa's Cape Bojador, through and beyond Guinea, "all the way to the Indians."[8]

Thus the efforts of Prince Henry were able to proceed without fear of competition, at least legal competition, from another Christian power. Columbus's discoveries in the Indies, near what was then still thought to be Asia, triggered a renewal of tension between Spain and Portugal with respect to overseas territorial poaching. With a Spaniard occupying the pope's throne at the time it is not surprising that Spain was given papal sanction for the exclusive right to acquire land and conduct trade west of a line 100 leagues beyond any of the Azores or Cape Verde Islands. The idea of Portugal having a prior claim to exclusive control "all the way to Indians" or islands lying off the eastern coast of Asia continued to trouble the affairs of Christendom, however. To quiet arguments still being heard on this score, the pope expanded his earlier decree to say that if the Spanish, by following Columbus's western route, should discover lands in Indian seas these would also belong to them.

In 1494, Portugal persuaded Spain to sign a treaty at Tordesillas which provided for a new and more westerly line of demarcation to separate their spheres of influence in the Atlantic. The Tordesillas Line of Demarcation was established as the meridian located 370 leagues west of the Cape Verde Islands. Given the difficulty of establishing longitude and the ongoing debates concerning the length of a degree of longitude, it is not surprising to find that uncertainty and misunderstanding became hallmarks of the

Line of Demarcation in the years following rati-
fication of the Treaty of Tordesillas. In spite of
its uncertain location, the Line of Demarcation
became a fixture on the maps of the Age of Discovery and influenced the location of national
political boundaries still functioning in South
America.

Suspicions that the lands Cabot had coasted
were on their side of the Line of Demarcation
triggered a quarter-century identified by Samuel Eliot Morison as the period of Portuguese
supremacy in the exploration of the North Atlantic. Although the first firmly documented
date of commercial fishing on the Newfoundland Banks places the French there in 1504, it
can be safely assumed that secretive Portuguese
fishermen from the Azores were taking catches
even earlier. One reason for believing this is the
fact that Portuguese fishermen operating in the
home waters fishery found it necessary to have
the king place a 10 percent tax on fares being
brought to market from the distant banks.[9] Morison points to this action as the first European attempt to protect home industries from American competition.

In the vanguard of the fishing interests were
explorers such as João Fernandes, an Azorean
who sailed from the Azores island of Terceira in
1499. Fernandes was a landed proprietor who
appears to have rented out his land to support
voyaging. Because of his identity as a farmer,
Fernandes was known as the *lavrador* to his
more professional seagoing comrades. In the
autumn of 1499 the King of Portugal issued a
patent to João Fernandes in response to his petition to be allowed to "seek out and discover at
his own expense some Islands lying in our
sphere of influence."[10]

Samuel Eliot Morison felt that the only evidence recording Fernandes's successful voyage
existed in the form of legends and inscriptions
found on maps of the early 1500s. One of the
most important of these is the world map made

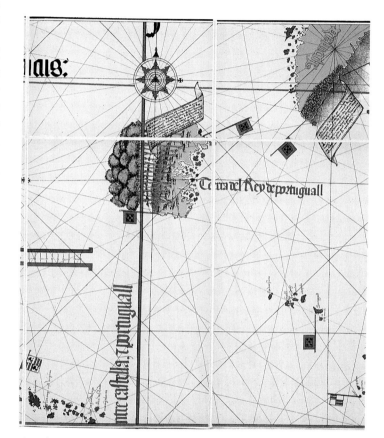

An enlargement of the section of the 1502 Cantino Map showing the discoveries made by the early Portuguese explorers in the North Atlantic. Notice that
the forested land labeled "Terra del Rey de Portuguall" is east of the Line of
Demarcation. It represents the island of Newfoundland. In his letter to his patron in Italy Cantino told of how the Corte Real brothers reported the island to
be a region with numerous large rivers where they found "luscious and varied
fruits, and trees and pines of such measureless height and girth, that they would
be too big as a mast for the largest ship that sails." This photograph was made
from the colored facsimile of the Cantino Map prepared by Henry Harrisse (Geography and Map Division).

in 1502 by Alberto Cantino for the Duke of Ferrara (illustrated in Chapter 5). The colored photographs included here are made from the facsimile of the Cantino Map that is included in the Henry Harrisse Collection in the Library of Congress Geography and Map Division. Fortunately the original map survives in Italy in spite of the fact that, for a time during the nineteenth century, it was used as a screen in a Modena butcher shop.

Cantino had the map painted while in Portugal and it clearly emphasizes that country's view of where the Line of Demarcation lay with respect to the discoveries being made in the North Atlantic and what would later become known as South America. The heavily forested island marked "Terra del Rey de Portugall" represents the island now called Newfoundland. From a map gloss Morison deduced that the farmer João Fernandes gave the "Land, ho!" announcement when Cape Farewell was first sighted. In commemoration of the irony of a farmer making the discovery, the land sighted was named, in Fernandes's honor, "Tierra del Lavrador." In time, the "Land of the Farmer" changed its position on maps to designate first Newfoundland and finally the northeasternmost coast of Canada where it identifies the mainland portion of the modern Province of Newfoundland, Labrador.

Hard on the heels of the "Lavrador" were two Portuguese brothers, Gaspar and Miguel Corte Real, who lost their lives but gained a place in history as the discoverers of Newfoundland and coastal Labrador. Gaspar Corte Real was reported to have discovered a land that was very cool and covered with big trees at about 50 degrees north latitude. He named his discovery "Terra Verde." The tall trees shown on Cantino's "Land of the King of Portugal" are an appropriate hallmark for the first cartographic depiction of the island that eventually came to be known as Newfoundland.

Returning to Lisbon from his first voyage, Gaspar set to work almost immediately to outfit a second expedition. The Cantino Map legend placed on the "Land of the King of Portugal" appears to summarize, in capsule form, the history of the voyage. Samuel Eliot Morison translated it to say that the island was discovered "by command of his most excellent majesty D. Manuel, King of Portugal, by Gaspar de Corte Real, a gentleman of the royal household, who sent thence a ship with both male and female natives, and stayed behind, but never returned . . . There are many mast trees."[11]

A fuller account of the Corte Real's 1501 landing on Newfoundland can be gleaned from a letter Cantino sent to his patron, the Duke of Ferrara. According to Cantino, the expedition consisted of "two well-equipped ships" sent "for the sole purpose of finding out if it were possible to discover in that region any lands or islands."[12] When Cantino wrote, one of the ships had already returned safely to Lisbon and reported finding:

a very large country which they approached with very great delight. And since throughout this region numerous large rivers flowed into the sea, by one of these they made their way about a league inland, where on landing they found abundance of most luscious and varied fruits, and trees and pines of such measureless height and girth, that they would be too big as a mast for the largest ship that sails, but the men of that country say they live altogether by fishing and hunting animals, in which the land abounds, such as a very large deer, covered with extremely long hair, the skins of which they use for garments and also make houses and boats thereof, and again wolves, foxes, tigers and sables. They [the explorers] affirm that there are, what appears to me wonderful, as many falcons as there are sparrows in our country, and I have seen some of them and they are extremely pretty.[13]

Like fellow-explorer Christopher Columbus far to the south, Gaspar Corte Real showed no hesitation in seizing natives of the land he discovered. Cantino continued his narration to the duke, stating that:

They forcibly kidnapped about fifty men and women of this country and he brought them to the king. I have seen, touched and examined these people, and beginning with their stature, declare that they are somewhat taller than our average, with members corresponding and well-formed. The hair of the men is long, just as we wear ours, and they wear it in curls, and have their faces marked with great signs and these signs are like those of the [East] Indians. Their eyes are greenish and when they look at one, this gives an air of great boldness to their whole countenance. Their speech is unintelligible, but nevertheless is not harsh but rather human. Their manners and gestures are most gentle: they laugh considerably and manifest the greatest pleasure. So much for the men. The women have small breasts and most beautiful bodies, and rather pleasant faces. The colour of these women may be said to be more white than otherwise, but the men are considerably darker. In fine, except for the terrible harsh look of the men, they appear to me to be in all else the same form and image as ourselves. They go quite naked except for their privy parts, which they cover with a skin of the above-mentioned deer. They have no arms nor iron, but whatever they work or fashion, they cut with very hard sharp stones, with which they split in two the very hardest substances.[14]

Cantino concluded his letter by mentioning that Gaspar Corte Real had remained behind with his ship to sail far enough along the newly discovered coast to determine whether it was an island or mainland shore.

While Cantino omitted the word slavery in his letter, the Venetian ambassador stationed in Lisbon was not so circumspect in his report of the arrival of the first of the Corte Real ships. The ambassador, Pietro Pasqualigo, like Cantino, wrote at some length on the appearance and demeanor of the Indian captives from Newfoundland and concluded:

They have also great store of wood above all of pines for making masts and yards of ships. On this account his Majesty here intends to draw great advantage from the said land, as well by the wood

for ships of which they are in want, as by the men, who will be excellent for labour and the best slaves that have hitherto been obtained.[15]

In spite of Pasqualigo's optimism concerning the economic potential of Newfoundland's forest and human resources, the area could not compare with the other overseas opportunities that were beginning to unfold for the Portuguese in Asia. Gaspar and brother Miguel Corte Real both disappeared in the northern waters without a trace. Voyages continued to be made to the north but the record is confusing concerning where they went and what they found. It was not until the voyages of another Portuguese, João Alvares Fagundes, in the 1520s, that new verifiable discoveries were made in the north. Fagundes's voyage to the south of Newfoundland and into the Gulf of St. Lawrence was responsible for several of the place-names found there. Some early maps named today's Cape Breton "Cap Fagundo," for example.[16]

By the early 1520s most European geographers and cartographers were convinced that the discoveries centering on Newfoundland in the north and the Caribbean Rimlands in the south were not extensions of eastern Asia. The burning question that was beginning to form in their minds dealt with the degree of insularity of the discoveries. Were they quite separate entities that were emerging in the sea known to lie between Western Europe and Eastern Asia? Or, were the explorers encountering islands, coasts, and peninsulas that were in some way connected but not part of Asia? If the latter were the case, were there straits or passages allowing sea connections to Asia? Asia, after all was said and done, remained the goal of European interest. Exploration might be a risky business but it was a business and the wealth of Asian spices and exotics as well as gold and treasure remained the prime objectives in the minds of expedition backers who bought and equipped the ships.

VERRAZANO LINKS NORTH AND SOUTH

If the first two decades of the sixteenth century saw Portugal take the lead in the northern Atlantic exploration, that position passed to France for the next two decades. Giovanni da Verrazano was an Italian from the Renaissance center Florence who joined the service of Francis I of France for a voyage of exploration in the years 1523–1524. His voyage was one of signal importance in defining the outline of North America's coasts from Florida to Newfoundland.

Verrazano in his person reflected the virtues of the archetypical upper-class, well-educated, Renaissance man. Unlike many professional navigator-mariners, who were largely unlettered, Verrazano left an eloquent and detailed description of what he saw. That verbal record was further elucidated by maps prepared by his brother, Girolamo Verrazano, who sailed with him on the voyage.

After surviving a harrowing hurricane in February, Verrazano's ship came within smelling distance of fragrant Indian-set fires on the coast of the Carolinas in early March 1524. As Verrazano wrote in his report to King Frances, "we realized that it was inhabited, for huge fires had been built on the seashore."[17] It was not long before Verrazano had his first encounter with the people whose fires helped guide his ship to a safe anchorage near the sand dune-backed beach. At first the Indians fled as the ship's boat approached them, but finally they responded to reassuring gestures and drew near the strangely attired white-skinned arrivals. Verrazano was doubtless relieved when "they showed us by various signs where we could most easily secure the boat, and offered us some of their food."

Rather than describing these Carolina Indians as white or nearly so, as Corte Real described the Beothuk Indians of Newfoundland, Verrazano wrote that they were "dark in color, not unlike the Ethiopians."[18] Like Corte Real, however, he was impressed by the physiques of the men whom he described as "well proportioned, of medium height, a little taller than we are." In certain respects, Verrazano opined, "they resemble the Orientals, particularly those from the farthest Sinarian regions." It should not be forgotten, that his goal was to sail "to the place called the Indies in Kathaye," as he styled China.

Continuing his course north along the shore, Verrazano was struck with the beauty and diversity of the, "beautiful fields and plains full of great forests, some sparse and some dense," that could be seen behind the low sand dunes. Many of the trees were aromatic and emitted "a sweet fragrance over a large area," even many miles at sea when burning. Such trees, he became convinced, "belong to the Orient by virtue of the surroundings, and they are not without some kind of narcotic or aromatic liquor." Probably thinking of placer gold deposits found in the sand and gravels of rivers, Verrazano predicted that gold should be found in the sandy Coastal Plain soils.

Farther to the northeast, Verrazano's attention was again drawn to the many signal fires the Indians lit along the shore. The heavy surf made it impossible for the ship's boat to make a landing, but one of the young sailors swam to shore with some trinkets for the Indians who were beckoning to them. After a hair-raising bashing in the surf he was rescued and kindly treated by the Indians who helped him to return to the boat.

By this time Verrazano's hopes that he was skirting some Asian shore had doubtlessly begun to dim. He was no Columbus blindly bent on fitting every new finding into his preconceived world view and map, no matter how grotesque the fit. His heart must have leaped, however, as he directed the ship to deeper water and rounded Cape Lookout to begin a long course paralleling the Outer Banks of North Carolina.

Here, he wrote, was "an isthmus a mile in width and about 200 long, in which from the ship, was seen the oriental sea between the west and north. Which is the one without doubt, which goes about the extremity of India, China and Cathay."[19] "We navigated along the said isthmus with the continual hope of finding some strait or true promontory at which the land would end toward the north in order to penetrate to those blessed shores of Cathay," Verrazano wrote his royal patron.

Some readers may find it strange that Verrazano failed to find a break or inlet in the barrier beaches separating him from Pamlico Sound, the broad expanse of waters which he termed the oriental sea—the Pacific Ocean of today. There are probably good reasons for this oversight which in no way diminish Verrazano's stature as an explorer. For one thing the number and position of Outer Bank inlets has never remained constant for very long. Perhaps even more important is the hazardous character of the coastal waters off the Outer Banks. Cape Hatteras, it will be recalled, has the dubious honor of being the "Graveyard of the Atlantic" as a result of the incredible number of shipwrecks that have occurred there. Verrazano doubtlessly tacked his way cautiously well clear of the shoals and breakers stretching seaward from the low barrier beaches he was skirting. Under such conditions, and with no charts or hydrographic information of any kind, the truly amazing thing is that he did not founder and become the first European whose ship went to the "Graveyard of the Atlantic."

Proceeding north for another fifty leagues, and possibly on Maryland's Eastern Shore, another landing was made in an area "which seemed much more beautiful and full of great forests." A party went inland to find the inhabi-

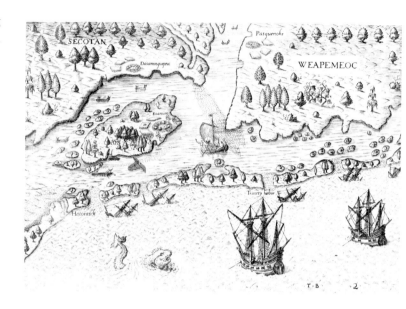

Verrazano mistakenly identified the Carolina Outer Banks as "an isthmus a mile in width and about 200 long, in which from the ship, was seen the oriental sea . . . which goes about the extremity of India, China and Cathay." Sir Walter Raleigh sponsored the founding of a colony there. For this engraving Theodor de Bry employed one of John White's maps to prepare a pseudoperspective view of the Carolina Outer Banks, Roanoke Island, and the adjacent North Carolina coast. In the text accompanying the engraving the often inconspicuous breaks in the barrier islands called "inlets" were described as "shallowe, and full of dangerous flatts." Although some scholars have severely criticized Verrazano for not reporting the breaks in his "isthmus a mile in width" there seem to be good reasons for his missing them (Rare Book and Special Collections Division).

tants who had fled as they approached the shore. Only two women with some small children were found. When the sailors presented food to them the old woman accepted it "with great pleasure" but the young woman "threw it angrily to the ground." Rather than return to the ship empty handed, a decision was made to kidnap a boy and the young woman "who was very beautiful and tall." The tawny Amazon proved to be their match, however, and they found it to be "impossible to take her to the sea because of the loud cries she uttered." Being still a long way from their boat they "decided to leave her behind, and took only the boy."[20]

Verrazano marveled at the ingenuity of the Indians living on the broad Atlantic Coastal Plain. He described their many "little boats made out of a single tree, twenty feet long and four wide, which are put together without stone, iron or any other kind of metal. For the whole country, in the area of two hundred leagues that we covered, we did not see a single stone of any kind." He told King Francis how they "use the fourth element [fire] and burn the wood as much as necessary to hollow out the boat; they do the same for the stern and prow so that when it sails it can plow through the waves of the sea."[21]

Naming the area "Arcadia on account of the beauty of the trees" Verrazano sailed on for another hundred leagues where he noted the outflow of "a very great river." This river was later named the Hudson. Today the Verrazano Narrows suspension bridge is one of the most impressive man-made features seen as one approaches New York from the sea. New York's upper bay was likened to "a very beautiful lake with a circuit of about three leagues; through which they [the Indians] went, going from one and another part to the number of 30 of their little barges, with innumerable people, who passed from one shore and the other in order to see us."[22] Unfortunately a sudden shift in the wind direction made it necessary for the ship to sail seaward so no opportunity for a Contact encounter with the Indians of New York was realized.

Sailing north, Verrazano sighted a "triangular-shaped island, ten leagues from the mainland, similar in size to the island of Rhodes; . . . we baptized it in the name of your illustrious mother." It is interesting to note that while experts identify this island as present day Block Island, the name Rhode Island is now applied to the nearby state. After sailing past the triangular island, the ship entered Narragansett Bay to a safe anchorage.

When the Indians of the locality approached the ship, trinkets and bells were thrown to them as gestures of goodwill. Thus reassured they "confidently came on board ship." Verrazano was greatly impressed by the Indians, as

The initials "T.B." near the feet of this impressive Indian identify the source as an engraving by the prolific Frankfurt map and print publisher Theodor de Bry. This print was titled "An Aged Manne In His Winter Garment" and was prepared to illustrate de Bry's 1590 edition of Thomas Harriot's Briefe and true report . . . of Virginia. The likeness of the Indian is based on John White's painting titled "The aged man in his wynter garment." The landscape details were adapted from other White sketches and added by de Bry to compose this interesting and favorable visual statement of Native American lifeways in the sixteenth century. It is included here to give some impression of what Verrazano may have seen and described when he explored the American East Coast in the early part of that century. Even when one discounts the Roman senatorlike posture and visage de Bry imparted to John White's Indian portrait and the geometric regularity of what appear to be fields of European wheat rather than American maize, what remains accords well with what Verrazano and other explorers reported (Rare Book and Special Collections Division).

can be seen in the following passage from his letter to the King of France:

Among them were two kings, who were as beautiful of stature and build as I can possibly describe. The first was about XXXX years old, the other a young man of XXIIII, and they were dressed thus: the older man had on his naked body a stag skin, skillfully worked like damask with various embroideries; the head was bare, the hair tied back with various bands, and around the neck hung a wide chain decorated with many different-colored stones. The young man was dressed in almost the same way. These people are the most beautiful and have the most civil customs that we have found on this voyage. They are taller than we are; they are a bronze color, some tending more toward whiteness, others to a tawny color; the face is clear-cut; the hair is long and black, and they take great pains to decorate it; the eyes are black and alert, and their manner of the ancients. I shall not speak to Your Majesty of the other parts of the body, since they have all the proportions belonging to any well-built man. Their women are just as shapely and beautiful; very gracious, of attractive manner and pleasant appearance; their customs and behavior follow womanly custom as far as befits human nature; they go nude except for a stag skin embroidered like the men's, and some wear rich lynx skins on their arms; their bare heads are decorated with various ornaments made of braids of their own hair which hang down over their breasts on either side. Some have other hair arrangements such as the women of Egypt and Syria wear, and these women are older and have been joined in wedlock. Both men and women have various trinkets hanging from their ears as the Orientals do; and we saw that they had many sheets of worked copper which they prize more than gold. They do not value gold because of its color; they think it the most worthless of all, and rate blue and red above all other colors. The things we gave them that they prized the most were little bells, blue crystals, and other trinkets to put in the ear or around the neck. They did not appreciate cloth or silk and gold, nor even any other kind, nor did they care to have them; the same was true for metals like steel and iron, for many times when we showed them some of our arms, they did not admire them, nor ask for them, but merely examined the workmanship. They did the same with mirrors; they would look at them quickly, and then refuse them, laughing. They are very generous and give away all they have.[23]

It should be kept in mind that Verrazano was writing long before the "Noble Savage" myth became popular in Europe. He writes his description from the perspective of a well-educated Italian gentleman of the Renaissance addressing the monarch of France about the marvels he has seen in a part of the world heretofore entirely unknown to the Europeans. We are indeed fortunate to be able to share his Contact encounter experiences and gain a rich insight into the lives of the Native Americans of one of the most densely settled regions of North America at the time. After an extended visit, which provided Verrazano with the opportunity to observe and describe the homes and life-styles of these Indians, whom he considered "very compassionate and charitable" toward one another, the explorer sailed onward on May 6, 1524.

Continuing his course and keeping within sight of the coast whenever possible, he skirted the sand banks and hazards of Nantucket Shoals and Cape Cod to sail into the Gulf of Maine. On the rocky coasts of Maine a very different Indian culture was encountered. Verrazano's unfavorable description of those people was outlined in Chapter 1. His disapproval of the Maine Indians lends credibility to his descriptions of Indians overall. Clearly all Indians were not admirable to Verrazano merely by virtue of being Indians.

In summarizing his voyage near the end of his report to the king, Verrazano verifies our earlier surmise that he came eventually to realize that he had not reached Asia. In what he termed an effort to promote science, he confided:

My intention on this voyage was to reach Cathay and the extreme eastern coast of Asia, but I did not expect to find such an obstacle of new land as I have found.[24]

Verrazano continued his informative remarks to King Francis I with a summary of the European world view current at the time he sailed:

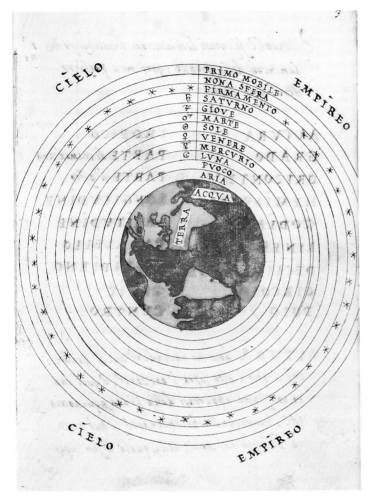

This revealing sketch is from an early sixteenth-century manuscript text intended for use in teaching the science of navigation. Titled "L'Arte de Navigare," it is written in Italian on paper and is bound in parchment. Notice that this diagram shows the earth-centered universe that Europeans believed existed during the centuries preceding the acceptance of the work done by Nicholas Copernicus. The orbits of the heavenly bodies are shown as concentric rings beginning with the Moon (Luna) and ending with Saturn (Saturno)—notice that the Sun (Sole) was located between Venus (Venere) and Mars (Marte). The eighth ring was believed to be the Firmament (Firmamento) where all the fixed stars were located. The earth, at the center of the universe, was made up of earth, water, air, and fire (Terra, Acqua, Aria, and Fuoco). Notice the world map drawn on this circa 1540 earth. Africa, Europe, and Asia are easily recognized in the Eastern Hemisphere. The Western Hemisphere, however, shows a South American continent connected to Eastern Asia by a thin isthmus while North America is shown as a narrow extension of Asia thrusting toward Northern Europe. Far to the south the theorized continent of Terra Australis is shown as a reality separated from South America (Medieval and Renaissance Manuscript Collection, Manuscript Division).

I estimated there would be some strait to get through to the Eastern Ocean. This was the opinion of all the ancients, who certainly believed that our Western Ocean was joined to the Eastern Ocean of India without any land in between. Aristotle supports this theory by arguments of various analogies, but this opinion is quite contrary to that of the moderns, and has been proven false by experience.[25]

As pointed out above, Verrazano was a true product of the Renaissance and, unlike Columbus, his mind was no slave to tradition or dogma. Listen to the ring of dogma-shattering modernity in his words as he concluded:

Nevertheless, land has been found by modern man which was unknown to the ancients, another world with respect to the one they knew, which appears to be larger than our Europe, than Africa, and almost larger than Asia, if we estimate its size correctly. All this land or New World, which we have described above is joined together, but is not linked with Asia or Africa (we know this for certain), but could be joined to Europe by Norway or Russia; this would be false according to the ancients, who declare that almost all the north has been navigated from the promontory of the Cimbri to the Orient, and affirm that they went around as far as the Caspian Sea itself. Therefore the continent would lie between two seas, to the east and west.[26]

Given what information he had concerning the eastern extension of the new land in the Arctic, Verrazano reasoned incorrectly that it must be connected to Europe. This was a concept that was eventually broken by navigators bent on finding the Northwest and Northeast Passages to Asia.

Some historians of discovery have been critical of Verrazano and have implied that his descriptions of the New World were less than accurate and written more to impress his royal patron than to reflect accurately what he saw. After reading these extracts from his letter to the King of France it is not difficult to see how a casual reading could lead to such an opinion.

However, when read and tested in light of Verrazano's background there appears to be much of substance and value to be learned from his descriptions of the aboriginal landscapes and peoples he encountered on the eastern seaboard of North America in 1524.

His hopes of persuading the king to support a follow-up voyage were never realized. Francis I had led his country into a disastrous war in Italy and was taken prisoner by the emperor. With no hope of support in France, the Verrazano brothers traveled to Portugal and became involved in Franco-Portuguese enterprises on the African coast. Giovanni was killed by Indians in Brazil while collecting a load of brazilwood in 1528.

CARTIER PLANTS THE SEED OF NEW FRANCE

Just as Giovanni da Verrazano recorded the first detailed description of the North American coasts between Florida and Nova Scotia, so a decade later another French expedition provided the first narratives describing the northern interior of the continent. Information concerning the north had been expanding but most of what was being learned was confined to the fishermen sailing from French coastal ports to the banks off Newfoundland. Fishermen then as now were notoriously guarded in revealing where and when they fished. There is evidence, however, that they were frequenting the Strait of Belle Isle, the long narrow arm of the sea separating Labrador from northern Newfoundland by the 1530s.

In 1534 a mariner from Saint-Malo, a small port on the coast of Brittany, received a royal commission from King Francis I of France to sail to China by way of the "baye des Chasteaulx," as the Strait of Belle Isle was then known. He was Jacques Cartier who sailed on April 20,

1534, with two ships to penetrate the areas Verrazano thought might link the New World with Scandinavia. Land was sighted at Cape Bonavista, Newfoundland, on May 10, 1534; a very swift westward passage had been Cartier's good fortune.

After resting and rigging the longboats, the expedition headed north to the Strait of Belle Isle. The "incredible" number of sea birds on the small islands they passed drew comments of amazement from Cartier. Indians were first encountered on the mainland side of the Strait at the place he named "Blanc Sablon." In his account of the voyage Cartier wrote:

There are people on this coast whose bodies are fairly well formed but they are wild and savage folk. They wear their hair tied up on top of their heads like a handful of twisted hay, with a nail or something of the sort passed through the middle and into it they weave a few birds' feathers. They clothe themselves with furs of animals, both men as well as women; but the women are wrapped up more closely and snuggly in their furs; and have a belt about their waists. They [all] paint themselves with certain tan colours. They have canoes made of birch-bark in which they go about, and from which they catch many seals. Since seeing them [the Indians] I have been informed that their home is not at this place but that they come from warmer countries to catch these seals and to get other food for their sustenance.[27]

More Indians were sighted as the reconnaissance of the Gulf of St. Lawrence proceded, but another encounter did not unfold until Cartier reached the Bay of Chaleur on the south side of the Gaspé Peninsula.

When the Micmac Indians at the Bay of Chaleur spied the French longboat, they immediately signalled their desire to trade by holding up furs on sticks. Being vastly outnumbered, the longboat party decided to return to the ships rather than begin trading on the beach. The Indians, however, were so intent on bartering their furs that they attempted to intercept the longboat with their canoes. The alarmed

French were forced to shoot their two small cannons over the Indians' heads and then shoot off two "firelances" to frighten them away from the encircled longboat.

On the next day a session of trading got underway on the beach and Cartier described how:

The savages showed a marvellously great pleasure in possessing and obtaining . . . iron wares and other commodities, dancing and going through many ceremonies, and throwing salt water over their heads with their hands. They bartered all they had to such an extent that all went back naked without anything on them; and they made signs to us that they would return on the morrow with more furs.[28]

It is clear that these Indians were no novices when it came to bartering furs for European metal and other trade goods. They had doubtless gained experience in trading with French or other fishing vessels before Cartier entered their world. Unlike the hostile group encountered by Verrazano in Maine, however, they do not appear to have suffered through those contacts.

For Cartier the Bay of Chaleur proved to be a disappointment when it terminated and he realized it was not a strait leading to Asia. Sailing out of the bay he turned north along the Gaspé coast. At Gaspé Harbour another large group of Indians, numbering about three hundred, with some forty canoes were fishing for mackerel. Cartier recognized that they were very different from the people he had traded with earlier. He wrote:

This people may well be called savage; for they are the sorriest folk there can be in the whole world, and the whole lot of them had not anything above the value of five sous, their canoes and fishing nets excepted. They go quite naked except for a small skin, with which they cover their privy parts, and for a few old furs which they throw over their shoulders. They are not at all of the same race or language as the first we met.[29]

Cartier continued his narrative with many further ethnographic details concerning these Huron Indians who had traveled to the coast for the fishing. He learned that in their home territory they grew "Indian corn like pease, the same as in Brazil, which they eat in place of bread, and of this they had a large quantity with them. They call it in their language, Kagaige." Cartier should have realized that, being far from home on a fishing expedition, these Indians were traveling with a bare minimum of necessary equipment and probably were not as sorry and poverty-stricken as they appeared at first glance.

As the expedition prepared to leave, Cartier had a thirty-foot-high cross set up at the entrance to the harbor. Three fleurs-de-lis on a shield and an engraved board with Gothic letters spelling out "Long live the King of France" were fastened to the cross and the Frenchmen knelt and prayed in the presence of the fascinated Indians. When they returned to their ships the Frenchmen received a visit from a not too happy Indian Chief. Cartier described the episode:

When we had returned to our ships, the chief dressed in an old black bear-skin, arrived in a canoe with three of his sons and his brother; but they did not come so close to the ships as they had usually done. And pointing to the cross he [the chief] made us a long harangue, making the sign of the cross with two of his fingers; and then he wished to say that all this region belonged to him, and that we ought not to have set up this cross without his permission. And when he had finished his harangue, we held up an axe to him, pretending we would barter it for his furskin. To this he nodded assent and little by little drew near the side of our vessel, thinking he would have the axe. But one of our men, who was in our dinghy, caught hold of his canoe, and at once two or three more stepped down into it and made the Indians come on board our vessel, at which they were greatly astonished. When they had come on board, they were assured by the captain that no harm would befall them, while at the same time every sign of affection was shown to them; and they were made to eat and to drink and to be of good cheer. And then we explained to them by signs that the cross had been set up to serve as a land-mark and guide-post on coming into the harbour, and that we would soon come back and would bring them iron wares and other goods; and that we wished to take two of his [the chief's] sons away with us and afterwards would bring them back again to that harbour. And we dressed up his two sons in shirts and ribbons and in red caps, and put a little brass chain round the neck of each, at which they were greatly pleased; and they proceded to hand over their old rags to those who were going back on shore. To each of these three, whom we sent back we also gave a hatchet and two knives at which they showed great pleasure. When they had returned on shore, they told the others what had happened. About noon on that day, six canoes came off to the ships, in each of which were five or six Indians, who had come to say good-bye to the two we had detained, and to bring them some fish. These made signs to us that they would not pull down the cross, delivering at the same time several harangues which we did not understand.[30]

With his two young Indian passengers, "Dom Agaya" and "Taignoagny," onboard Cartier encountered one last group of Indian fishermen at Natashquan Point, north of Anticosti Island, before sailing through the Strait of Belle Isle and home to St. Malo.

Cartier had found no passage to China but had every reason to be pleased with the results of his first voyage. In five months he had circuited the Gulf of St. Lawrence and encountered Indians eager to trade rich stocks of northern furs for goods of small value. On his follow-up expedition he entered and ascended the St. Lawrence River to the Indian town Hochelaga, site of the modern metropolis Montreal. Thanks to his explorations, Cartier is credited with planting the first seeds of the French colonial empire that evolved into today's Francophone Canadian Province of Quebec.

In the month following his return to St. Malo, Cartier received a second commission to "conduct, lead, and employ three ships equipped and victualed for fifteen months, for the perfec-

tion of the navigation of lands by you already begun."[31] His flagship, *La Grande Hermine*, was a three-masted ship of the type the French used on Grand Bank fishing expeditions and a very practical vessel for his purposes.

The Strait of Belle Isle was entered without bothering to land at Newfoundland. On July 15, 1535, the flagship anchored at "Blanc Sablon" where the first Indians had been encountered the year before. Back in their home country the two young Indian captives began to act as guides for the expedition. Early in the exploration Cartier mentioned that "the two Indians whom we had captured on our first voyage" were providing important information and geographical intelligence.[32] They had told him that not far from a cape they were near on the Quebec shore, north of Anticosti Island, "began the kingdom of Saguenay."[33] A few days later "the two Indians assured us that this was the way to the mouth of the great river of Hochelaga and the route towards Canada, and that the river grew narrower as one approached Canada, and also that farther up, the water became fresh, and that one could make one's way so far up the river that they had never heard of anyone reaching the head of it."

It would appear that Cartier's young Indian captives were honest as well as informed concerning the nature of the upper river which they assured him could only be penetrated in small boats. In light of these revelations Cartier decided to keep searching for a strait on the northern side of the gulf rather than entering the St. Lawrence River. Finally, after thoroughly exploring the north shore to no avail, Cartier was ready to make his way "towards Canada" on the river he was to style "Chemin de Canada."

At the mouth of the Saguenay River an Indian fishing party showed "great fear and trembling" until one of the young captives onboard "gave his name and told who he was." Thus reassured they approached the ships with "all confidence." Farther upstream they sighted fish Cartier described as being as large as a porpoise but without a fin and "very similar to a greyhound about the body and head and is as white as snow, without a spot on it." These were the beluga whales of the St. Lawrence estuary that the Indians called "adhothuys."

As they neared the location of Quebec City, Cartier took his two Indian captives ashore. The first Indians they encountered took flight and "would not come near, until our two Indians had spoken to them and told them that they were Taignoagny and Dom Agaya." When they realized that their chief's sons had been returned the local Indians "began to welcome them, dancing and going through many ceremonies."[34] Gifts of fish, eels, Indian corn, and large melons were showered on the Frenchmen by the appreciative kinsmen of the young returnees. Cartier was gracious and freely presented the Indians with trinkets and "small presents of little value."

The following day "the Lord of Canada, named Donnacona" came to the ships with a large company in twelve birchbark canoes. Cartier described the colorful scene:

He then sent back ten of these and came alongside our ships with only two canoes. And when he was opposite to the smallest of our three ships (Emerillon), this Agouhanna [Donnacona] began to make a speech and to harrangue us, moving his body and limbs in a marvellous manner as is their custom when showing joy or contentment. And when he came opposite to the Captain's vessel on board of which were Taignoagny and Dom Agaya, the chief spoke to them and they to him, telling him what they had seen in France, and the good treatment meted out to them there. At this the chief was much pleased and begged the Captain to stretch out his arms to him that he might hug and kiss them, which is the way they welcome one in that country.[35]

Cartier then got into Donnacona's canoe and shared French bread and wine with the Indians.

After this ceremonial welcome the Indians took their leave. Cartier proceeded upstream along the north shore of Ile d'Orleans to "a forking of the waters, which is an exceedingly pleasant spot, where there is a small river and a harbour with a bar, on which at high tide, there is a depth of from two to three fathoms." They named the tributary that is now known as the St. Charles River, the St. Croix, and laid up their ships in its safe waters.

Donnacona and his people lived near the site of modern Quebec City in the village called Stadacona. Cartier was obviously favorably impressed with what he saw and described:

This region is as fine land as it is possible to see, being very fertile and covered with magnificent trees of the same varieties as in France, such as oaks, elms, ash, walnut, plum trees, yew trees, cedars, vines, hawthorns bearing a fruit as large as a damson, and other varieties of trees. Beneath these grows as good hemp as that of France, which comes up without sowing or tilling it.[36]

The Isle d'Orleans impressed him with its fertility and profusion of wild grapevines so favorably that he named it "Bacchus's Island." Cartier missed no opportunity to present gifts and ingratiate himself with the Indians. The two former captives were, however, not friendly now that they were free. Cartier was upset to find them "altogether changed in their attitude and goodwill." Not surprisingly they refused to come onboard the ships even when "many times begged to do so." One free trip to France had been their fill. They had, while still his prisoners, promised to guide the expedition to Hochelaga far upstream where the city of Montreal would be built in the next century. Cartier was most upset with their refusal to carry out this promise.

Cartier and a small party pushed on to Hochelaga which he described as being in the midst of a populous and productive region. When he reached the town's landing he described being met by "more than a thousand persons . . . who

COMPETITION IN THE NORTH

gave us as good a welcome as ever father gave to his son, making great signs of joy, for the men danced in one ring, the women in another and the children also apart by themselves." After the dance of welcome "they brought us quantities of fish, and of their bread, which is made of Indian corn, throwing so much of it into our long-boats that it seemed to rain bread."[37]

When Cartier's party left the boats to march to the town they discovered "that the path was as well trodden as it is possible to see." The fortified town of Hochelaga was described as follows:

The village is circular and is completely enclosed by a wooden palisade in three tiers like a pyramid. The top one is built crosswise, the middle one perpendicular and the lowest one of strips of wood placed lengthwise. The whole is well joined and lashed after their manner, and is some two lances in height. There is only one gate and entrance to this village, and that can be barred up. Over this gate and in many places about the enclosure are species of galleries that are provided with rocks and stones for the defence and protection of the place. There are some fifty houses in this village, each about fifty or more paces in length, and twelve or fifteen in width, built completely of wood and covered in and bordered up with large pieces of the bark and rind of trees, as broad as a table, which are well and cunningly lashed after their manner. And inside these houses are many rooms and chambers; and in the middle is a large space without a floor, where they light their fire and live together in common. Afterwards the men retire to the above-mentioned quarters with their wives and children. And furthermore there are lofts in the upper part of their houses, where they store the corn of which they make their bread.[38]

The construction details of Hochelaga's palisade wall and village layout were made clearer by the engraving Ramusio prepared and printed in 1556.

Before leaving Hochelaga, Cartier gleaned as much geographical intelligence as he could from the residents. He was particularly interested in the nature of the upper St. Lawrence beyond the extensive rapids he could see from

the nearby mountain he named "Mount Royal." Cartier explained how the Indians assured him "by signs that after passing the rapids, one could navigate along the river for more than three moons." The course of the Ottawa River joining the St. Lawrence from the north was also described by the Indians for the eager French explorers. Cartier and his fellows were doubtlessly amazed when "without our asking any questions or making any sign, they seized the chain of the Captain's whistle, which was made of silver and a dagger handle of yellow copper gilt like gold . . . and gave us to understand that these came from up that river (Ottawa)."[39] When Cartier showed them copper and "asked by signs if it came thence? They shook their heads to say no, showing us that it came from the Saguenay, which lies in the opposite direction."

The spontaneous volunteering of information concerning the place where silver and gold could be found suggests that Cartier's two young Indian former captives were secretly advising the Hochelaga Indians. The account reads like a classic "tell them what they want to hear and send them away" strategy episode. This seems all the more likely in light of the fact that the Saguenay region to the east, rather than Lake Superior in the west, was named as the source of the Indians' copper.

Returning down river to the place where the ships had been berthed, Cartier and his party prepared for the onset of winter near the site of present day Quebec City. The Canadian winter amazed the Frenchmen with its ferocity. Being at a latitude that was considerably south of that of Paris they were anticipating a winter of the sort they were familiar with if not even milder. When relationships with Donnacona and his former captive sons began to sour visibly, Cartier strengthened his fortified camp with "large, wide, deep ditches and with a gate and drawbridge, and with extra logs of wood set crosswise to the former."

All might have gone well for the Frenchmen if "the pestilence" had not broken out among the local Indians. In December Cartier learned that over fifty of the tribesmen of Stadacona had already died of the unnamed scourge. Cartier reacted by barring the Indians from entering the fortified encampment for any reason. In all likelihood the Indians were falling prey to an introduced European infection to which the Frenchmen were largely immune so the strict quarantine was an unnecessary precaution. As it turned out it was a precaution that spelled death for many of Cartier's party who expired from a virulent attack of scurvy. Cut off from the Indians and the supplies of fresh game and fish they brought to the camp, the French were reduced to eating stale ship's biscuit, and rancid salt meat.

Unaware of the impact of their now vitamin-deficient diet, Cartier felt that the pestilence had spread from the Indians in spite of his stringent quarantine. His description of the manifestations of the scurvy among practically the whole of his party is graphic and gruesome. With no remedy available or known, they resorted to prayer and Cartier had "an image and figure of the Virgin Mary carried across the ice and snow and placed against a tree about a bow-shot from the fort." [40] In desperation Cartier performed an autopsy on one twenty-two-year-old member of the party who had expired. The description of the internal organs he examined matched for gruesomeness his clinical description of the external symptoms of scurvy.

Cartier continued to keep the Indians at a distance in spite of the fact that almost all of his men were desperately ill and too weak to bury the corpses of their dead fellows. Finally he called on one of the Indians he had taken to France earlier to find out how he had been cured. The Indian, Dom Agaya, told him that the juice of the leaves of certain trees was the only remedy for the sickness. Cartier, keeping up his subterfuge, pretended that he needed to prepare some of the remedy for his servant "who had caught the disease when staying in Chief Donnacona's wigwam." Two squaws gathered several branches and showed Cartier's men how to grind the bark and leaves and boil them in water. The curative tree was called "Annedda" by the Indians.

At first the sick Frenchmen were relcutant to drink the Indian decoction but eventually a few tried it. As they began to benefit from the ascorbic acid in the needles and bark, the recovering scurvy victims ascribed miraculous powers to the decoction. A clue as to the identity of the "pestilence," which some Indians may have contracted from their French visitors, is revealed by Cartier when he enthusiastically mentioned that the sailors who had been suffering from the "French pox" (syphilis) had been "cured completely" by the Indians' scurvy remedy. "When this became known, there was such a press for the medicine that they almost killed each other to have it first; so that in less than eight days a whole tree as large and tall as any I ever saw was used up, and produced such a result that had all the doctors of Louvain and Montpellier been there, with all the drugs of Alexandria, they could not have done so much in a year as did this tree in eight days; for it benefited us so much that all who were willing to use it, recovered health and strength thanks be to God," Cartier concluded. [41]

In addition to the spruce bark and needle tea, Cartier should have mentioned the beneficial return of the Indians who brought "fresh fish which they bartered for a good price" to the recovering French explorers. Their prices were high because their own supply of food was low after what had been a long and hard winter even by Indian standards. As he prepared to return to France, Cartier used his considerable wile once again and carefully laid a plot to kidnap chief Donnacona to take him back to France with several other Indians. Cartier had resolved earlier that Donnacona should be brought along so that "he might relate and tell the king all he had seen in the west of the wonders of the world; for he assured us that he had been to the land of the Saguenay where there are immense quantities of gold, rubies and other rich things."[42] If Donnacona had, as is suspected, been engaging in the strategy of "tell them what they want to hear" the table had been radically turned on him. On July 16, 1536, Cartier, the survivors of the scurvy-racked Canadian winter, and their ten or a dozen Indian captives reached St. Malo. They had accomplished a long and detailed reconnaissance of what was to become the heart of New France, the lower St. Lawrence River Valley. Unfortunately none of the Indian captives ever saw their homes again. By the time Cartier was ready to return on his third voyage they had all died or disappeared from the pages of history somewhere in France. Space limitations will not permit a review of the ill-fated Canadian settlement attempts undertaken by Cartier and Jean Francis de Roberval during the 1540s. Once again the unbridled ferocity of the Canadian winter combined with Indian hostilities to hammer the colonists and force their retreat. The permanent settlement of the St. Lawrence valley by French colonists was forestalled until the early seventeenth-century plantings of Samuel de Champlain.

A FRENCH COLONY IN FLORIDA

In spite of the failed colonial attempts of Cartier and Roberval, France did not abandon entirely the idea of establishing a colony in eastern North America. A strong push factor was developing within the community of Protestants known as Huguenots. The Huguenots were an influential minority who were increasingly coming under

stress in predominantly Catholic France. The Huguenots' protector in the monarchy was Gaspard de Coligny, the Admiral of France, with authority over the merchant and naval fleets. In the 1560s persecution of Huguenots erupted into religious wars which were strongly tinged with politics and took on the character of civil war. Almost one-half of the French nobility were Protestants as these conflicts were breaking out.

Coligny was adroit in combining French rivalry with Spain and the interests of the Huguenots in a scheme to establish a colony on the Atlantic coast of La Florida. His ambitions were further assisted as it became known that Philip II of Spain had decided that the mainland of the Southeast of the present United States was not suitable for a Spanish colony. Coligny reasoned that an overseas colony on the Florida coast would form an excellent French base for attacks on the exclusivist Spaniards, whose official policy barred all other Europeans from dealings with southern North America. Further, a colony in more southerly latitudes would be spared the rigors of the Canadian winters that dealt so bitterly with the colonies attempted by Cartier and Roberval.

In February 1562, two French ships under the command of Jean Ribault and René de Laudonnière made an easy passage from the port of Le Havre to the mouth of Florida's St. Johns River which they named River of May. Like Verrazano before them, the French voyagers experienced "an inspeakable pleasure of the odoriferous smell and bewtye [beauty]" of the forested shores of La Florida. As also had been the experience of many Europeans before them, the Huguenots received a friendly reception from the Indians they encountered on landing. In his report to Admiral Coligny, Jean Ribault described how:

Thus entered, we perceived a good numbre of the Indians, . . . coming alonge the sandes and seebanck somewhate nere unto us, without any token of feare or doubte, shewing unto us the easiest landing place . . . fourthewith one of the best of appearance amonges them, brother unto one of there kinges or governours, comaunded one of the Indians to enter into the water . . . to showe us the easiest landing place.[43]

As was almost always the case with Contact encounters, the European arrivals were overwhelmed by the hospitality and generosity shown by the Indians. As Ribault wrote, they "receaved us verry gentilly with great huymanytie, putting us of their fruites, even in our boates, as mulberies, respices [raspberries] and suche other frutes as they found redely by the waye."[44]

In 1562 Jean Ribault and his French Huguenot colonists enjoyed a typical cordial Contact encounter with the Indians living in the vicinity of the St. Johns River in northern Florida. An earlier French attempt to found a colony in Brazil had met with disaster. Before leaving Florida to sail north to establish a post at Port Royal Sound in today's South Carolina, Ribault erected "a piller or colume of hard stone, our kinges armes graven therin" on the south side of the St. Johns River. On "a littell hill compassed with cipers, bayes, palmes, and other trees, and swete pleasaunt smelling shrubbes . . . we planted the first bounde or lymete of his majestie," wrote Ribault. In this engraving Theodore de Bry has attempted to follow a painting by Jacques Le Moyne, the artist-cartographer who joined the colony in 1564. The scene shows René de Laudonnière being taken to the boundary marker column by the Indian Chief Athore (Rare Book and Special Collections Division).

After describing the verdant Florida landscape in the superlatives typical of all newly arrived explorers, Ribault told how they lost no time in interrogating their Indian hosts:

As we nowe demaunded of them for a certen towne called Sevola [Cibola], whereof some have wrytten not to be farr from thence, and to be scituate within the lands and towards the southe sea, they shewed us by signes which we understoode well enough, that they might go thither with there boates by rivers in xxiie [twenty] days.[45]

Before sailing farther up the coast, the French marked their landing by setting up "a piller or colume of hard stone, our kinges armes graven therein . . . at the entrye of the port in some high place wher yt might be easelly sene."[46] Ribault's column establishing the basis for a "prior discovery" claim was the subject of a painting by Huguenot artist-cartographer Jacques Le Moyne. Le Moyne was not a member of Ribault's original crew but sailed to America with René de Laudonnière in 1564 as the expedition's recording artist.

One of the true treasures of the New York Public Library is a small painting by Le Moyne inscribed "Laudonnierus Et Rex Athore Ante Columnam A Praefecto Prima Navigatione Locatam Quamque Venerantur Floridenses." In English it is usually titled "Athore shows Laudonnière the Marker Column Set Up By Ribault."[47] What the painting shows is a somwehat stylized depiction of Laudonnière being shown the marker column by the Indian Athore. A large number of Indians are kneeling and worshipping the column which is festooned with garlands of flowers and surrounded with votive offerings of Indian baskets and bowls filled with foodstuffs, a bundle of large corn ears, and a quiver of arrows. The scene is far better known through the engraved version published by Theodor De Bry in 1591 illustrated in this chapter. De Bry prepared and published over forty different engravings based on Le Moyne's original

American artwork but only the original painting of the marker column scene is known to exist.[48]

De Bry published captions with the engravings that are attributed to the French artist. Le Moyne's caption for the marker column engraving states:

When the French had landed in the province of Florida, on the second voyage made under Laudonnière's leadership, he went down on shore himself, accompanied by twenty-five arquebusiers, and was received in greeting by the Indians (for these had come up in crowds to see them). Even the chief Athore came, who lives four or five miles from the seashore; and when they had exchanged gifts and all manner of courtesies he indicated that he wished to show them something special and asked them for this reason to go along with him. They agreed, but because they were aware that he was surrounded by a great number of his subjects, they set out with caution and vigilance in his company. In fact he led them to the island on which Ribault had placed on top of a certain mound a marker of rock carved with the arms of the King of France. Drawing close they noticed that the Indians were worshipping this stone as if it were an idol. For when the chief himself had saluted it and shown it the sort of reverence he was accustomed to receive from his subjects, he kissed it; his people copied him and encouraged us to do the same. In front of the stone were lying various offerings of fruits of the district and roots that were either good to eat or medicinally useful, dishes full of fragrant oils, and bows and arrows; it was also encircled from top to bottom with garlands of all kinds of flowers, and with branches of their most highly prized trees. After witnessing the rites of these poor savage people they returned to their comrades with the intent to search out the most suitable site for building a fort.

This chief Athore is an extremely handsome man, intelligent, reliable, strong, of exceptional height, exceeding our tallest men by a foot and a half, and endowed with a certain restrained dignity, so that in him a remarkable majesty shone forth. He married his mother and by her raised more children of both sexes whom he produced for us by slapping his thigh; and indeed, after she had been betrothed to him, his father Satouriwa did not touch her any more.[49]

Jacques Le Moyne was clearly a gifted and dedicated artist. His were the first widely cir

In this engraving from de Bry's America, Part 2, published in 1591, the construction of the fort the French built in Florida in 1591 is shown. The scale of the figures, fort, and island are clearly unrealistic but the construction techniques and plan are probably close to authentic. Fort Caroline was named in honor of the King of France and a replica built by the U.S. National Park Service downstream from Jacksonville, Florida, on the St. Johns River is open for visitation. Jacques Le Moyne, who drew the sketch on which the engraving is based, wrote of how the local Indian chief sent eighty of his "strongest men, who were well used to work," to aid the French in building Fort Caroline (Rare Book and Special Collections Division).

listic conventions become apparent and require that caution be applied in their interpretation.

In addition to his maps and drawings of the Huguenot explorations, Le Moyne prepared a lengthy narrative that was also published by De Bry in 1591.[50] Space limitations will restrict us to only one of the many colorful descriptions included in Le Moyne's narrative. It deals with the visit of the powerful Indian chieftain called Satouriwa to the French force as they were beginning the construction of Fort Caroline on the banks of the St. Johns River near present day Jacksonville, Florida. Le Moyne wrote of how:

The chief was escorted by seven or eight hundred splendid-looking men, strong, hardy, athletic and highly trained as runners, who were carrying their weapons in the way they usually do when about to go to war. He was preceded by fifty youths carrying javelins or spears in their hands. Nearer to him were twenty pipers who were playing some primitive thing discordantly and raggedly, merely blowing the pipes as hard as they could. These pipes are no more than extremely thick reeds with two holes, an upper one where they blow and a lower one where the breath comes out, as with the pipes or tubes of organs. Flanking the chief on the right with the sorcerer and on his left his leading counsellor, for he undertakes nothing without these two. Going alone into the place which had been made ready, he sat down in Indian fashion, that is, on the ground itself, like a monkey or other animal. Then looking all around him and seeing our tiny company drawn up, he ordered Laudonnière and Ottigny, his deputy, to be called into the pavilion and made them a long speech, which they understood only in part. But eventually he enquired who we were, why we had entered his territory rather than anyone else's, and what our intentions were. Laudonnière answered through Captain La Caille—who had picked up something of the language of that region, as we have said above—that he had been sent by a very powerful king, who was called the King of France, to invite him to make a treaty with him, by which he would be a friend to him and his allies and an enemy to his enemies; and this idea pleased him much. Then gifts were presented and the chief came nearer to us and admired our weapons, especially our arquebuses; and coming up to the ditch of our fort, he explored it outside and in, and when he saw earth being removed from the ditch and the

culated images to provide a visual account of North America's native people and their landscapes. Little is known about his training or background beyond the fact that he was from Dieppe, an important center of cartographic development in the early sixteenth century. The so-called "Dieppe School" of cartographers was famed for artistically embellished maps showing details of the flora and fauna of newly discovered places as well as their geographical configurations and locations. As one studies the De Bry engravings of Le Moyne's work, European sty-

bank being constructed, he asked what purpose these things served.

He received the reply that a building was being put up to accommodate us all and that many huts were to be built in it. Impressed by this, he said it was his wish that this building of ours should soon be finished. Consequently he agreed to our request to provide some of his men to help ours with the construction and thereupon sent eighty of the

strongest men, who were well used to work, by whose efforts we were greatly relieved. Our fort was quickly built and the huts finished; but Satouriwa, for his part, left us.[51]

The Spanish, already well aware of the Huguenots' activities in La Florida, were incensed by a rebellious breakaway faction of Laudon-

This attractively hand-colored engraving shows the Spanish town of St. Augustine, Florida, under attack by Sir Francis Drake's fleet in 1586. This is the earliest printed depiction of any town of European construction within the United States. The town is made up of the eleven rectangular-shaped blocks and associated gardens shown in the upper left corner of the print. Located north of the town is the six-sided log fort built to command the inlet from the Atlantic Ocean to the Matanzas River. Both the fort and town are shown to be under attack by Drake's forces. A close look will reveal that an armed soldier has gained the top of "a high scaffold" the Spanish had built for the town watchman. At this early date the cedar log and sand fort was named "Saint John de Pinos." It was burned by the English during the conflict pictured here. In 1642 Spain began a stone castillo built from the local shellstone known as coquina. At the present time the Castillo de San Marcos overlooking St. Augustine and the Matanzas River is a popular historic site administered by the U.S. National Park Service (Drake Collection, Rare Book and Special Collections Division).

nière's colonists who took up piracy. Not surprisingly it was resolved that the French should be expelled from the region altogether. In the late summer of 1565, Fort Caroline was attacked and captured by a Spanish force under the command of Pedro Menéndez de Aviles. Most of the Frenchmen were quickly killed and a short while later disaster in the form of a hurricane wrecked a reinforcing fleet under the command of Jean Ribault. The fleet's survivors, who washed up on the coast to the south, had begun to make their way along the beach to Fort Caroline when they were intercepted by Menéndez's men. What followed was an orgy of slaughter. Only a few French Catholics were spared to tell of Menéndez's brutality against the unarmed shipwreck victims.

With the French menace to Spain's vital Gulf Stream sea route eliminated, Menéndez took steps to found a permanent Spanish outpost on the coast of La Florida. Ultimately he established St. Augustine, Florida, south of the St. Johns River. This attractive north Florida city now boasts its history as the oldest continuously occupied European settlement in the United States.

ENGLAND CHALLENGES SPAIN'S MONOPOLY

As might be expected, English Protestant eyes were no less attracted to New Spain than those of the French Huguenots. The reign of Henry VIII's daughter by Catherine of Aragon, Mary, had seen the restoration of Roman Catholicism in England in the 1550s. Mary's marriage to Philip II of Spain in 1554 went far toward insuring that her subjects would refrain from challenging Spain's exclusive control of the Indies, New Spain, and La Florida. It is not an exaggeration to view the period of Mary's ill-starred reign as a prolonged period of frustration for England's burgeoning maritime community. Voyages to

the north in search of a Northwest Passage around northern North America or a Northeast Passage around northern Eurasia to the Orient, voyages with no threat to Spain's claims, were sent out during this period. They did little, however, to satisfy the growing English ambitions articulated by publicists like Richard Eden who, in 1555, exhorted his fellows "for owre owne commoditie to attempte summe vyages into these coastes, to doo for owr partes as the Spaniards have doone for theyrs, and not ever lyke sheepe to haunte one trade, and to doo nothynge woorthy of memorie among men or thankes before god . . ."[52]

When Protestant-reared Elizabeth ascended to England's throne in 1558, there was no quick or radical shift in policy insofar as poaching on Spain's New World claims was concerned. Elizabeth repealed the Catholic legislation of Mary and reenacted her father's laws relating to the church but did nothing to break or weaken relations with Spain by overtly challenging its American hegemony. As her government grew in strength, however, Elizabeth proved to be less than cowed by the might of Spain under Philip II.

England, like all other leading European states of the time, was committed to the ideals of mercantilism in its national economic life. Mercantilism was the economic counterpart of political unification. In practice the aim of mercantilist leaders was twofold. They endeavored first, to strengthen the state by concentrating the national economic life under the direction of a powerful central government; and second, to increase the strength of his or her state against that of other national states. When it came to the second aim of the mercantilists, the best means of promoting the power of the state was believed to be the accumulation of wealth. Wealth, it should be understood, was defined in terms of gold and silver rather than productive capability. In the mercantilists' thinking this was because precious metals were not perishable, or so "mutable as other commodities," but were wealth "at all times and in all places." "Money," mercantilists proclaimed "is the sinews of war." In the seventeenth century an English writer expressed the same thought thus: "in the common opinion, that state that abounds in money hath courage, hath men, and all other instruments to defend itself and offend others."[53]

By the midsixteenth century it was clear that only in New Spain and Peru were to be found the rich mines that would produce precious metals in the quantities needed to insure great national power on a world scale. The hope of finding treasure continued to spur countries outside of Spain to sponsor voyages and exploration, but hard-headed mercantilist realists increasingly turned toward trade as the only feasible means of accumulating specie and increasing national wealth.

In this period the Spanish colonists in and around the Caribbean Sea had two demands that were not being met by Spain's tightly controlled system of commerce. These were the demand for good textiles and the demand for slaves. The first outsider to systematically exploit the economic opportunity provided by these demands was an English adventurer who had the tacit encouragement of Elizabeth's government, John Hawkins. In his youth Hawkins had voyaged to the Canary Islands and learned of the great demand for slaves on Hispaniola and the other islands where Spanish mining and plantation agriculture were flourishing. Hawkins, as every Englishman, was aware that England excelled in cloth production and that slaves could be obtained on the coast of West Africa.

The story of Hawkins's profitable voyages to the African coast for slaves and their delivery and sale on the Spanish Main and islands is well known and not strictly part of the history of discovery. Hawkins is, however, connected to the narrative of that history through the ex-

This striking portrait of England's Queen Elizabeth I was engraved as a frontispiece for Christopher Saxton's 1579 collection of maps of the counties of England and Wales. As the power of her realm grew, Elizabeth's government promoted the mapping of the home country as well as overseas discoveries. After some false starts, England and Wales were surveyed by Saxton in the years 1574–79. When he published his work with this regal frontispiece in 1579, members of Elizabeth's court could at last boast a set of county maps "after the manner that Ortelius hath dealt wyth other countries . . . to the great benefits of our nation." In truth it can be argued that Saxton's atlas of England and Wales was the first national atlas ever produced. In the pose pictured here the queen is shown as the patron of geography and astronomy flanked on the left by Strabo and on the right by Ptolemy (Geography and Map Division).

ploits of his cousin and fellow West Country-man, Francis Drake.

In 1567, Drake sailed with Hawkins on another profit-seeking venture to the African slave coast and the Indies. The six-ship fleet sought refuge and repairs in the Spanish port of San Juan de Ulúa near Vera Cruz, Mexico, before returning to England with the rich rewards of what had been a lucrative but technically illegal trading enterprise interspersed with a bit of piracy. While helpless in the harbor, the Englishmen were surprised and overwhelmed by the arrival of a Spanish flotilla of thirteen great ships with the new Viceroy of Mexico onboard.

After some hectic negotiations an agreement was reached by which Hawkins's men were allowed to repair their ships and purchase provisions needed for the voyage to England. The pact was treacherously broken, according to Hawkins and Drake, by the viceroy's order, and the English ships came under attack. Only two of the smaller ships, the *Minion* with Hawkins, and the *Judith,* with Drake in command managed to escape. Over five hundred men and almost all of the proceeds of the expedition were lost.

To say that Drake harbored a bitter resentment against the Spanish for the double cross at San Juan de Ulúa would be an understatement. He was consumed with rage and a determination to avenge his comrades' murders and recoup his and Hawkins's losses. In 1570 and 1571 he returned to the Indies on brief voyages about which little is known. With the intelligence gained, he formulated a plan to strike the Spanish in the jugular of their empire—the point on the isthmus of Panama at which the gold and silver from Peru was sent overland to the Caribbean Sea.

Drake sailed from Plymouth in May 1572 with two small vessels and a force of seventy-three. His scheme to seize the treasure came very close to succeeding but failed when he was wounded. He remained in the Caribbean teaming up with French buccanneers to raid Spanish shipping and landing positions. By August of 1573 he returned to Plymouth with a hoard of gold and silver estimated to be worth 20,000 pounds.

The lure of such treasure drew many of Queen Elizabeth's highest officials to contribute to Drake's next expedition. Although it cannot be proven beyond doubt, most experts feel certain that Queen Elizabeth secretly backed Drake in the voyage's financing.[54] The company of five vessels sailed from Plymouth on December 13, 1577. Publicly it had been announced that they were bound for the eastern Mediterranean and even now the true objectives of the voyage remain obscure. William Markham, master of the *Elizabeth*, later complained that "Master Drake hired him for Alexandria, but had he known that this [the Strait of Magellan] had been the Alexandria he would have been hanged in England rather than have come on this voyage."[55]

FROM REVENGE TO CIRCUMNAVIGATION

At the Cape Verde Islands Drake took his first prize, a Portuguese ship, and kidnapped its navigator who was familiar with the Atlantic coast of South America. A tedious crossing to the Rio de la Plata was followed by a long stop at bleak Port St. Julian, on the coast of southern Argentina where Magellan, the first circumnavigator, had anchored fifty-eight years before. It was here that Drake, like Magellan, was faced with a challenge to his authority that led to the trial and execution of one of his chief officers.

Finally, after Drake quelled an attempted mutiny by devising a policy of equality before the mast that an authority on Tudor naval history termed "a new tradition in English leadership," the fleet was ready to traverse the fearsome Strait of Magellan. Favorable winds saw them through to the Pacific in only sixteen days. Violent weather was encountered when they entered, what for Drake's expedition was a misnamed ocean, the Pacific. Storms tore the fleet, sinking the smaller vessels and forcing the *Elizabeth* with its master William Markham to retrace the course through the Strait and return to England. Drake in his flagship, the famous *Golden Hind,* was driven far to the south beyond the latitude of Tierra del Fuego. As a result of this harrowing experience he came to the conclusion that the hypothetical southern continent named Terra Australis did not reach so far north as many of the maps then showed.

Until Drake's arrival, the Pacific rim of Spain's American empire had been virtually immune to attack thanks to its remoteness from Europe. Once his presence became known, it caused a near panic from Chile to Mexico. The eastern Pacific had been a Spanish lake for two generations and very little in the way of port defense had been built or even deemed necessary.

The *Golden Hind,* Drake's only ship in the Pacific was, in itself, not overly impressive. It bore the name *Pelican* when the expedition left Plymouth in December, but Drake had renamed her in August while at Port St. Julian. Nor was the *Golden Hind* unusual in any way; according to one expert it "was probably not much more than eighty or ninety feet overall, a small vessel for so tremendous a voyage."[56] She did, of course, carry a crew of nearly eighty well-picked men trained in the school of sixteenth-century piracy and armed with eighteen carriage guns. The perils of the sea rather than anything the Spanish could bring to bear posed the greatest challenge for the *Golden Hind* on the western coasts of South and North America. The fact that she completed the world's second circumnavigation attests to her seaworthiness and the competence of her master and crew.

As Drake sailed slowly north along the island-strewn coast of Chile there was probably no idea in his or anyone else's mind that this voyage would end as a circumnavigation of the globe. His goal at that point appears to have been Spanish treasure and sweet revenge for the treatment Hawkins and he had suffered with their expedition on the coast of Mexico. The turning point of the voyage is thought to have come at Valparaiso. The town itself was a mean place and hardly worth the time it would take to plunder, but a ship was in the harbor which Drake captured. Drake had learned of the presence of the Spanish ship from "an Indian in a Canoa, who thinking us to have bene Spaniards, came to us and told us, that at a place called S. Iago, there was a great Spanish ship laden from the Kingdome of Peru, for which good newes our Generall [Drake] gave him diverse trifles, whereof he was glad, and went along with us and brought us to the place which is called the port of Valparizo."[57]

Drake kidnapped the ship's pilot "one John Grego a Greeke borne, whom [he] carried with him for his Pilot to bring him into the haven of Lima."[58] Also seized was "a good store of the wine of Chile, and 25,000 pezoes of very pure and fine gold of Baldiuia [Valdivia], amounting in value to 37,000 duckets of Spanish money and above." More treasure was gathered from Spanish settlements and ships on the way to Lima. Among these were "three small barkes" which yielded "57 wedges of silver, each of them weighing about 20 pound waight, and every one of these wedges were of the fashion and bignesse of a brickbat."

Lima's port proved to be an easy prize with "about twelve sayle of ships lying fast moored at an anker, having all their sayles carried on shore, for the masters and merchaunts were here most secure, having never bene assaulted by enemies, and at this time feared the approach of none such as wee were."[59] While he "rifled these shippes" Drake learned that a treasure-laden ship irreverently called the *Cacafuego* had recently left port for the Isthmus of Panama. Cutting the cables of the ships without completing the plunder of their cargoes, Drake took leave of Lima's port Callao in chase of *Cacafuego*.

So eager was Drake to overhaul this prize that he offered "his chaine of gold" to the first onboard to spot the *Cacafuego*. Off a place called "Cape Francisco, about 150 leagues from Panama," the gold chain was won by a young cousin of the captain, John Drake. The *Cacafuego* was boarded and "great riches, as jewels and precious stones, thirteen chestes full of royals of plate, four score pound weight of gold, and five and twentie tunne of silver" was taken aboard the *Golden Hind*, now truly deserving of her name. After casting adrift the plundered *Cacafuego*, Drake soon overhauled a merchantman laden "with linnen cloth and fine China dishes of white earth, and great store of China silks, of all which wee tooke as we listed."[60] The ship owner, "a Spanish Gentleman," who had the misfortune to be onboard was personally relieved of "a Fawlcon [Falcon] of golde with a great emeraude [emerald] in the breast thereof," by Drake.

The pilot of the ship was kidnapped by Drake, who by now was doubtlessly thinking of returning to England by way of the Pacific and Indian Oceans. After taking still more treasure Drake told his crew that he felt that both England and he were now amply repaid and revenged for the "contempts and indignities" that the Spaniards had inflicted at Vera Cruz. Therefore he proposed that they "continue no longer upon the Spanish coasts, but beg[in] to consider and consult of the best way for [their] country."[61] A return through the Strait of Magellan was ruled out for two reasons:

the one least [lest] the Spaniards should there waite, and attend for him [Drake] in great number and strength, whose hands he being left but one shippe, could not possibly escape. The other cause was the dangerous situation of the mouth of the Streights in the south side, where continuall, stormes, raining and blustering, as he found by experience . . .[62]

Rather than immediately heading west and crossing the Pacific to the "Islands of the Moluccaes and . . . the course of the Portingals [Portuguese]," Drake was forced to sail "a Spanish course . . . somewhat northerly to get a wind" that would carry him over the earth's widest ocean and home to England. Some experts feel that he sailed farther north than needed simply to encounter favorable winds. In their view, Drake may have been hoping to discover a rumored strait that would allow him to sail east around the north side of the still vaguely-known continent of North America. If this was the case Drake was careful never to mention anything concerning such an intention.

ENCOUNTER IN NOVA ALBION

When they sailed to latitude 42° North it became so cold "that our men being greevously pinched . . . complained of the extremitie thereof" and Drake decided to head south and make a landing on the coast of what is now northern California. At what Drake reckoned to be 38° North latitude, they found "a faire and good Baye, with a good winde to enter the same." Here, close to present day San Francisco, the *Golden Hind* came to anchor within sight of an Indian settlement on the shore. Drake was reported to have "curteously intreated them, and liberally bestowed on them necessarie things to cover their nakedness." According to the account published by Richard Hakluyt in 1589, the Indians "supposed us [the English] to be gods and would not be persuaded to the contrarie."[63]

The Indians lived in conical houses that were tightly built and "very warme." The men went

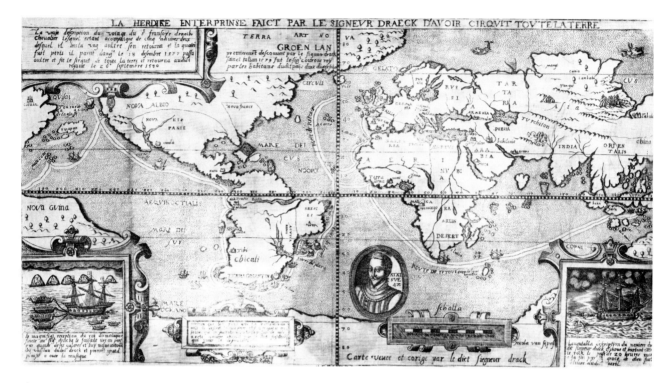

This map was prepared to show Francis Drake's circumnavigation route shortly after his return to England. It is probably the first printed map to illustrate this momentous voyage. According to the legend printed below the scale bar near the medallion portrait of Drake at age forty-two, this is "A map seen and corrected by the aforesaid Sir Drake." Nicola van Sype probably engraved the plate for the map during the winter of 1580–1581, immediately after Drake's return to cash in on the large European demand for cartographic confirmation of his extraordinary accomplishment. Although the great map Raleigh gave to Queen Elizabeth is no longer extant, there is good reason to believe that this printed map is very close to that original. Notice the small heraldic symbols placed to the south of South America and in western North America. These are representative of the "Crowne, Garter, and Armes" and designate the two New World areas Raleigh claimed for England. Raleigh named land south of Tierra del Fuego "Elizabeth Island" and California "New Albion" (Nova Albio on the map). An eye witness who described Queen Elizabeth's great Raleigh map when it was hanging in the palace at Whitehall drew attention to the fact that similar arms were affixed to it (Drake Collection, Rare Book and Special Collections Division).

naked while the women "take bulrushes and kenbe [trim] them after the manner of hempe, and thereof make their loose garments, which being knit about their middles hang downe about their hippes, having also about their shoulders a skinne of Deere, with the haire upon it." To the Englishmen the Indian women appeared to be "very obedient and service-able to their husbands." News of the arrival of the *Golden Hind* and her crew quickly spread through the country beyond the bay and before long a throng of Indians came to see them.

Surprisingly little that is readily available to the general reader has been written concerning the California Indians encountered by Drake in 1579. For this reason portions of the description of Drake's Indian encounter included in the narrative titled *The World Encompassed by Sir Francis Drake . . . Carefully Collected Out of the Notes of Master Francis Fletcher Preacher In This Employ-*

ment, and Divers Others His Followers In the Same are quoted here. This account was first published in London in 1628, some thirty-nine years after Richard Hakluyt published "The Famous Voyage of Sir Francis Drake Into the South Sea, and There Hence About the Whole Globe" in his book, *The Principall Navigations* (London: 1589). In its essentials the *The World Encompassed* account agrees with Hakluyt's earlier version but is richer in details concerning the encounter.

That narrative, written by the *Golden Hind*'s chaplain, leaves no doubt that Drake and his comrades interpreted the reactions displayed by the Indians as worshipping and treating them like "gods." Even before they landed, an Indian emissary was described as coming from the shore "with great expedition to us in a Canow." The account continues:

Who being yet but a little from the shoare, and a great way from our shippe, spake to us continually as hee came rowing on. And at last at a reasonable distance staying himselfe, hee began more solemnely a long and tedious Oration, after his manner: using in the delivery thereof, many gestures and signs: moving his hands, turning his head and body many wayes: and after his Oration ended, with great shew of reverence and submission, turned backe to shoare againe. Hee shortly came again the second time in like manner, and so the third time: When hee brought with him (as a present from the rest) a bunch of Feathers, much like the Feathers of a blacke Crow, very neatly and artificially gathered upon a string, and drawn together into a round bundle; being very cleane and finely cut, and bearing in length an equall proportion one with another; a speciall cognisance (as wee afterwards observed) which they that guard their Kings person, weare on their heads. With this also hee brought a little basket made of Rushes, and filled with an herbe which they called *Tobáh*. Both which being tyed to a short rodde, he cast into our Boat. Our Generall intended to have recompensed him immediately with many good things, hee would have bestowed upon him: but entring into the Boat to deliver the same, hee would not bee drawne to receive them by any meanes: save one Hat, which being cast into the water out of the shippe, hee tooke up (refusing

utterly to meddle with any other thing, though it were upon a board put off unto him) and so presently made his returne. After which time, our Boat could row no way, but wondring at us as at Gods, they would follow the same with admiration.[64]

The *Golden Hind* had "received a leake at Sea" and was brought to anchor as near to the shore as Drake's crew could tow her with the ship's boat. Once the cargo and movable tackle had been brought to shore the ship was ready for careening to allow serious hull repairs to be made. Drake insured the safety of the expedition by erecting tents in an enclosure that the author of *World Encompassed*, Francis Fletcher, styled a "Fort." Such preparations signaled their intention to remain to the Indians who were observing from nearby higher ground. Fletcher described how they "in great haste . . . with such weapons as they had . . . came downe unto us; and yet with no hostile meaning or intent to hurt us."

Fletcher's next statement provides an important clue to what the Indians were thinking as their Contact encounter with Drake's crew continued to unfold. Recall that the Englishmen had no doubt that they were being apprehended as "gods" by the locals. Fletcher wrote of how the Indians drew near and stood "as men ravished in their mindes." That his interpretation of this behavior was cast in the "Englishmen as God" model can be perceived clearly when his following words are read:

they came downe unto us; and yet with no hostile meaning, or intent to hurt us: standing when they drew neere, as men ravished in their mindes, with the sight of such things as they never had seene or heard of before that time: their errand being rather with submission and feare to worship us as Gods, than to have any warre with us as with mortall men.[65]

Fletcher's use of the phrase "mortall men" may be evidence that he deduced or intuited the true motivations underlying the Indian behavioral pattern which he stated "did partly show itselfe at that instant, so did it more and more manifest it selfe afterward during the whole time of our abode amongst them." The length of that "abode," it should be noted, extended over the five-week period from June 17 until July 23, 1579.

By signs and gestures the Englishmen urged the Indians to leave their bows and arrows at home, a wish they readily complied with. Even when large numbers from the surrounding region came to Drake's encampment they left their weapons some distance off. According to Reverend Fletcher, Drake and "all his company, used all means possible, gently to intreat them . . . to cover their nakednesse." To persuade them to adopt habits of modesty, the Englishmen told the uncomprehending Indians that "wee were no Gods but men, and had neede of such things to cover our owne shame . . . for which cause also wee did eat and drinke in their presence, giving them to understand that without that wee could not live, and therefore were but men, as well as they."[66] With some exasperation Fletcher concluded that "nothing could persuade them, nor remove that opinion . . . that wee should be Gods."

The Indians returned to their village on the hill overlooking Drake's encampment and "began . . . a kind of most lamentable weeping and crying out." Even at three-quarters of a mile distance the Englishmen heard their laments "very plainly . . . the Women especially extending their voices in a most miserable and dolefull manner of shrieking."[67] Drake was clearly mystified by the Indians' behavior but took no chances. As Fletcher wrote, "wee thought it no wisdome too far to trust them" and the company set to work strengthening their position "with walls of stone."

After three days had elapsed the Indians made another ceremonial visit to the English camp. The women and children stayed behind on the hill and only the unarmed men entered the enclosure "in such sort as if they had appeared before a God." When they approached Drake himself "they thought themselves nearest unto God," according to Fletcher. While the Indian men were pressing gifts and tokens on Drake and the other Englishmen, the women were described as acting "as if they had been desperate." They "used unnaturall violence against themselves, crying and shreeking piteously, tearing their flesh with their nailes from their cheekes in a monstrous manner, the blood streaming downe along their breasts; besides despoiling the upper parts of their bodies . . ." As well as self-laceration, the Indian women "with fury cast themselves upon the ground, never respecting whether it were cleane or soft, but dashed themselves in this manner on hard stones, knobby hillockes, stockes of wood, and pricking bushes, or what ever else lay in their way, iterating the same course againe and againe: Yea women great with childe, some nine or tenne times each, and others holding out till fifteene or sixteene times (till their strengths failed them), exercised this cruelty against themselves: . . ."[68]

The Englishmen were mystified and shaken by these displays of "cruelty against themselves" on the part of the Indians. The English response was to begin praying and "by signes in lifting up our eyes and hands to Heaven, signified unto them, that the God whom we did serve, and whome they ought to worship was above." The prayers, Fletcher explained, sought the Christian God's assistance in opening "by some meanes their [the Indians] blinded eyes; that they might in due time be called to the knowledge of Him, the true and everliving God, and of Jesus Christ whom he had sent, the salvation of the Gentiles." The prayers were followed by "singing of Psalmes, and reading of certaine Chapters in the Bible."

The singing and scripture reading was pleasing to the Indians who "sate very attentively" and cried "*Oh*" at every pause "greatly rejoycing in our exercises." It is clear from Fletcher's narrative that the uncomprehending audience appreciated most the English sailors' singing voices. He noted, "Yea they tooke such pleasure in our singing of Psalmes, that whensoever they resorted to us, their first request was commonly this *Gnaáh*, by which they entreated that wee would sing." [69]

By this time the reader may feel as mystifified as Drake and his men were by the strange behavior of the California Indians whom later day anthropologists suggest were the ancestors of the people known today as the Coast Miwok Indians. What was going on in the minds of these people the Englishmen found to be "of a free, and loving nature, without guile or treachery"? The clearest and most succinct answer to this intriguing question was provided by Alfred L. Kroeber, author of the Bureau of American Ethnology's *Handbook of the Indians of California*. Kroeber wrote "the simplest explanation is that the Indians regarded the whites as the returned dead." "Such a belief," Kroeber continued, "would account for their repeated wailing and self-laceration, as well as the burned 'sacrifice' of feathers." [70]

On June 26, 1579, Drake's encampment received an impressive formal visit from a large body of Indians that Fletcher construed to be the retinue and subjects of the region's "King" or paramount chief. Before the arrival of the chief two messengers visited Drake to announce the approach of their "*Hióh*, that is, their King." After hearing out their formally orated "Proclamation," Drake complied with their wish that he provide a token to signify "that his coming might be in peace."

Before long the whole body of Indians moved toward the gathered English crew in the manner here described by Reverend Fletcher:

In their coming forwards they cryed continually after a singing manner with a lusty courage. And as they drew nearer and nearer towards us, so did they more and more strive to behave themselves with a certaine comelinesse and gravity in all their actions.

In the forefront came a man of a large body and goodly aspect, bearing the Scepter or royall Mace (made of a certaine kind of black wood and in length about a yard and a halfe) before the King. Whereupon hanged two crownes, a bigger and a lesse, with three chaines of a marvellous length, and often doubled; besides a bagge of the herb *Tobáh*. The Crownes were made of knitworke, wrought upon most curiously with Feathers of divers colours, very artificially placed, and of a formall fashion: The chaines seemed of a bony substance: every linke or part thereof being very little, thin, mostly finely burnished, with a hole pierced through the middest. The number of linkes going to make one chaine, is in a manner infinite: but of such estimation it is amongst them, that few be the persons that are admitted to weare the same: and even they to whom it is lawful to use them, yet are stinted what number they shall use; as some ten, some twelve, some twenty, and as they exceed in number of chaines, so are they thereby knowne to be the more honourable personages.

Next unto him that bare this Scepter, was the King himselfe with his guard about him: His attire upon his head was a Cawle of knitworke, wrought upon somewhat like the Crownes, but differing much both in fashion and perfectnesse of worke; upon his shoulders hee had on a Coat of the skinnes of Conies, reaching to his waste: His guard also had each coats of the same shape, but of other skins: some having Cawles likewise stucke with Feathers, or covered over with a certain downe, which groweth up in the Country upon an herbe much like our Letuce; which exceeds any other downe in the World for finenesse, and being layed upon their Cawles by no windes can bee removed: Of such estimation is this herbe amongst them, that the Downe thereof is not lawful to bee worne but of such persons as are about the King (to whom also it is permitted to weare a Plume of Feathers on their heads, in signe of honour) and the seeds are not used but only in sacrifice to their Gods. After these in their order, did follow the naked sort of common people; whose haire being long, was gathered into a bunch behind, in which stucke Plumes of Feathers, but in the forepart only single Feathers like hornes, every one pleasing himselfe in his owne device. This one thing was observed to be generall amongst them all; that every one had his face painted, some with white, some blacke, and some with other colours, every man also bringing in his hand one thing or other for a gift or present: Their traine or last part of their companie consisted of women and children, each woman bearing against her breast a round basket or two, having within them divers things, as bagges to *Tobah*, a roote which they call *Petah*, whereof they make a kind of meale, and either bake it into bread, or eate it raw; broiled fishes like a pilchard; the seed and downe aforenamed, with such like.

Their baskets were made in fashion like a deepe boale, and though the matter were rushes, or such other kind of stuffe, yet was it so cunningly handled, that the most part of them would hold water; about the brims they were hanged with pieces of the shels of pearles, and in some places with two or three linkes at a place, of the chaines forenamed: thereby signifying that they were vessells wholly dedicated to the onely use of the gods they worshipped: and besides this, they were wrought upon with the matted downe of red feathers, distinguished into divers works and formes.

In the meantime, our Generall having assembled his men together (as forecasting the danger, and worst that might fall out), prepared himselfe to stand upon sure ground, that wee might at all times be ready in our owne defence, if any thing should chance otherwise than was looked for or expected.

Wherefore every man being in a warlike readiness, hee marched within his fenced place, making against their approach a most warlike show (as he did also at all other times of their resort) whereby if they had been desperate enemies, they could not have chosen but have conceived terrour and feare, with discouragement to attempt anything against us, in beholding of the same.

When they were come somewhat neere unto us, trooping together, they gave us a common or a generall salutation: observing in the meane time a generall silence. Whereupon, hee who bare the Scepter before the King, being prompted by another whom the King assigned to that office, hee pronounced with an audible and manly voyce, what the other spake to him in secret: continuing, whether it were his oration or proclamation, at the least half an houre. At the close whereof there was a common *Amen*, in signe of approbation given by every person: and the King himselfe with the whole number of men and women (the little children onely remaining behind) came further downe the hill, and as they came, set themselves againe in their former order.

And being now come to the foot of the hill and neere our fort, the Scepter bearer, with a composed countenance and stately carriage began a song, and answereable thereunto, observed a kind of measures in a dance: whom the King with his guard and every other sort of person following, did in like manner sing and dance, saving onely the women, who danced but kept silence. As they danced they still came on: and our Generall perceiving their plaine and simple meaning, gave order that they might freely enter without interruption within our bulwarkes: Where after they had entered, they yet continued their Song and Dance a reasonable time: their women also following them with their wassaile boales in their hands, their bodies bruised, their faces torne, their dugs, breasts, and other parts bespotted with blood, trickling down from the wounds, which with their nailes they had made before their comming.

After that they had satisfied, or rather tired themselves in this manner, they made signes to our Generall to have him sit downe; Unto whom both the King and divers others made several Orations, or rather indeed if wee had understood them, supplications, that hee would take the Province and Kingdom into his hand, and become their King and Patron: making signes that they would resigne unto him their right and Title in the whole Land, and become his vassals in themselves and their posterities: Which that they might make us indeede believe that it was their true meaning and intents; the King himselfe with all the rest, with one consent and with great reverence joyfully singing a Song, set the Crown upon his [Drake's] head; enriched his neck with all their Chaines; and offering unto him many things, honoured him by the name of *Hyóh*. Adding thereunto (as it might seeme) a Song and Dance of Triumph: because they were not only visited of the gods (for so they still judged us to be) but the great and chief God was now become their God, their King and Patron, and themselves were become the only happie and blessed people in the World.

These things being so freely offered, our Generall thought not meet to reject or refuse the same: both for that hee would not give them any cause of mistrust or disliking of him (that being the onely place, wherein at this present, we were of necessitie enforced to seeke relief of many things) and chiefly, for that hee knew not to what good end God has brought this to passe, or what honour and profit it might bring to our Country in time to come.

Wherefore in the same and to the use of her most excellent Majesty, hee tooke the Scepter,

Crowne, and Dignity, of the said Country into his hand; wishing nothing more, than it had layen so fitly for her Majesty to enjoy, as it was now her proper owne, and that the riches and treasures thereof (where with in the upland Countries it abounds) might with a great conveniency be transported, to the enriching of her Kingdome here at home, as it is in plenty to be attained there: and especially, that so tractable and loving a people, as they showed themselves to bee, might have meanes to have manifested their most willing obedience the more under her, and by her meanes, as a Mother and Nurse of the Church of Christ, might by the preaching of the Gospell, bee brought to the right knowledge, and obedience of the true and ever-living God.[71]

After reading Fletcher's colorful and detailed account of Drake's acceptance of "Sceptor, Crowne and Dignity" of the Indians' country "in the name and to use of her most excellent Majesty," the question of Indian understanding and intentions remains. Did the ceremony described signal the cession of the land Drake christened "Albion" in acknowledgement of its "white banckes and cliffes, which lye toward the sea" and general resemblence to his homeland? Or, was it a ceremony of initiation the Indians felt to be necessary in coming to terms with a group of fair-skinned apparitions who had entered their lives from the western sea where the daily sun disappeared and dead spirits were known to reside?

Fletcher provides an important clue to the correct answer to these conundrums in his next paragraph:

The ceremonies of this resigning and receiving of the Kingdome being thus performed, the common sort, both of men and women, leaving the King and his guard about him, with our Generall, dispersed themselves among our people, taking a diligent view or survey of every man; and finding such as pleased their fancies (which commonly were the youngest of us) they presently enclosing them about, offered their sacrifices unto them, crying out with lamentable shreekes and moanes, weeping, and scratching, and tearing with their very flesh off their faces with their nailes, neither were it the women alone which did this, but even old men, roaring and crying out, were as violent as the women were.[72]

Robert F. Heizer, expert on California Indian ethnohistory, is clear and unequivocal in his interpretation of the events that transpired between the Indians and English on the shores of "New Albion" on the 26th day of June 1579. Heizer wrote:

The close scrutiny of the English by the Indians following the "crowning" ceremony indicates that the main business of the day (i.e., the ceremonial crowning by secret society initiates) was over, and that the general public could now take part in the festivities. Of great interest are Fletcher's statements to the effect that the most youthful Englishmen were repeatedly selected as recipients of personal sacrifice, and adoration which took the form of lamenting, moaning, weeping, wailing, and self-lacerating. Only one conclusion can be drawn: the Indians supposed that they were looking upon relatives returned from the dead, and hence performed the usual mourning observances.[73]

Heizer went on to make the point that "except for the sole occasion, at the conclusion of the ceremony on June 26, when the Indians embraced the youthful Englishmen, the natives seem to have avoided touching the whites." To Heizer, this behavior was further proof of the "dead returned" explanation, "for bodily contact with a dead person or spirit was certain, in their minds, to have disastrous results."[74] It is also significant that one of the handful of Indian terms recorded by members of Drake's company is the phrase "*Nocaro mu*," which translates to "touch me not" in English. Heizer hypothesizes that the reason this phrase was one of so few recorded was "the simple fact that the English heard this phrase uttered a great many times, and it stuck in their memory." Heizer continued his argument, "in view of the fact that the natives held the English in fear as dead people, the phrase 'touch me not' might often have been used toward amorous sailors, or against any form of bodily contact."[75]

Perhaps the reason why Drake's contact interactions with the California Indians have been largely ignored outside anthropology and ethnohistory circles is to be found in the way that the results of the circumnavigation generally were received on his return to England. There can be no mistaking the fact that while Queen Elizabeth treated Drake and his crew as national heroes, as evidenced by his knighthood bestowed on the quarterdeck of the *Golden Hind,* she kept the enormous wealth of geographical and cartographic intelligence he had collected a tightly held state secret. In the words of map scholar Helen Wallis: "Drake . . . entered the ranks of the great explorers and navigators in a very different way from that of his predecessors."[76] As Wallis pointed out, Columbus's and Magellan's accomplishments were published with dispatch in languages that were read widely in every corner of Europe. Drake, on the other hand, was a heroic circumnavigator without a true history; his accomplishments being deemed secret and essential to Elizabeth I of England's government. Wallis correctly concluded, "national pride was ill served by such a policy," and "claims of priority of discovery have to be made in good time to gain general recognition." The secrecy, rumors, and false reports that Elizabeth's policy engendered had the effect of perplexing the circle of Age of Discovery professional geographer-cartographers such as Gerard Mercator and Abraham Ortelius, whose maps and publications might otherwise have placed Drake firmly in the heroic pantheon of exploration where he belonged.

The long-term impact of Elizabeth's policy of secrecy and suppression probably resulted in the destruction or loss of Drake's detailed log and maps of the circumnavigation. The historical record makes it amply clear that he presented his queen with "a diary of everything that had happened during the three years and a very large map."[77] From the recollections of the Portuguese pilot he took prisoner early in the voyage, it is learned that Drake's "diary" or journal was itself a richly illustrated document. The pilot, Nuño da Silva, reported:

Francis Drake kept a book in which he entered his navigation and in which he delineated birds, trees and sea-lions. He is an adept at painting and has with him a boy, a relation of his, who is a great painter. When they both shut themselves up in his cabin they were always painting.[78]

The mind almost boggles at the thought of what the discovery of Drake's lost maps and journal could add to humankind's knowledge of the world and its people in the late sixteenth century! If nothing else the knowledge of such lost or misplaced geographical and cartographical treasure makes clear the fact that the full history of the Age of Discovery is still to be written.

Map of the part of Ontario, Canada, extending from Lake Ontario to Georgian Bay (Partie du Grand Lac des Hurons) and from Lake Huron in the west to Lake Simcoe (Lac Oventarenk) in the east. The map's 1631 date was corrected to read 1651. It is an unsigned manuscript map that may have been prepared by a missionary-priest living among the Huron Indians. Whoever the author of the map was, he probably gained much if not most of his information from Indian maps and informants. Maps like this often resulted from Relationship encounter situations. It may have served as the basis for the map "Huronum Explicata Tabula" signed by G. F. Pesca, F[ecit], that formed an inset to a large Italian copperplate showing New France with drawings of Indians, animals, bark lodges, canoes, and an idealized Christian Indian family. The copperplate is thought to have been commissioned by the church for missionaries in North America in the late seventeenth century. This manuscript map was bequeathed to the Library of Congress by Henry Harrisse, the distinguished student of the history of discovery and exploration of North America (Harrisse Collection, Geography and Map Division).

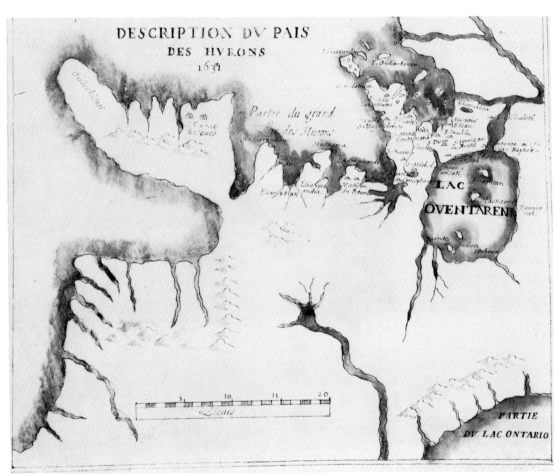

CHAPTER 1. INTRODUCTION: THE AGE OF DISCOVERY, FOCUS AND PERSPECTIVE

1. J. H. Parry, *The Age of Reconnaissance* (New York: New American Library, 1964).
2. Dan O'Sullivan, *The Age of Discovery, 1400–1550* (New York: Longman, 1984).
3. Cornelius J. Jaenen, *Friend and Foe: Aspects of French-Amerindian Cultural Contact in the Sixteenth and Seventeenth Centuries* (New York: Columbia University Press, 1976), 10.
4. Ann F. Ramenofsky, *Vectors of Death: The Archaeology of European Contact* (Albuquerque: University of New Mexico Press, 1987).
5. *New American World: A Documentary History of North America to 1612*, ed. David B. Quinn (New York: Arno Press and Hector Bye, Inc., 1979), 1: 285.
6. Louis De Vorsey, Jr., "The New Land: The Discovery and Exploration of Eastern North America," in Robert D. Mitchell and Paul A. Groves, *North America, The Historical Geography of a Changing Continent* (Totowa, N.J.: Rowman and Littlefield Publishers, 1987), 27.
7. Bernard G. Hoffman, *Cabot to Cartier* (Toronto: University of Toronto Press, 1961), 113.
8. *New Iberian World: A Documentary History of the Discovery and Settlement of Latin America to the Early Seventeenth Century*, ed. John H. Parry and Robert G. Keith (New York: Times Books and Hector and Rose, 1984), 1: 9–10.
9. Chrestien Le Clercq, *New Relation of Gaspesia* [Paris, 1691], ed. and trans. William F. Ganong (Toronto: Champlain Society, 1910), 109.
10. James Axtell, *After Columbus* (New York: Oxford University Press, 1988), 127.
11. Fray Bernardino de Sahagún, *General History of the Things of New Spain: Book II—Earthly Things*, trans. from the Aztec into English, with notes and illus. by Charles E. Dibble and Arthur J. O. Anderson (Salt Lake City: University of Utah, 1963), 19.
12. Bernal Diaz del Castillo, *The True History of the Conquest of Mexico*, trans. from the original Spanish by Maurice Keatinge, Esq., reprint of the London edition of 1800 (La Jolla: Renaissance Press, 1979), 114.

CHAPTER 2. WORLDS APART: EUROPEAN WORLD VIEWS BEFORE COLUMBUS

1. Halford J. Mackinder, *Democratic Ideals and Reality* (London: Henry Holt and Co., 1919), 186.
2. H. G. Wells, *The Outline of History Being a Plain History of Life and Mankind*, 2 vols. (New York: Macmillan Company, 1921), 2: 185.
3. Fernando Colón, *The Life of the Admiral Christopher Columbus*, trans. and annotated by Benjamin Keen (New Brunswick: Rutgers University Press, 1959), 10.
4. Christopher Columbus, *Four Voyages to the New World*, bilingual ed., trans. and ed. R. H. Major (New York: Corinth Books, 1961), 136.
5. Ibid.
6. Samuel Eliot Morison, *Admiral of the Ocean Sea: A Life of Christopher Columbus* (Boston: Little Brown and Company, 1942), 1: 374.
7. Robert H. Fuson, *The Log of Christopher Columbus* (Camden, Maine: International Marine Publishing Company, 1987), 9.
8. Ibid., 53.
9. Morison, *Admiral of the Ocean Sea*, 240.
10. T. Bentley Duncan, *Atlantic Islands Madeira, the Azores and the Cape Verdes in the Seventeenth Century* (Chicago: University of Chicago Press, 1972), 11.
11. Colón, *Life of . . . Columbus*, 25.
12. Ibid., 24.
13. J. H. Parry, *The Age of Reconnaissance* (New York: New American Library, 1964), 23.
14. Colón, *Life of . . . Columbus*, 18.
15. Parry, *Age of Reconnaissance*, 167.
16. Colón, *Life of . . . Columbus*, 11.
17. R. A. Skelton, Thomas E. Marston, and George D. Painter, *The Vinland Map and the Tartar Relation* (New Haven and London: Yale University Press, 1965), dust jacket.
18. Henri Pirenne, *Medieval Cities: Their Origins and Revival of Trade* (Garden City: Doubleday and Company, 1956), 67.
19. Skelton, *Vinland Map*, 140.
20. *Proceedings of the Vinland Map Conference*, ed. Wilcomb E. Washburn (Chicago: University of Chicago Press, 1971), ix.

CHAPTER 3. WORLDS APART: NATIVE AMERICAN WORLD VIEWS IN THE AGE OF DISCOVERY

1. C. F. Volney, *A View of the Soil and Climate of the United States*, trans. with occasional remarks by C. B. Brown (New York: Hafner Publishing Co., Inc., 1968), 363.
2. William P. Cumming, *The Discoveries of John Lederer* (Charlottesville: University of Virginia Press, 1958), 12.
3. Ibid., 13.
4. John Collier, *Indians of the Americas* (New York: New American Library, 1964), 102.
5. Tzvetan Todorov, *The Conquest of America*, trans. from the French by Richard Howard (New York: Harper and Row Publishers, 1984), 75.
6. Ibid.
7. Miguel Leon-Portilla, *Aztec Thought and Culture* (Norman: University of Oklahoma Press, 1963), 155.

8. Eulalia Guzman, "The Art of Map Making Among the Ancient Mexicans," *Imago Mundi*, 3 (1964): 1.

9. Hernando Cortés, *Letters from Mexico*, trans. and ed. Anthony Pagden (New Haven: Yale University Press, 1986), 340.

10. Peter Martyr D'Anghera, *De Orbe Novo*, trans. from the Latin with Notes and Introduction by Francis Augustus MacNutt (New York: Burt Franklin Reprint, 1970), 2: 201.

11. Ibid., 193.

12. Cortés, *Letters from Mexico*, 105.

13. Fray Diego Durán, *Book of the Gods and Rites and the Ancient Calendar*, trans. and ed. F. Horcasitas and Doris Heyden (Norman: University of Oklahoma Press, 1971), 75.

14. Ferdinand Colón, *The Life of the Admiral Christopher Columbus*, trans. and annotated by Benjamin Keen (New Brunswick: Rutgers University Press, 1959), 235.

15. Garcilaso de la Vega, El Inca, *Royal Commentaries of the Incas and General History of Peru*, trans. with an Introduction by Harold V. Livermore (Austin: University of Texas Press, 1966), xii.

16. Ibid., 116.

17. Ibid., 117.

18. Ibid.

19. Ibid., 124.

20. Ibid., 422.

21. *New Iberian World: A Documentary History of the Discovery and Settlement of Latin America to the Early Seventeenth Century*, ed. John H. Parry and Robert G. Keith (New York: Times Books and Hector and Rose, 1984), 1: 186.

22. Charles Hudson, *The Southeastern Indians* (Knoxville: University of Tennessee Press, 1976), 120.

23. James Mooney, "Myths of the Cherokee," *Nineteenth Annual Report of the Bureau of American Ethnology* (Washington: Government Printing Office, 1900), 239.

24. Chrestien Le Clercq, *New Relation of Gaspesia* [Paris: 1691], ed. and trans. William F. Ganong (Toronto: Champlain Society, 1910), 84.

25. Ibid., 85.

26. Hartley Burr Alexander, *The World's Rim: Great Mysteries of the North American Indians* (Lincoln: University of Nebraska Press, 1967), 22–23.

27. John Smith, *Travels and Works of Captain John Smith President of Virginia, and Admiral of New England 1580–1631*, ed. Edward Arber with a Biographical and Critical Introduction by A. G. Bradley, parts 1 and 2 (Edinburgh: John Grant, 1910), 396.

28. Ibid.

29. Ibid.

30. Ibid., 398–399.

31. Peter H. Wood, Gregory Waselkov, and M. Thomas Hatley, *Powhatan's Mantle* (Lincoln: University of Nebraska Press, 1989), 308.

32. Helen C. Rountree, *The Powhatan Indians of Virginia, Their Traditional Culture* (Norman and London: University of Oklahoma Press, 1989), 120.

33. Smith, *Travels and Works of Captain John Smith*, 1: xli.

34. Ibid., xlii.

35. Ibid., xliv.

36. Ibid., xlvi.

37. Le Clercq, *New Relation of Gaspesia*, 100.

38. Ibid.

39. Ibid., 136.

40. Ibid.

41. De Vorsey, "Amerindian Contributions," 71.

42. *Works of Samuel De Champlain*, 1: 335.

43. Ibid.

44. Ibid., 336.

45. Ibid., 340.

CHAPTER 4. CHRISTOPHER COLUMBUS FINDS THE WAY: FIRST ENCOUNTERS ON THE ISLANDS IN THE OCEAN SEA

1. John Kirtland Wright, *The Geographical Lore of the Time of the Crusades*, an unabridged and corrected republication of the 1925 edition with an Introduction by Clarence J. Glacken (New York: Dover Publications, 1965), 285.

2. Fernando Colón, *The Life of the Admiral Christopher Columbus*, trans. and annotated by Benjamin Keen (New Brunswick: Rutgers University Press, 1959), 19.

3. Ibid., 20.

4. Ibid., 35.

5. Ibid., 36.

6. Ibid., 37.

7. Ibid., 38.

8. Ibid., 39.

9. Ibid., 40.

10. Ibid., 42.

11. Ibid., 44.

12. W. G. Kendrew, *Climatology* (Oxford: At the Clarendon Press, 1949), 133.

13. *The Journal of Christopher Columbus*, trans. Cecil Jane with an Appendix by R. A. Skelton (New York: Bramhall House, 1960), 3.

14. Robert H. Fuson, *The Log of Christopher Columbus* (Camden, Maine: International Marine Publishing Company, 1987), 12.

15. R. H. Major, *Christopher Columbus Four Voyages to the New World: Letters and Selected Documents*, bilingual ed. trans. and ed. R. H. Major (New York: Corinth Books, 1961), 2.

16. Louis De Vorsey, Jr. and John Parker, *In the Wake of Columbus: Islands and Controversy* (Detroit: Wayne State University Press, 1985).

17. Joseph Judge, "Where Columbus Found the New World," *National Geographic Magazine*, vol. 170, no. 5 (November, 1986): 568.

18. Ibid., 599.

19. Oliver Dunn and James E. Kelley, Jr., *The Diario of*

Christopher Columbus's First Voyage to America 1492–1493 (Norman and London: University of Oklahoma Press, 1989), 65.

20. Samuel Eliot Morison, *Admiral of the Ocean Sea: A Life of Christopher Columbus* (Boston: Little Brown and Company, 1942), 1: 305.

21. Dunn, *Diario of . . . Columbus's First Voyage*, 67–69.

22. *The Letter of Columbus on the Discovery of America*, a facsimile of the Pictorial Edition, with a New and Literal Translation, and a Complete Reprint of the Oldest Four Editions in Latin (New York: Lenox Library, 1892), 6–7.

23. Morison, *Admiral of the Ocean Sea*, 1: 440.

24. Bartolomé de Las Casas, *Historia de las Indias*, ed. Agustin Millares Carlo and Lewis Hanke (Mexico and Buenos Aires: Fondo de Cultura Economica, 1951), 1: 325.

25. *Letter of Columbus*, 7.

26. Dunn, *Diario of . . . Columbus's First Voyage*, 71.

27. Colón, *Life of . . . Columbus*, 48.

28. Dunn, *Diario of . . . Columbus's First Voyage*, 57.

29. Tzvetan Todorov, *The Conquest of America*, trans. from the French by Richard Howard (New York: Harper and Row, 1984), 9.

30. Dunn, *Diario of . . . Columbus's First Voyage*, 331.

31. Ibid., 71.

32. Ibid., 75.

33. Ibid.

34. Helen Rand Parish, *Las Casas As a Bishop* (Washington: Library of Congress, 1980), xi.

35. *New Iberian World*, ed. John H. Parry and Robert G. Keith (New York: Times Books, 1984), 2: 49.

36. Dunn, *Diario of . . . Columbus's First Voyage*, 341.

37. Colón, *Life of . . . Columbus*, 101.

38. Parry, *New Iberian World*, 2: 38.

39. Alfred W. Crosby, *The Columbian Exchange* (New York: Greenwood Press, 1972), 66.

CHAPTER 5. IN THE WAKE OF COLUMBUS: CONQUEST AND EMPIRE

1. Fernando Colón, *The Life of the Admiral Christopher Columbus*, trans. and annotated by Benjamin Keen (New Brunswick: Rutgers University Press, 1959), 119.

2. Peter Martyr D'Anghera, *De Orbe Novo*, trans. from the Latin with Notes and Introduction by Francis Augustus MacNutt (New York: Burt Franklin Reprint, 1970), 1: 95.

3. Ibid., 106.

4. Tzvetan Todorov, *The Conquest of America* (New York: Harper and Row, 1984), 47–48.

5. Colón, *Life of . . . Columbus*, 176.

6. Ibid., 185.

7. Ibid., 191.

8. *New Iberian World*, ed. John H. Parry and Robert G. Keith (New York: Times Books, 1984), 2: 235.

9. Colón, *Life of . . . Columbus*, 232.

10. Justin Winsor, *Christopher Columbus* (Cambridge: Riverside Press, 1892), 442.

11. *New American World: A Documentary History of North America to 1612*, ed. David B. Quinn (New York: Arno Press and Hector Bye, Inc., 1979), 1: 236.

12. Ibid., 235.

13. Bernal Diaz del Castillo, *The True History of the Conquest of Mexico*, trans. from the original Spanish by Maurice Keatings, Esq., reprint of the 1800 London ed. (La Jolla: Renaissance Press, 1979), 2.

14. Ibid., 4.

15. *Hernan Cortes Letters from Mexico*, trans. and ed. Anthony Pagden (New Haven: Yale University Press, 1986), 51.

16. Ibid., 57.

17. Ibid., 58.

18. Ibid.

19. D'Anghera, *De Orbe Novo*, 2: 258.

20. Paul E. Hoffman, *A New Andalucia and a Way to the Orient* (Baton Rouge: Louisiana State University Press, 1990).

21. *New American World*, 1: 261.

22. Ibid., 2: 6.

23. Ibid., 19.

24. Ibid.

25. Ibid., 20.

26. Ibid., 22.

27. Ibid., 23.

28. Ibid.

29. Ibid., 24.

30. Ibid., 25.

31. Ibid., 29.

32. Ibid., 54.

33. *Narratives of the Coronado Expedition 1540–1542*, ed. George P. Hammond and Agapto Rey (Albuquerque: University of New Mexico Press, 1940), 60.

34. Ibid., 66.

35. Ibid.

36. Ibid., 75.

37. Ibid., 79.

38. Ibid., 141.

39. Ibid., 159.

40. Jesse Green, *Zuni, Selected Writings of Frank Hamilton Cushing* (Lincoln: University of Nebraska Press, 1979), xii.

41. Ibid., 174.

42. *Narratives of the Coronado Expedition*, 170.

43. Ibid., 219.

44. George P. Winship, *The Coronado Expedition, 1540–42; Fourteenth Annual Report of the Bureau of Ethnology, 1892–93* (Washington: Government Printing Office, 1896), 1: 581.

45. *Narratives of the Coronado Expedition*, 336.

46. *New American World*, 2: 93.

47. Ibid., 95.

48. Charles Hudson, *The Juan Pardo Expeditions* (Washington: Smithsonian Institution Press, 1990).

49. *New American World*, 2: 110.
50. Ibid., 113.
51. Ibid.

CHAPTER 6. COMPETITION IN THE NORTH: PORTUGAL, FRANCE, AND ENGLAND

1. Samuel Eliot Morison, *The European Discovery of America: The Northern Voyages, A.D. 500–1600* (New York: Oxford University Press, 1971), 166.
2. *New American World: A Documentary History of North America to 1612*, ed. David B. Quinn (New York: Arno Press and Hector Bye Inc., 1979), 1: 94.
3. Ibid., 95.
4. Morison, *European Discovery of America*, 191.
5. W. F. Ganong, *Crucial Maps in the Early Cartography and Place-Nomenclature of the Atlantic Coast of Canada* (Toronto: University of Toronto Press, 1964).
6. *New American World*, 1: 140.
7. Ibid., 97.
8. Frances Gardiner Davenport, *European Treaties Bearing on the History of the United States and Its Dependencies to 1648* (Gloucester: Peter Smith, 1967), 31.
9. Morison, *European Discovery of America*, 225.
10. *New American World*, 1: 145.
11. Morison, *European Discovery of America*, 217.
12. *New American World*, 1: 148.
13. Ibid., 149.
14. Ibid.
15. Ibid., 151.
16. Morison, *European Discovery of America*, 231.
17. *New American World*, 1: 281.
18. Ibid., 282.
19. William P. Cumming, R. A. Skelton, and D. B. Quinn, *The Discovery of North America* (New York: American Heritage Press, 1972), 81.
20. *New American World*, 1: 283.
21. Ibid., 284.
22. Cumming, *Discovery of North America*, 82.
23. *New American World*, 1: 285.
24. Ibid., 288.
25. Ibid.
26. Ibid., 288–89.
27. Ibid., 295.
28. Ibid., 300.
29. Ibid., 301.
30. Ibid., 302.
31. Morison, *European Discovery of America*, 388.
32. *New American World*, 1: 307.
33. Ibid.
34. Ibid., 309.
35. Ibid., 309–10.
36. Ibid., 310.
37. Ibid., 314.
38. Ibid., 315.
39. Ibid., 317.
40. Ibid., 322.
41. Ibid., 324.
42. Ibid., 325.
43. *New American World*, 2: 288.
44. Ibid., 289.
45. Ibid.
46. Ibid., 290.
47. Jacques Le Moyne De Morgues, *The Work of* (London: British Museum Publications Limited, 1977), 2: plate 6.
48. Ibid., 1: 162.
49. Ibid., 140.
50. Ibid., 119.
51. Ibid., 120–21.
52. *New American World*, 1: 227.
53. Rice Vaughan, *A Discourse of Coin and Coinage*, reprint of the London 1675 ed. (New York: S. R. Publishers Limited and Johnson Reprint Co., 1970), 59.
54. Hans P. Kraus, *Sir Francis Drake: A Pictorial Biography*, with an Historical Introduction by Lt. Commander David W. Waters and Richard Boulind, and a detailed Catalogue of the Author's Collection (Amsterdam: N. Israel, 1970), 65.
55. *Sir Francis Drake and the Famous Voyage, 1577–1580*, ed. Norman J. W. Thrower (Berkeley and Los Angeles: University of California Press, 1984), 4.
56. Ibid., 6.
57. Kraus, *Sir Francis Drake*, 73.
58. Ibid., 74.
59. Ibid.
60. Ibid.
61. Ibid., 75.
62. Ibid.
63. Ibid.
64. *New American World*, 1: 470.
65. Ibid.
66. Ibid., 471.
67. Ibid.
68. Ibid., 472.
69. Ibid.
70. Alfred L. Kroeber, *Handbook of the Indians of California: Bureau of American Ethnology Bulletin 78* (Washington: Government Printing Office, 1925), 277.
71. *New American World*, 1: 472–74.
72. Ibid., 474.
73. Robert F. Heizer, "Francis Drake and the California Indians, 1579," *University of California Publications in American Archaeology and Ethnology*, vol. 42 (1945–1951): 250–296.
74. Ibid., 273.
75. Ibid.
76. *Sir Francis Drake*, 137.
77. Ibid., 121.
78. Ibid., 123.

SELECTED CHRONOLOGY

B.C.

c. 50,000–11,000	Waves of Paleo-Siberians cross Beringia and disperse throughout North and South America
c. 10,000–8,000	Pleistocene epoch (last Ice Age) ends with retreat of continental glaciers
c. 3,000–1,000	Aleuts and Eskimos migrate from Siberia to North America
c. 2,500–1,500	Permanent agricultural villages spread in Middle America
c. 1,500	Olmec civilization in Middle America
c. 168–90	Claudius Ptolemy living in Alexandria

A.D.

c. 300–900	Mayan civilization flourishing
711	Moslems invade Iberian Peninsula
c. 860	Norsemen discover Iceland
985/6	Eric the Red colonizes Greenland
c. 1001	Leif Ericson explores Vinland
c. 1010	Thorfinn Karlsefni in Vinland
c. 1117	Bishop Eric Gnupsson visits Vinland
1126	Greenland Bishopric established
c. 1150	Pueblo of Oraibi founded—oldest continuously occupied settlement in the United States
c. 1240	Inca rule begins in Peru
1295	Marco Polo returns from China
c. 1325	Aztecs reach Lake Texcoco and begin building Tenochtitlan
c. 1345	Greenland's Western Settlement wiped out
1402	Franco-Castilian colonization of Lanzarote in the Canary Islands
1406	Ptolemy's *Geography* translated into Latin
1410	Latin Ptolemy appears with maps
1410	Last Greenland ship reaches Iceland
1415	Portugal takes Ceuta in Morocco
1418	Prince Henry begins program of exploration
1425	Portuguese land in the Madeira Islands

1433/34	Portuguese succeed in rounding Cape Bojador on Western Saharan Coast of Africa—Azores discovered
1438	Yupanqui displaces his brother as Pachacuti reigns over and enlarges Inca Empire
1439	Prince Henry authorized to colonize the "seven islands of the Azores"
1441	Slave Trade begins in Rio do Ouro region of Africa
1444	Portuguese navigators reach Senegal River on coast of Africa
c. 1451	Birth of Columbus in Genoa—Mayan center Mayapan destroyed—abandonment of Uxmal and Chichen Itza
1453	Constantinople falls to Mohammed the Conqueror—End of Eastern Empire
1454	Gutenberg prints his first Bible
1456	Cadomosto, a Venetian in Prince Henry's service, explores Senegal and Gambia Rivers and discovers Cape Verde Islands
1460	Prince Henry dies—Portuguese reach Sierra Leone
1469	Marriage of Isabela of Castile to Ferdinand of Aragon
1472	Fernando Po discovers island and Rui de Sequeira reaches 2° south latitude
1474	Toscanelli's first letter to Columbus—Bartolomé de Las Casas born
1477	First complete printed edition of Ptolemy's *Geography* with twenty-six copper plate maps—Columbus residing in Lisbon
1481	Papal Bull *Aeterni Regis* sanctions Portugal's exclusive rights in Guinea
1482	Portuguese explorers reach Congo River—Columbus living in Madeira Islands
1483–84	Columbus proposes plan to sail west to King John II of Portugal
1484–85	Columbus moves to Castile
1486	Columbus received at Spanish court and presents plan
1488	Bartolomew Dias rounds Cape of Good Hope
1489	Queen Isabela promises to have Columbus's plan reevaluated after reconquest of Granada
1492	Spanish take Granada, last Moorish area of the Iberian Peninsula—Spiritual reconquest in form of expulsion of Jews and later the Moors—Columbus embarked on his first voyage and made landfall at Guanahani-San Salvador in the Bahama Islands
1493	Columbus returns to Palos on March 15—Line of Demarcation 100 leagues west of Azores and Cape Verde Islands—Columbus begins second voyage with seventeen ships on September 25
1494	Treaty of Tordesillas established Line of Demarcation at meridian located 370 leagues west of Cape Verde Islands
1496	Santo Domingo founded on Hispaniola
	Columbus returns from Second Voyage

1497 John Cabot discovers land in the west for England—Vasco da Gama sets out from Lisbon for India

1498 John Cabot disappears on second voyage—Vasco da Gama reaches India—Columbus begins Third Voyage

1499 Vasco da Gama returns to Portugal—Alonso de Ojeda and Amerigo Vespucci explore coast of northeastern South America

1500 Francisco de Bobadilla arrests Columbus on Hispaniola and sends him to Spain—World map showing discoveries prepared by Juan de la Cosa—Pedro Alvares Cabral sailing for India took possession of Brazil for Portugal—João Fernandes the "Lavrador" sights land in northwest—Corte Real brothers kidnap Indians on Newfoundland and bring to Portugal

1501 African slaves introduced to Hispaniola

1502 Montezuma becomes Aztec ruler—Columbus leaves Cadiz on fourth voyage on May 11—Cantino World Map showing discoveries in north—All Moslems to convert or leave Castile

1503 Columbus attempts colony on coast of Mosquito Gulf in Panama—Columbus suffers shipwreck on Jamaica

1504 Columbus returns to Spain from last voyage November 7—Queen Isabela dies in late November

1505 First engravings of American Indians appear in Europe

1506 Death of Columbus, May 20

1507 Martin Waldseemüller's world map names the new southern continent "America"

1508 Juan Poncé de Leon begins colonization of Puerto Rico

1512 Jamaica colonization begun—Pope decrees that Indians are descended from Adam and Eve

1513 Juan Poncé de Leon names La Florida and encounters the Gulf Stream—Vasco Nuñez de Balboa crosses Panama from Caribbean Sea to Pacific Ocean

1517 Francisco Hernandez de Córdoba finds traces of cities and wealth in Yucatan

1518 Juan de Grijalva makes reconnaissance of Yucatan and Mexican coast to the Panuco River and applies name "New Spain"

1519 Ferdinand Magellan begins first circumnavigation of the earth under banner of Spain—Hernando Cortés lands in Mexico—Alvárez Pineda explores Gulf of Mexico from Vera Cruz to Florida—Smallpox epidemic on Hispaniola wipes out one out of three Indians

1520 Aztecs of Tenochtitlán rebel and force Cortés and army to flee city

1521 Poncé de Leon fatally wounded by Indians while trying to colonize Florida—Cortés and Indian allies retake and raze Tenochtitlán—Mexico City constructed on ruins—Magellan killed in Philippines

1522 Elcano completes first circumnavigation with Magellan's ship *Victoria*

1524 Giovanni de Verrazano explores coast from Georgia to Nova Scotia for France

1526 Lucas Vásquez de Ayllón attempts to establish colony San Miguel de Gualdape on Georgia coast

1528	Panfilo de Narvaez leads Florida entrada which ends in disaster
1531	Atahualpa the Inca captured at Cajamarca
1532	Francisco Pizarro leads conquest of the Inca Empire for Spain
1534	Jacques Cartier explores Gulf of St. Lawrence for France
1535	Jacques Cartier explores St. Lawrence River to Hochelaga—Pizarro founds Lima—Cortés attempts a colony in Lower California
1536	Cabeza de Vaca, Estevan the Moor, and two others reach Mexico and are only survivors of Narváez Entrada
1539	Fray Marcos de Niza and Estevan begin search for evidence of Cibola—Estevan killed by Zuni Indians—Ferdinand Columbus dies
1540	Hernando de Soto leads Entrada into area of Southeastern United States—Francisco Vásquez de Coronado leads Entrada into area of Southwestern United States—Roberval attempts colony in Canada
1542	Hernando de Soto dies and is interred in Mississippi River—Spanish king promulgates "New Laws" respecting treatment of Indians
1543	Survivors of Soto Entrada reach Mexico
1544	Valparaiso, Chile, founded
1546	Mayan revolt crushed
1547	Archbishopric of Mexico founded
1549	Fray Luis Cancer killed by Indians on Florida Gulf Coast
1553	Richard Hakluyt born—Queen Mary crowned
1554	Marriage of Mary of England to Philip of Spain
1558	The Inca returns to Lima
1559	Don Tristán de Luna attempts colony in Alabama
c. 1560	Huron prophet Deganawaida founds Iroquois League of Five Nations
1562	Jean Ribault builds Charlesfort on Port Royal Sound—Huguenots form political party and religious wars begin in France—John Hawkins sells African slaves in Indies
1564	René de Laudonniére builds Fort Caroline on St. Johns River—Spain occupies the Philippines
1565	Pedro Menendez de Avilles captures Fort Caroline and founds St. Augustine
1576–78	Martin Frobisher encounters Eskimos
1577	Drake begins his world encompassing voyage
1578	Drake enters Pacific
1579	Drake claims California as "New Albion"

1580	Drake returns from second circumnavigation
1582	Hakluyt publishes *Divers Voyages*
1583	Sir Humphrey Gilbert claims Newfoundland for England
1584	Amadas and Barlow explore and name "Virginia"
1585	First Virginia colony
1586	Francis Drake sacks Santo Domingo and Carthagena and rescues second Virginia colony
1587	John White leads "Lost Colony" to Virginia
1588	Spanish Armada defeated—Hariot's account of Virginia published with White's map
1590	De Bry begins publishing *Voyages*
1598	French colony attempted on Sable Island—Indian insurrection in Mexico
1599	Acoma Pueblo Indians battle Spanish
1600	East India Company chartered—French colony attempted at Tadoussac on St. Lawrence River—Sheep introduced into U.S. Southwest

NAMING AMERICA

COSMOGRPHIAE

Capadociam/Pamphiliam/Lidiam/Ciliciã/Arme
nias maiorẽ & minorẽ.Colchiden/Hircaniam/Hi≠
beriam/Albaniã:et prẽterea m̃tas quas singilatim
enumerare longa mora esset.Ita dicta ab eius nomi
nis regina.

Nũc ỹo & hẽ partes sunt latius lustratẽ/& alia
quarta pars per Americũ Vesputiũ(vt in sequenti
bus audietur)inuenta est/quã non video cur quis
iure vetet ab Americo inuentore sagacis ingenij vi

Ameri≠
ca
ro Amerigen quasi Americi terrã / siue Americam
dicendã:cũ & Europa & Asia a mulieribus sua sor
tita sint nomina.Eius situ & gentis mores ex bis bi
nis Americi nauigationibus quæ sequunt liquide
intelligi datur.

Hunc in modũ terra iam quadripartita cogno≠
scit:et sunt tres primẽ partes cõtinentes/quarta est
insula:cũ omni quaꝗ mari circũdata conspiciat.Et
licet mare vnũ sit quẽadmodũ et ipsa tellus/multis
tamen sinibus distincctum/& innumeris replẽtum

Priscia≠
nus.
insulis varia sibi noĩa assumit:quẽ et in Cosmogra
phiæ tabulis cõspiciunt/& Priscianus in tralatione
Dionisij talibus enumerat versibus.

Circuit Oceani gurges tamen vndiꝗ vastus
Qui ꝗuis vnus sit plurima nomina sumit.
Finibus Hesperijs Athlanticus ille vocatur
At Boreẽ qua gens furit Armiaspa sub armis
Dicit ille piger necnõ Satur,ide Mortuus est alijs;

A page from the 1507 St. Die edition of Martin Waldseemüller's book, Cosmographiae Introducto. On this page Waldseemüller engages in a bit of male chauvenist humor in justifying the name "America." A translation of the paragraph next to the word America reveals this for the nonreader of Latin: "Now, really these parts of the earth [Europe, Africa, and Asia] have been more extensively explored and another fourth part has been discovered by Amerigo Vespucci. . . . Inasmuch as both Europe and Asia received their names from women, I see no reason why anyone would rightly object to calling this part Amerige, i.e., the land of Amerigo, or America, after Amerigo, its discoverer, a man of great ability. Its position and the customs of its inhabitants may be clearly understood from the four voyages of Amerigo, which are subjoined." (Thacher Collection, Rare Book and Special Collections Division).

Without any doubt Amerigo Vespucci is the most honored figure in the annals of geographical discovery. Two great continents embracing a third of the earth's land surface bear his name. Who was Amerigo and why should his name, above all others, apply to the American arc from Cape Horn in the south, to Cape Columbia in the north? Was he correctly accused by Ralph Waldo Emerson? In 1856 Emerson wrote, "Strange that broad America must wear the name of a thief! Amerigo Vespucci, the pickle-dealer at Seville, who went out in 1499, a subaltern with Hojeda, and whose highest naval rank was boatswain's mate, in an expedition that never sailed, managed in this lying world to supplant Columbus, and baptize half the earth with his own dishonest name!"

Like Columbus, Vespucci was an Italian, but unlike the humble son of Genoa, Amerigo was the scion of an old and distinguished family of Florentine aristocrats. He was baptized in 1454, and so was probably a few years junior to Columbus. In keeping with his station, Amerigo received an excellent education in part gained at the feet of an uncle who ran a school for the sons of local nobles. With the death of his father in 1482, Amerigo went to work for the Medici organization in a position of considerable trust and responsibility. After several prosperous years in the service of this wealthy house he was posted in Spain and set up residence in Seville in 1492.

Amerigo Vespucci was thus centrally placed and personally involved in the events that unfolded when Columbus returned in 1493 with news of his discoveries. Columbus was acquainted with him and wrote about him in complimentary terms in at least one letter.

Apparently convinced that Columbus had not discovered a sea passage to India as he claimed, Vespucci decided to use his good family and business connections to undertake his own search. In 1499 he joined an expedition being organized by Alonso de Hojeda, an aristocrat who served as a lieutenant in

NAMING AMERICA

Columbus's second voyage to the Indies. According to the contemporary historian Herrera, Amerigo served as "one who knew cosmography and matters pertaining to the sea" as well as in the role of representative of the moneyed group backing the enterprise.

After successfully exploring the coast of northern South America with Hojeda for Spain, Vespucci entered the service of the King of Portugal as the Royal Geographer. In the opening years of the sixteenth century he made two more voyages along the Atlantic coast of Brazil and southward. Like Columbus, Vespucci labored to fit the discoveries he and others were making into the world geographic framework of Ptolemy. The more he learned about the Spanish discoveries in the west and the Portuguese findings in the east, the more dissatisfied he became with the Ptolemaic world view. Unlike Columbus, however, Vespucci's mind was able, in the light of the mass of empirical evidence he was accumulating, to break out of the constraints of that ancient world view.

Colored facsimile of Martin Waldseemüller's large (54 by 96 inches) map, regarded to be the first naming the New World discoveries "America." Described as representing the earth "with a grandeur never before attempted," the map was discovered in 1901 in a castle in Württemberg, Germany. The original map is composed of twelve printed sheets designed to be laid together (Geography and map Division).

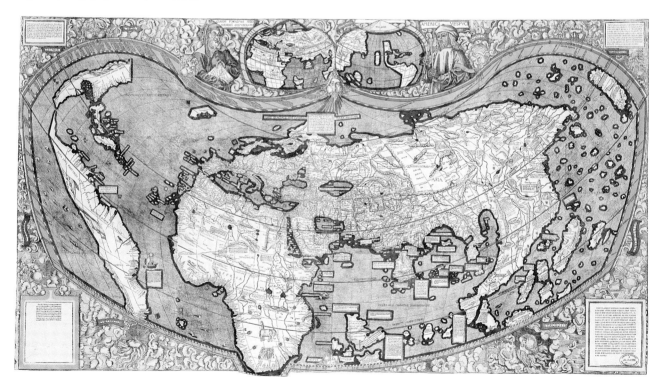

A close-up view of the decorative portraits of Claudius Ptolemy and Amerigo Vespucci. Notice the small inset hemispheric maps Waldseemüller placed between them. Ptolemy is gazing at the tripartite Old World, while Amerigo studies the New World, which is shown quite separate and removed from Asia. It is interesting to see how the southern and northern New World landmasses are shown to be connected on the inset map but unconnected on the main map (Geography and Map Division).

Upon his return to Lisbon, after his voyage along the Brazilian coast far into the Southern Hemisphere, Vespucci wrote to Lorenzo de Medici, "We arrived at a new land which, for many reasons that are enumerated in what follows, we observed to be a continent."

In his own mind, Amerigo Vespucci was convinced that the discoveries in the west comprised an inhabited "new land," a new land sufficiently large and diverse and positioned independently of Asia so that it could only be considered a "continent." Such speculations were, however, not unique to the explorer alone. Peter Martyr, as early as 1494, had used the term "new world" in reference to Columbus's descriptions of what he had found in the Indies. Certainly it would take something more than Amerigo's personal judgement of what he had discovered before the world would accept and name that "new land" in his honor.

NAMING AMERICA

■ THE POWER OF THE PRINTED WORD

Europe's thirst for information concerning the overseas discoveries was increasingly being satisfied by the recently established printing industry. Like the early letters of Columbus, Amerigo Vespucci's letter to Lorenzo de Medici was quickly translated into Latin and published. A second edition came off the press with the added title "Mundus Novus," thus linking Amerigo Vespucci's name with the emerging idea that something heretofore unknown, possibly even a "New World," was being revealed by European discoverers.

In 1505 someone, perhaps Amerigo or an over-zealous publisher, brought out a new letter that told of the discoveries he made on an alleged "fourth voyage" to the New World. This claim was disputed by his contemporaries, as well as later scholars, and brought forth the uncharacteristically harsh criticism from Ralph Waldo Emerson quoted above.

It is doubtful that the linkage with the New World Amerigo Vespucci gained through the publication of his colorful letters was sufficiently strong to suggest naming, in his honor, the lands that were slowly emerging in the consciousness of well-informed Europeans during the first decades of the sixteenth century. What then was the flux that welded his name so firmly to North and South America?

■ THE POWER OF THE PRINTED MAP

Even greater than the thirst for printed accounts of the discoveries, was Europe's craving for maps to clarify, locate, and explain the reported landfalls and coastlines in graphic form. It is no accident that the maps produced during the Age of Discovery are universally recognized as fundamental documents for the historical interpretation and understanding of that period.

At about the time Amerigo Vespucci's letters were being published, a circle of scholars was gathered at the Cathedral of St. Die, in the Vosges Mountains, in what is today Alsace-Lorraine. They had been re-cruited by the cathedral's canon to produce a new edition of Ptolemy's *World Atlas* that would include the new discoveries being reported by Spanish and Portuguese expeditions. Among the St. Die scholars was a German-born priest from the diocese of Constance named Martin Waldseemüller. The atlas and other publication projects were already underway when Vespucci's letter arrived at St. Die.

One of these ongoing projects was a primer or introductory text on cosmography. The book that appeared from the St. Die press in 1507 was titled, *Introduction to Cosmography . . . to which are added The Four Voyages of Amerigo Vespucci, A Representation of the Entire World, Both in the Solid and Projected on the Plane, Including Also Lands Which Were Unknown to Ptolemy, and Have Been Recently Discovered.*

In chapter 7 of *Introduction to Cosmography*, headed "Of Climates," Amerigo Vespucci's discoveries on the southern coast of South America were mentioned as follows:

In the sixth climate toward the antarctic there are situated the farthest part of Africa, recently discovered, the islands, Zanzibar, the lesser Java, and Seula, and the fourth part of the earth, which, because Amerigo discovered it, we may call Amerige, the land of Amerigo, so to speak, or America.

Commenting on this quotation from *Introduction to Cosmography*, the historian of discovery and benefactor of the Library of Congress, John Boyd Thacher, was moved to write, "This then, is that simple sentence composed by an unknown geographer and printed in an obscure town in a remote corner of the earth, which christened a new world and fixed on it forever its pleasant sounding name." Thacher, however, was writing in the era before the discovery of surviving examples of the two maps that were originally published with *Introduction to Cosmography*. Recall, the maps were mentioned on the book's title page.

NAMING AMERICA

Clearly more effective in fixing that "pleasant sounding name" were the two world maps prepared by Martin Waldseemüller to accompany the St. Die edition of *Introduction to Cosmography.* One of those maps took the form of a set of gores for a globe or map "in the Solid" as it was described on the title page. The second map was an elegant and very large (7½ feet by 4 feet) twelve-sheet map of the world, printed on paper from woodblock engravings. The full title of this richly decorated cordiform (heart-shaped) map is, "Universalis Cosmographia Secundum Ptholomaei Traditionem Americi Vespucci Alorum Que Lustrationes" (A Drawing of the Whole Earth According to the Tradition of Ptolemy and the Travels of Amerigo Vespucci and Others). Long felt to be lost, copies of both the large sheet map and globe gores were discovered in 1901 by the German geographer Josef Fischer while he was researching in Wolfegg Castle in southern Germany.

On both these 1507 maps there is shown a new landmass named "America" lying between the island-fringed coast of a Ptolemaic eastern Asia and an easily recognizable western coast of Europe and Africa. To further emphasize the importance they attached to Amerigo Vespucci's contributions to this new and revolutionary image of the world, Waldseemüller and the St. Die scholars included his engraved portrait along with that of Claudius Ptolemy in a place of honor at the top of "Universalis Cosmographia." The discoverer of the one surviving example of this map was correct when he wrote that it "represents the earth with a grandeur never before attempted." The vulnerability of such large, unbound maps is attested to by the fact that although sheets for at least one thousand copies were originally pulled, only one copy appears to have survived the vicissitudes of the long period since 1507. The smaller globe gores, however, exist in at least three known sets.

Waldseemüller's map was quickly copied by other cartographers and the name America began to take root in Europe. The author of *Cosmographiae Introducto* provided an explanation for the original choice of the name that may also help to explain its ready adoption by those outside of St. Die. In Chapter 9, headed "Of Certain Elements of Cosmography," Waldseemüller or one of his associates wrote:

Now, really these [three] parts of the earth [Europe, Africa, and Asia] have been more extensively explored and another fourth part has been discovered by Amerigo Vespucci. . . . Inasmuch as both Europa and Asia received their names from women, I see no reason why anyone would rightly object to calling this part Amerige, i.e., the land of Amerigo, or America, after Amerigo, its discoverer, a man of great ability. Its position and the customs of its inhabitants may be clearly understood from the four voyages of Amerigo, which are subjoined.

Thus the earth is now known to be divided into four parts. The first three parts are continents, while the fourth is an island, inasmuch as it is found to be surrounded on all sides by the ocean.

It can be seen that Waldseemüller and the St. Die circle, unlike Vespucci himself, were giving Amerigo credit for discovering a "fourth part" of the world that was an "island" as distinct from a "continent." In a period when numbers of islands were being discovered in the ocean sea, naming one, even as large as the one shown on Waldseemüller's maps, was not an extraordinary thing to do.

A close-up of the New World landmasses as shown on this facsimile of Waldseemüller's main map. The word "America" is located where the Tropic of Capricorn crosses the southern New World landmass (Geography and Map Division).

RESEARCHING THE AGE OF DISCOVERY IN THE LIBRARY OF CONGRESS

Compiled by LOUIS DE VORSEY, JR.

With the Assistance of the

Library's Special Collections

Reference Staff

Many of the original European explorers who came to the northern part of the new world were searching for a Northwest Passage to the Pacific. The French philosopher Michel Serres has described the attempt in our time to reunify the humanities and the sciences, old books and new technologies, as the new "Northwest Passage" that we must both discover and learn to navigate. The custodians of books can be models as well as guides for gratifying man's basic instinct that things be whole and comprehensive.

Books and the World, James H. Billington

INTRODUCTION

The Library of Congress was first created to aid our early senators and congressmen as they made the laws needed for the country to function. Through the decades it grew to become the world's largest library, and over a century ago Congress began sharing its resources with the nation and world.

The Library is approaching its two hundredth birthday. It was founded in 1800, when the government moved from New York City to the new District of Columbia, and when the Library was begun it had but one purpose: to gather the information the members needed for their day-to-day work on the floors of the Congress. But about three generations into its life, the Library took on a second responsibility: to capture the history of the American people. It set out to accumulate and store the record of the nation's life. It sought to get a better understanding of where the American people came from in "The Old Country," and it began to be recognized as the nation's memory, the place where the story of the American Experience was kept. By the time the Library reached the twentieth century, it had made *all* knowledge its province and was trying to accumulate everything that was known by *all* cultures. It was trying to build a single treasury where creative and questioning Americans could go to find "all the answers stored in a single place."

The combination of these three purposes has led to the superlatives that seem to cling to the Library like filings to a magnet. It *is* the largest library in the world. It does have more phonograph records, more manuscripts, more Stradivari violins, more flutes, more letters by George Washington, more newsreels, more cookbooks, and more writings about the North and South Poles than any other place on earth. It has over twenty million books, but these represent less than a fourth of the holdings of the Library. Of the more than twenty million books, less than a fourth are in English, with the other three-quarters in some 470 languages (the majority of which—like Japanese, Chinese, Thai, Arabic, Hebrew, and Hindi—are in scripts that are unfamiliar to most Americans).

The library employs close to five thousand staff members. About half of these acquire, process, and make the Library's material available to the public, but the other half are occupied in the production of new materials or the provision of services quite removed from the books and documents of the Library's collections. There are some nine hundred specialists who work exclusively for Congress providing cost projections, pro and con studies, and legislative analyses related to the routine work of the legislature. Another group provides services to the blind and the physically handicapped of the nation under a multi-million-dollar program which distributes records, tapes, and braille to those who cannot use printed materials. The Library houses the Copyright Office of the United States; it also contains the nation's largest preservation laboratory, provides computerized bibliographic data to libraries around the world, makes music recordings, and stages concerts, literary programs, and similar activities several steps removed from what is usually expected of a typical public or university library.

When I began working on this book I soon realized that the Library of Congress lived up to every superlative I had ever heard or read about it. Until that time my experience as a researcher at the Library had been limited almost exclusively to just one of its many divisions with brief forays into the collections of two others. To me the Library of Congress had come to mean the precincts and personnel of the Geography and Map Division (G&M).

My first opportunity to work in the G&M Reading Room came in the early 1960s when the division was housed in the Library's Adams Building (then called the Annex) located immediately behind the green-domed Jefferson Building. In the 1970s, visits to the G&M Division took one across the Potomac River to Virginia. This came about because by the autumn of 1969 the division's collection of maps and charts had outgrown the space then available on Capitol Hill, and temporary quarters were secured in a warehouse complex on the outer fringe of Alexandria. Patrons and staff who drove to the division enjoyed the ease of parking, but such a remote site had little else to commend it.

I once tried to use public transport to reach the Alexandria facility. After receiving directions from a transit authority employee manning the toll-free advisory telephone service, I made my way by Metro, Washington's subway system, to the bus plaza at the Pentagon Building. After spending a futile, very hot and frustrating hour trying to find the bus that would take me to the warehouse district where G&M was housed, I decided to telephone for a cab. Walking to the telephone kiosk I passed a stationary bus and decided to ask the driver where I had gone wrong. As I explained to him that I had received detailed routing instructions by calling the transit authority telephone hotline service, he began to nod and smile sympathetically. When I finished my mild diatribe on the inadequacies of the service, he invited me to board the bus and started the engine. As we began to pull out of the plaza he told me that he heard many similar complaints and, as a member of the transportation system, he apologized most sincerely for the inconvenience I had experienced. He then drove me as a solitary passenger to the warehouse district, explaining that he had been on call at the Pentagon in the event that a bus on one of the many routes converging there was to break down. He said it was a boring assignment and it pleased him to be able to make amends for the incorrect information I had been given.

Needless to say, I was delighted to reach my destination in such an unusual way. Leaving the bus, I told the driver that I planned to write to the transit authority and report his generous and courteous service. He asked me not to and explained that his supervisor might not understand. I agreed, and did not write at that time, but hope that he will read this while he sits waiting for a Pentagon-bound bus to break down.

After their long spell in the Alexandria warehouse, G&M patrons and staff were pleased when the division moved into the new, gleaming white Madison Building in 1980, on Capitol Hill adjacent to the Jefferson and Adams Buildings of the Library of Congress. Their decade in the wilderness had ended.

NOT A LIBRARY BUT A UNIVERSITY

At the outset of this project I realized that I would need to find out more about the Library's other divisions holding materials of interest to the many and varied readers and researchers who might wish to investigate some aspect or other of the Age of Discovery. To this end, I spent several weeks visiting the reading rooms and talking to staff members of many, but by no means all of the Library's divisions.

One morning while engaged in these visitations and interviews I happened to be walking from my hotel, across the Capitol Building grounds toward the Library, when I had a flash of insight. That insight was that I was not approaching a "library" at all, at least not in the usual sense of the familiar word. No, I had been working in and was now entering what correctly could only be termed a university. Yes, this complex in the shadow of the Capitol Building is a large and diverse university. There is no charter in a glass case or bronze plaque proclaiming this identity, but it is a fact nonetheless. The architecture, the facilities, the books and documents, the readers and, most importantly, the knowledgeable staff specialists and support personnel, all combine to form one of the world's truly great universities. It was not planned to be one but thank heaven it had evolved as one in my lifetime.

Like most large, diverse universities, wherever they are found, the Library of Congress is possessed of institutional strengths and, unfortunately, institutional weaknesses. Try as it will it cannot be all things to all people. To put it another way, the first-time user of the Library of Congress shares much in common with the small-town or rural freshman in his first days of attendance as a naive stranger at a huge and impersonal university.

To use the jargon of the computer age, such campus experiences are far from what we usually term "user friendly." The story of the freshman who was already at home when his or her parents returned from having driven the young scholar along with his or her personal computer, posters and pennant, and dorm room furniture to "Any State U." is a familiar anecdote across the land. Large institutions, such as universities, often seem to exist as clubs for the welfare of insiders. At the university the insiders are upperclass men and women who are sometimes not above adding to the discomfort and feelings of intimidation being suffered by the freshman.

To the freshman, or first-time researcher-visitor, the Library of Congress can seem an equally intimidating place. This is especially true if readers arrive expecting to find simply a bigger and better library than the one they are familiar with. Things will probably go much more easily if the first-time reader recognizes that the many divisions of the Library of Congress resemble and function in ways that are very similar to those of the academic departments, schools, and colleges of a large and diverse university. Just as the faculty members and secretarial staff of a department like physics may have only the vaguest awareness of a department like geography, in a neighboring building, so the specialists in one of the Library of Congress's divisions may be unaware, sometimes annoyingly so, of the holdings and interests of other divisions, even those in the same building.

READER PREPARE

The best way for a freshman, or first-time reader-visitor, to lower the potential frustration level in his or her encounters with the Library of Congress is, strange as it may seem, by reading. Ideally one should arrive at the Library having exhausted the resources available in one's local libraries. If this is the case one will have acquired a good working knowledge of one's research topic. This, in turn, should enable one to communicate more clearly one's needs and desires to the specialists in the Library's various divisions.

Be prepared to take copious notes when you are conversing with Library specialists. Reference work titles and names of published authors and researchers are almost impossible for most of us to remember, so jot them down as you hear them. Generally speaking, information so offered is deemed important by the spe-

cialist and to neglect to note it and follow up on it is potentially insulting and wasteful of her or his time and energy. Be especially attentive when the specialist tells you about the particular indexes, lists, catalogs, or other finding aids that are available in a specific division. These are the keys with which you can begin to open the metaphorical treasure vaults containing the many collections which any particular division of the Library holds and maintains.

SECURITY, SECURITY!

Be prepared also to abide by the security and access rules and regulations that may be required by the division you are in. These precautions vary from strict entrance security maintained by uniformed guards to the sort of relaxed supervision maintained by librarians in most school and community libraries. In certain divisions the use of ink pens of any sort is not allowed so be prepared to utilize old-fashioned pencils when taking notes. In some instances you may even be required to wear protective gloves before you are allowed to handle certain rare materials. The reason for such strict security and handling procedures is the obvious one—many of the Library's holdings are exceedingly rare and fragile. If they are defaced, damaged, or lost they cannot be replaced and represent the loss of a national treasure.

For this reason also, you may be presented a microfilm or some other form of facsimile of the document you plan to study. Only when it is clearly necessary for the original material to be examined at first hand will certain very rare or vulnerable items be made available, and then only under secure conditions as determined by the responsible specialist in charge. None of this should come as a surprise. The Library of Congress is in the business of not only collecting the treasures of civilization, but also of maintaining, conserving, and interpreting them so that they are available to all who need to consult them now and in the future.

BUILDINGS AND FACILITIES

The main facilities of the Library of Congress are housed in three large buildings clustered near the southeast corner of the U.S. Capitol Building's parklike grounds. Closest to and facing the Capitol Building is the Library's main and first facility, the Thomas Jefferson Building, rightly termed "the mecca of the young giant Republic" by its ambitious architects of more than a century ago. Only a short distance to the north along Washington's First Street is the Jefferson Building's neighboring edifice, also an architectural gem, the familiar U.S. Supreme Court Building. When it comes to prestigious locations the Library is unquestionably upscale. Immediately to the east and behind the Jefferson Building is the Library's second major component, the John Adams Building. First known simply as "The Annex," the Adams Building was built during the mid-1930s and, while severely functional, reflects the art deco style of the period. It is far less decorated than the flamboyant Renaissance-style Jefferson Building, in keeping with the Depression-decade of its creation. The third building of the Library of Congress is the James Madison Memorial Building. It is located immediately south of the Jefferson Building, across Independence Avenue, and diagonally across Second Street from the Adams Building. The Madison Building is only surpassed in size by the Pentagon and the FBI buildings among the vast number of U.S. government properties. In addition to accommodating a large number of Library of Congress collections and activities, the Madison Building houses the nation's memorial to our fourth president, James Madison.

Not only are the three Library buildings in close proximity, they are linked by tunnels beneath the busy Washington streets that provide surface access. The researcher needing to go from one building to another soon comes to appreciate these convenient subterranean pathways. When it is raining or the weather is harsh they are particularly welcome. Even in fine weather they are heavily used escapes from the hazards of Washington traffic and exhaust fumes.

Before leaving the topic of underground travel at the Library of Congress, the Washington Metro deserves mention. It is an extensive and very efficient underground railway system that provides a clean and cheap way of traveling throughout the Washington area and into neighboring Virginia and Maryland. The stop closest to the Library of Congress is the Capitol South station served by the Blue and Orange Lines. A first-time visitor to the Library not familiar with Washington would do well to request a Metro map and information brochure from the Washington Metropolitan Area Transit Authority at 800 Fifth Street, N.W., Washington, D.C. 20001.

The first-time visitor will also profit from a viewing of the twenty-two-minute video presentation "A Tour of the Library of Congress." The video is shown in the Orientation Theater in the Visitor Services Center every half hour from 8:30 A.M. to 5 P.M. on weekdays. On weekends and during the evening the video is self-activated. Even more informative than the video are the free one-hour guided tours that leave from the Visitor Center several times each weekday.

Once inside the Library complex there is no compelling reason to leave before the end of the work day. This is because there are plenty of facilities where lunch or coffee break needs can be satisfied within the Library itself. If a break and return to the outside world is needed there are plenty of snack bars and restaurants within a short walk of any of the three buildings. Library publications, facsimile maps and prints, and a range of tasteful souvenir-type items are available in the sales shops located in the Jefferson Building and the Madison Building.

DIVISIONS AND READING ROOMS

As mentioned above, the Library of Congress is the world's largest and most diverse library. Consequently, researchers interested in questions dealing with the Age of Discovery can be assured that answers to many, if not most, of them can be found somewhere in LC. It is the word *somewhere* that poses challenges and complications for anyone, be he or she a novice or senior scholar, using the vast and complex resources of this mega-library cum university on Capitol Hill. Librarians on the staff like to make this point by calling attention to the fact that, while a good university library might offer one hundred references to articles or books devoted to Christopher Columbus, LC has over five thousand on the Discoverer. A word of caution is in order when the Discoverer of America is the subject for research. Remember that the accepted style of his name has changed with time. In the older LC catalogs he appears as "Christoforo Colombo" while in the more modern indexes he is recorded as "Christopher Columbus."

It if were only a question of quantity, as implied by this simple comparison of the numbers of catalog entry cards, things might not be all that bad. Time spent flipping through the cards should enable the patient researcher to gain access to most if not all that the Library contains on the great Navigator. Unfortunately, such is not the case. Much, perhaps the most significant, material on Columbus in LC may not be mentioned in the reference catalog file drawers or on any computerized catalogs. This is because it may be in one of the almost three hun-

dred special collections held in the various Library of Congress divisions.

While it is probably true to state that the Age of Discovery is such a broad research focus one might reasonably expect to encounter something of interest in every division of the Library, it is probably equally true to say that the holdings of certain divisions are such that they should be singled out for priority treatment. In keeping with this realization, I have selected five divisions—the General Reading Rooms, Rare Book and Special Collections, Geography and Maps, Manuscript, and Hispanic—for priority treatment. Two others—Prints and Photographs, and Motion Picture, Broadcasting and Recorded Sound—will receive briefer mention.

GENERAL READING ROOMS DIVISION

The Main Reading Room has been described as the index to the whole encyclopedia of world knowledge that is the Library of Congress. It is from the Main Reading Room that you can tap the volumes you need from the Library's huge general collections. Many research projects begin and end in the Main Reading Room without the researcher ever finding it necessary to move beyond its domed confines in the Jefferson Building.

The first-time patron at the Library of Congress should begin her or his visit by calling in at the Research Guidance Office. Here, a reference librarian will acquaint you with the resources and facilities of the Main Reading Room, describe the procedures to follow in using it, or, if necessary, direct you to another division of the Library. There are also reference librarians strategically situated in the Reading Room to assist as problems arise. Should you have any questions on the use of the card or computer catalogs or any of the other information sources, seek out a member of the general reference staff to assist you. They are best equipped to guide you through the complexities of research in the Library of Congress.

The key to the Library's book collections is familiarity with the subject headings and various subdivisions used to narrow in on a given topic. The needed familiarity can be gained through studying the three-volume compilation, *Library of Congress Subject Headings*. This sensibly titled and useful guide is usually available in university and other large libraries for study before travelling to Washington. For a general study of the Age of Discovery begin with the heading "Discoveries (in geography)." Within that main entry, listed subdivisions cover particular aspects topically or geographically— "Discoveries, Maritime," "Exploration and discovery," "Exploring expeditions," "Explorers," "Man, Primitive-First contact with Occidental civilization," etc. One may also search under the name of some particular explorers, such as Sir Francis Drake, although headings for Coronado or Columbus and some others are not included. If you have a fairly specific subject in mind, it is best to begin by searching for it directly before consulting the broader subject headings.

The Library, like almost every other large institution, has been irreversibly impacted by the computer. The transition from the traditional card catalog to the computer catalog has created both advantages and problems for the researcher. At present, the computer catalog is best used for those publications that have been cataloged since 1968, though older materials may be located through a file that is undergoing bibliographic improvement. Unfortunately, however, this file currently contains outdated subject terms and may give false impressions with respect to the number of works on particular topics. To be certain that you have complete coverage of older works, you should search the card catalog, which contains cross references

not included in the computer entries. Visually browsing from category to category within a given subject area is more effective in the card catalog than with the computer. Always remember that for works cataloged by the Library *since 1980, the computer catalog is the only access point.*

There are two program approaches to the collections through the computer: SCORPIO, which involves a step-by-step process not unlike the steps in searching the card catalog; and MUMS, which has a key word capability for those terms that appear in a subject, title, or other searchable fields of a catalog entry. Each has its idiosyncrasies, and consultation with a librarian for the wisest approach is recommended.

As conditions change and terminology expands, the Library's subject headings attempt to adapt, but the overwhelming size of the collections frequently dictates that older headings continue to exist as new ones develop. Therefore, older editions of *Library of Congress Subject Headings* may contain subject terms that can be found in the card catalog. Also, the card catalog's cross references may help sort out such complexities. Through a MUMS approach, on the other hand, one can sometimes simplify complicated searches by entering all possible terms that may appear in subject headings or titles. Knowledge of Boolean Logic helps in streamlining such searches, but librarians can assist if problems occur.

Remember also that not everything in the Library's collections, especially the almost three hundred special collections, can be found through the main catalog (card or computerized). Many collections of potential interest to the student of the history of discoveries are cataloged only in the special reading room which has control of them. Nonbook materials may be controlled and identified in large chunks because of the incredible number of individual pieces involved. Books converted to microform (either acquired in that form as part of a larger collection or converted to a micro format for preservation) may or may not appear in the main catalog. The list of apparent inconsistencies and gaps in cataloging is longer but need not concern us here. The important thing is for the researcher to realize that these problems exist and not to conclude that a volume is not in the Library of Congress just because a check of entries in the general catalog has drawn a blank. Persist in your search by enlisting the aid of the reference staff. Do not, whatever you do, lose your temper. The cool determination of your favorite detective character, teasing out the clues to a seemingly insoluble mystery, is probably the best mental attitude and posture to assume. As all too many Washingtonians have learned, the Library of Congress is not the sort of place where you can pop in during lunchtime and expect to accomplish anything in the way of research.

Before closing this lengthy discussion of the General Reading Rooms, the forty thousand-plus-volume reference collection shelved on open stacks and readily available to readers should be mentioned. This collection is separately cataloged in the "Main Reading Room Reference Catalog." Here one will find, for example, the superb multivolume set edited with commentary by David B. Quinn and titled, *New American World: A Documentary History of North America to 1612*. As a glance at my notes at the end of the six chapters in this book will reveal, Quinn's collection of documents and journals, many in translation, is an indispensable source for the study of the discovery and early exploration of North America.

The General Reading Rooms Division as well as other divisions of the Library of Congress were somewhat disrupted and even relocated as the historic Jefferson Building was renovated in the period of the late 1980s and early 1990s. For this reason researchers planning to work at the Library were well advised to request the revised renovation edition of the free booklet titled *In-formation for Readers Using the Library of Congress*. You would be smart to obtain the current edition for study before you visit the Library. Request it from: Library of Congress, Central Services Division, Washington, D.C. 20540. There is no charge and the information it contains can save you hours of frustration. If time is short you might try ordering the booklet by telephone. The general number for the Library of Congress is (202) 707-5000.

RARE BOOK AND SPECIAL COLLECTIONS DIVISION

Perhaps the complexity of the Library of Congress as a whole can be better understood by reviewing the birth and genesis of one of its many constituent divisions. In the case of the Rare Book and Special Collections Division that birth was unplanned and came about almost accidentally. Early in the Library's history, the practice developed whereby books of great value and significance were located in the Librarian's office for safekeeping. In time such books were labeled "Office." Before the move of the Library from its original quarters in the Capitol Building to the Thomas Jefferson Building, the Librarian's office was described as "piled up with an almost inaccessible mass of rare books, pamphlets, letters and other papers."

Following the move in 1897, the "Office" collection was shelved in a large room assigned to the Chief Assistant Librarian, Ainsworth Rand Spofford. Mr. Spofford acted as the curator of rare boks in addition to his official administrative duties. Eventually the collection outgrew its original space and was moved to new quarters in the Jefferson Building and put under the administration of the Superintendent of the Main Reading Room.

The next stage in the collection's life coincided with the donation of the book and manuscript collection of a leading nineteenth-century authority on the history of discovery. He was John Boyd Thacher (1847–1909), who had amassed an impressive and valuable collection of incunabula, early Americana, and French Revolution material while pursuing his career as a New York manufacturer and politician.

The addition of the Thacher Collection to the Library's rare holdings was a dramatic sign that the original small nuclear collection had come of age. Accordingly, a separate Rare Book reading room, adjoining a section of locked stacks, was opened in 1927. The collections continued to grow through periodic selective cullings from other Library collections and bequests. By 1980 the Rare Book and Special Collections included more than 300,000 volumes and 200,000 broadsides, theater playbills, title pages, prints, manuscripts, posters, and photographs.

■ JOHN BOYD THACHER COLLECTION

This 5,193-item collection is composed of four distinct bodies of material—incunabula, early Americana, material pertaining to the French Revolution, and autographs. The early printed books include works produced by more than five hundred fifteenth-century presses and such outstanding items as a vellum copy of *Rationale Divinorum Officiorum* by Gulielmus Durantis (Mainz, 1459) and the only known American copies of *Brevigrium Morguntinum* (Marienthal, 1474) and *Vocabularius ex Quo* (Eltvil, 1476). Mr. Thacher drew upon his extensive collection of Americana for his publications on the history of discovery, *The Continent of America* (1896) and *Christopher Columbus* (1903–4). This and the incunabula segment of the Thacher Collection are certainly of most interest to researchers concerned with Age of Discovery topics and questions. Some of the highlights of the Thacher Americana and incunabula are:

Claudius Ptolemaeus—copies of thirty-four early editions of Ptolemy's *Geographia* dating from the early fifteenth century onward. Also in the incunabula collection are five fifteenth-century editions of Ptolemy's *Cosmographia* including the Rome, Arnoldus Buckinck, 1478 edition, containing the famous map of the world known to the Europeans on the eve of Columbus's voyage in 1492.

Bible. *O.T. Psalms. Polyglot*—Published in Genoa in 1516, this first polyglot Psalter is in Hebrew, Greek, Arabic, and Chaldean as well as Latin. It also contains the first biographical account of Christopher Columbus.

Angelo Trevigiano [Trevisan]-[Venice, 1503]. Letters written from Granada and Ecija in 1501 and 1502 to Domenico Malipiero at Venice, transmitting the seven books of "La Navigation de Colochut facta par Portugalesi 1501." This manuscript (sometimes called the Sneyd Codex) includes letters written by Trevisan, a friend of Columbus. He had transcribed Peter Martyr's Latin text describing Columbus's voyages a decade before they were published. Trevisan also provided the first description of Columbus's physical appearance when his notes were published in 1504, well before Martyr's *Decades.*

Cristoforo Colombo. *De insulis in mari Indico nuper inuentis.* [Basel] 1494–contains the woodcut illustration showing the first group of islands named by Columbus during his 1492–93 voyage (illustrated here in Chapter 4).

Bartolomé de Las Casas. *An Account of the First Voyages and Discoveries Made by the Spaniards in America. Containing the Most Exact Relation hitherto published, of their unparalleled Cruelties on the Indians, in the destruction of above Forty Millions of people . . .* London, 1699–An early English edition of Las Casas's exposé of Indian abuses in the West Indies.

Martin Waldseemüller. *Cosmographiae introductio.* [St. Die, Walter Lud, 1507]—The publication in which Waldseemüller and a St. Die group of scholars forward the suggestion that the new discoveries in the west form a continent that should be named "America" for Amerigo Vespucci, the supposed discoverer. Henry Harrisse purchased this copy in Rome and believed it to be the Vatican copy. (See "Naming America" herein for photographs of Waldseemüller's text and map).

Of particular value when utilizing the Thacher Collection is the published three-volume catalog: U.S., Library of Congress, John Boyd Thacher Collection. *The Collection of John Boyd Thacher in the Library of Congress* (Washington: Government Printing Office, 1931. 3 v. Z881.U51931).

■ HENRY HARRISSE COLLECTION

Of equal importance to researchers concerned with the Age of Discovery is the Rare Book and Special Collections Division's Henry Harrisse Collection. Henry Harrisse (1828–1910) was a highly regarded scholar and Americanist whose *Bibliotheca Americana vetustissima*, originally published in New York in 1866, remains a standard bibliographical guide. So thorough and accurate was this work that the great American bibliographer Joseph Sabin termed it an "indispensable necessary" for the study of early books pertaining to America.

Perhaps his finest work, and certainly his most important for the student of the Age of Discovery, is the exacting study Harrisse published entitled *The Discovery of North America* (Paris and London, 1892). As a contemporary reviewer noted "No praise could be too great for the immense research, prolonged and microscopic labour, and seemingly faultless accuracy, which are the chief characteristics of Mr. Harrisse's splendid volume. It sums up in one view the monographs already published by him on Columbus, on John and Sebastian Cabot, on the Cortereals and Verrazano, and on the first explorers of the American Seas."

Anyone familiar with Henry Harrisse's life and career at the time of his death might have been surprised to learn that his personal collection had been bequeathed to the Library of Congress. Having come to the United States from France at the age of eighteen, Harrisse was proud of his American citizenship but scath-

ingly critical of American scholars, publishers, wealthy collectors, and libraries for ignoring his works. Eschewing his early academic career for the practice of law, Harrisse spent the last forty years of his productive life in Paris representing and advising a largely American clientele. His successful Paris law practice provided the freedom he required to pursue his research and writing on the discovery of America.

The Henry Harrisse Collection came to the Library of Congress in 1915, more than five years after his death. Many of the more than two hundred volumes are printed on special paper with wide margins to accommodate his extensive annotations and most volumes have letters and other related material interleaved. There are also eighteen bound volumes of manuscripts and thirteen containers of unbound material related to Harrisse's writings. Works by others include a number of monographs by Harrisse's contemporaries, three rare works, one published in each of the sixteenth, seventeenth, and eighteenth centuries, and two sixteenth-century manuscripts. Original maps from the collection are in the Geography and Map Division of the Library of Congress. In the Rare Book vaults the Harrisse Collection occupies 25 linear feet.

The Henry Harrisse Collection includes:

Henry Harrisse, 1829–1910. *Le Corte-Real et leurs Voyages au Nouveau-monde . . .* 1883. The map has the title: *Fragment du planisphere envoyé de Lisbonne a Hercule d'Este duc de Ferrare avant le 19 novembre 1502, par Alberto Cantino. De la grandeur de l'original* (this beautifully colored facsimile is the part relating to the New World, together with the western portion of Europe and Africa, see herein, Chapters 5 and 6 for illustrations).

Karl Maria Seyppel. *Christoph Columbus Logbuch.* Dusseldorf, [1890]. (This secret log of Columbus, purportedly thrown overboard during a storm and later retrieved from the ocean depths, is an example of several similar versions in English and German that were offered as popular mementos of the Columbus anniversary a century ago. It seems safe to predict that the Quincentenary of Columbus's first voyage will spawn similar hoaxes).

Henry Harrisse. *The Discovery of North America.* London and Paris, H. Welter, 1892. (This monumental synthesis of Harrisse's extensive research on discovery focuses on early cartography, describing over two hundred fifty maps and globes made before 1536. Although rejected by American publishers as being too erudite, this work received an award at the World's Columbian Exposition as a "valuable contribution to science." It includes Juan de la Cosa's early map of the New World, which has religious and cosmological significance as well as political and cartographic importance, see the illustration in Chapter 4 herein.)

Henry Harrisse. *Christopher Columbus, his own book of Privileges, 1502. Historical Introduction.* London, 1893. (To commemorate the quatercentenary of Columbus's discovery, B. F. Stevens published an elaborate facsimile edition of the Paris copy of Columbus's 1502 Book of Privileges that had recently been discovered in the archives of the Foreign Office by the noted Columbus scholar Henry Harrisse. Harrisse's copy of his introduction to this important facsimile edition is enclosed in a facsimile of the dispatch bag Columbus used to send his privileges to Genoa. Harrisse maintained that the original bag was the only authentic relic of Columbus other than his books and letters. See the illustration in Chapter 4 herein.)

A detailed "Guide to the Henry Harrisse Collection" has been prepared by Rosemary F. Plakas, a member of the staff of the Rare Book and Special Collections Division. At present this excellent sixty-five-page guide and finding aid is available in typescript in the division's reading room. There are, however, efforts being made to publish Ms. Plakas's guide along with an essay on Harrisse written by Richard W. Stephenson of the Geography and Map Division. When complete, the proposed publication will include a long-needed catalog to the maps in the Henry Harrisse Collection.

■ HANS P. AND HANNI KRAUS SIR FRANCIS DRAKE COLLECTION

In 1980, Hans P. Kraus and his wife Hanni presented their superb Sir Francis Drake Collection of Drake manuscripts, printed books, medals, and portraits to the Library of Congress. The gift from the well-known collector and bibliophile and his wife followed by ten years another major donation by the Krauses, that of 162 manuscripts relating to the colonial period of Spanish America. The earlier gift will be mentioned in the description of the Library's Manuscript Division.

The Kraus Drake Collection, while officially housed in the Rare Book and Special Collections Division, was regarded as a major supplement to the resources of several other divisions in the Library, including the Geography and Map, Hispanic, and Manuscript Divisions.

A decade before the presentation of this unparalleled collection bearing on one of the most influential Elizabethans in the annals of discovery and exploration, Hans Kraus published *Sir Francis Drake, A Pictorial Biography,* with an Historical Introduction by Lt. Cdr. David W. Waters and Richard Boulind (Amsterdam: 1970). Included in the book is "a detailed Catalogue of the Author's Collection." This catalog continues to serve as the basic reference and finding aid for researchers working with the Kraus Drake Collection. Although selected items have been added since the 1970 "detailed Catalogue" appeared, anyone expecting to consult the collection at the Library of Congress can be assured that the preponderance of Drake material is described in detail in it.

This remarkable collection contains much material that had been unknown to most historians until 1970. Some of the items are unique and the collection, as assembled by Mr. Kraus, adds a fund of insights vital for a full appreciation of Drake's feats in the area of discovery and exploration. It represents one of the most desired fruits of collecting, that is the drawing together of otherwise scattered material into a coherent record which enables the scholar-researcher to arrive at and test fresh hypotheses and insights in the effort to advance knowledge.

Students of the Age of Discovery will be pleased to find that the most lengthy section of the "Pictorial Biography" portion of the 1970 publication is devoted to "The Famous Voyage: The Circumnavigation of the World 1577–1580." Included in this discussion are photographic facsimiles of the following collection items:

Richard Hakluyt's first published account of Drake's circumnavigation that appeared in his *The Prinicipall Navigations* (1589). [Item 27]

The title page and engraved world map that appeared with *The World Encompassed by Sir Francis Drake* (1628). This detailed account adds much to Hakluyt's original report. See Chapter 6 herein for quotations from *The World Encompassed*. [Item 42]

Gerard Mercator's autograph letter to Abraham Ortelius (1580). Rightly deemed "one of the crowning pieces of this collection," this correspondence between Europe's two leading cartographer-map publishers is unique. [Item 2A]

The southern portion of Levinus Hulsius's map "Nova et exacta delineatio Americae Partis Australiae" (1602). In this second edition of the map three islands have been inserted below the bottom border of the southern map, with the name "Francisci Draco Ins." They reflect the first of Drake's two principal geographical discoveries made during the circumnavigation. That was the insular nature of Tierra del Fuego. On most maps the islands bear the name "Elizabeth" which Drake designated the largest of the group in honor of his queen. [Item 52]

The passage relating to the map Drake had presented to Queen Elizabeth on his return from the circumnavigation as published in *Purchas his Pilgrimes* (1625). Purchas wrote of this map as "still hanging in His Maiesties Gallerie at White Hall, neere the Privie Chamber, and by that Map wherein is Cabotas Picture, the first and great Co-

lumbus for the Northerne World." It is assumed that this map was lost when Whitehall burned. [Item 40]

Nicola van Sype's engraved map "La Herdike (sic, for Heroique) Enterprinse Faict par le Signeur Draeck D'Avoir Cirquit Toute la Terre" (c. 1581). Nicola van Sype probably engraved this map immediately after Drake's return from the circumnavigation. It is considered to have been based on Drake's original map that hung in Whitehall (see the illustration in Chapter 6 herein). [Item 48]

Michael Mercator, A World Map in two hemispheres, engraved or struck on silver, and bearing the track of Drake's 1577–1580 circumnavigation of the earth. 68 mm diameter. Weight 383 grains Troy. In a red leather case (1589). This is a splendid example of the famous Drake Silver Map or Silver Medal, a piece commemorating Drake's circumnavigation. This is the only extant specimen bearing Michael Mercator's name and the location of his London workplace in a cartouche. [Item 58]

■ LESSING J. ROSENWALD COLLECTION

The Lessing J. Rosenwald Collection is one of the distinguished resources of the Rare Book and Special Collections Division. It is of significance in research agendas dealing with the Age of Discovery because Mr. Rosenwald collected pristine examples of books within his chosen field of interest—western illustrated books from the fifteenth through the twentieth centuries. Beginning his collecting in the late 1920s Mr. Rosenwald's earliest purchases were of fifteenth-century German illustrated books. Needless to say, his collection soon began to embrace many of the books from which the Europeans gained their initial descriptions and images of the new discoveries being reported from the far reaches of the Ocean Sea.

The Library of Congress's holdings of late sixteenth- and early seventeenth-century Latin and German editions and issues of the indispensable "Great Voyages" and "Small Voyages" of Theodor de Bry were immensely enriched by additions from the Rosenwald Collection, which also contains the second 1590 edition of Thomas Hariot's *A Briefe and True Report of the New Found Land of Virginia,* the first volume of de Bry. Many of the seventeenth-century and eighteenth-century books are milestones in the history of cartography, astronomy, and navigation.

The Rosenwald Collection sustains and stimulates research in several fields related to the history of discovery, such as bibliography, the history of printing, literature, geography, cartography, and art history. Researcher can gain a more comprehensive appreciation of the collection by consulting the several Library of Congress publications that have been devoted to it over the years. The essential guide to be consulted is the Library's *The Lessing J. Rosenwald Collection: A Catalog of the Gifts of Lessing J. Rosenwald to the Library of Congress, 1943 to 1975* (Washington: Library of Congress, 1977. xxi, 517 p. Z881.U5 1977).

■ OTHER COLLECTIONS

Space limitations preclude further detailed description of the several dozen additional collections maintained by the Rare Book and Special Collections Division. What can be included here is this listing of a few more of the treasures and the collections in which they are found:

Christopher Colombo. *Epistola de indulis nuper inventis.* [Rome, Stephan Planck, after 29 April 1493]. (This Latin translation of Columbus's letter to Sánchez was the edition that spread the news of his discovery throughout Europe, see the illustration in Chapter 4 herein. [Incunabula Collection]

[Oviedo y Valdés, Gonzelo Fernández de]. *La historia generale las Indias . . .* [1535]. (This is the first book that contains illustrations engraved from drawings made in the New World, see the illustrations in Chapter 4 herein.) [Rare Book Collection]

Joel Barlow. *The Vision of Columbus: A Poem in Nine Books.* Hartford, 1787. (This grandiose epic celebrating the discovery and the future hopes of America was later enlarged and embellished as Barlow's colossal *Columbiad* (1807). [American Imprints Collection]

Juan Bautista Muñoz. *Historia del Nuevo-Mundo.* Madrid, 1793. (In 1779 King Charles III of Spain requested Muñoz, chief cosmographer of the Indies, to write a history of Spanish discoveries and conquests in the New World using government and private archives previously unavailable to scholars. The portrait of Columbus, which Muñoz selected as best representing Ferdinand Columbus's description of his father, was engraved from an original painting belonging to the Duke of Berwick y Liria, illustrated in Chapter 4 herein). [Pre-1801 Collection]

The Rare Book and Special Collections Reading Room is located on the second floor of the Jefferson Building and is open to the public from 8:30 A.M. to 5:00 P.M. on weekdays only. For information write or telephone (202) 707-5434. Because so much of the division's material is ephemeral in format or is part of special collections which have been cataloged within the division, only a portion of the total holdings is represented in the Main Catalog of the Library of Congress. In the Rare Book and Special Collections Reading Room you will find a card catalog containing 650,000 cards that provide access to almost the whole of the division's collections by author or other form of main entry and in some instances by subject and title also. In addition to this central card catalog, the division has created over one hundred special card files describing individual collections or special aspects of books from many collections. These special aspect files provide access by means not available in the regular catalogs and so are well worth seeking out.

GEOGRAPHY AND MAP DIVISION

The roots of this division go deep, and today its collections cover a landscape larger than the earth itself. The modern location of the division in the James Madison Memorial Building is particularly fitting since the first historical roots of the Library of Congress and a division of the Library devoted to maps and geography can be traced to an ad hoc committee of the Continental Congress consisting of James Madison, Hugh Williamson and Thomas Mifflin. On January 24, 1783, the committee recommended the establishment of a congressional library. The report contained a list of books—309 titles arranged in thirteen classes according to subject—and was urgently but unsuccessfully supported by James Madison. Research reported by Loren Eugene Smith in his 1969 Ph.D. dissertation established that Madison was the author of the list and that later, when collaborating in writing *The Federalist*, he relied on a study of these listed sources.

As one might anticipate, many of the books Madison chose for his proposed congressional library dealt with politics, law, and history. His sixth category, however, was devoted to geography and included works by Anton Friedrich Busching, William Guthrie, Thomas Salmon, and Thomas Jeffreys.

Items 73 and 204 in Madison's list of recommended holdings dealt directly with maps and charts. Unfortunately the list provided only the headings "73. *Collections of best maps.*" and "204. *Collections of Best Charts.*" As Dr. Smith noted in his dissertation: Madison, had he chosen to do so, could have selected one of several good collections of maps and charts available at that time to qualify under his headings 73 and 204. There is no indication of why he did not do this but the speculation might be that he intended that care be taken to assure that members of Congress have only the "best" maps and charts

in their reference library when that library was established.

As described above, a Library of Congress came into being in 1800 when the government moved from New York to its new permanent home in the District of Columbia. At its establishment the Library lacked the collections of "best maps and charts" that Madison recommended seventeen years earlier. An inventory of the Library of Congress holdings at the time of its establishment included only three maps and four atlases! Two years later when the first *Catalogue of Books, Maps and Charts Belonging to the Library of the Two Houses of Congress* was published (1802) the cartographic collections had expanded to seven maps and six atlases. A decade later, the Library possessed some fifty maps and an unrecorded number of atlases. These and most of the other holdings of the Library were destroyed in 1814, when British forces burned the Capitol.

In the effort to reconstitute the Library, Thomas Jefferson offered his personal collection of books, maps and other reference materials. Fortunately, Congress approved the purchase and the collection was moved from Monticello to Washington in 1815. As a glance at the recent Library of Congress publication, titled *Thomas Jefferson's Library: A Catalog with the Entries in his Own Order* (1989), will demonstrate, a large number of Jefferson's books dealt with the history of geographical discovery. Ortelius's great atlas *Theatrum Orbis Terrarum*, Amerigo Vespucci's *Letters*, Hakluyt's *Voyages* (first edition), Wytfliet's *Universal History*, Garcilaso de La Vega's *La Florida*, Herrera's *History of the Indies* and *General History*, and Gomara's *Conquest of Mexico and New Spain* are a few of the many items bearing on the Age of Discovery that the Library of Congress acquired from Thomas Jefferson, third president of the United States and namesake of the Library's main building.

During the decades that followed the Jefferson reconstitution, the Library continued to acquire maps and books of a geographical nature. In 1851 a fire swept through the Library's rooms in the Capitol destroying some thirty-five thousand books and "nearly all our extensive collection of Maps." During the 1850s, three unofficial proposals to establish a separate map department in the Library were advanced. The first was made by Lt. Edward B. Hunt at the annual meeting of the American Association for the Advancement of Science, held in Cleveland from July 28 to August 2, 1853. Lieutenant Hunt, who was then on detail to the U.S. Coast Survey, complained that "no [map] collection exists in our land which furnishes full material for extensive investigations, such as are now more and more demanded by questions of history, science, commerce, and policy." He proposed, therefore, that there be established, preferably at the Library of Congress, "a complete and special geographical library . . . [which] would be a valuable aid to all . . . researchers." Because of the difficulties he experienced in conducting his personal research, Lieutenant Hunt further stressed the need "to arrange complete and systematic indexes and catalogs, which would at once make known all the materials so arranged as best to facilitate special research."

Johann Georg Kohl, an eminent German geographer and Americanist, reiterated two years later the need for a systematic cartographic collection. His "Substance of a Lecture delivered at the Smithsonian Institution on a Collection of Charts and Maps of America" was published in the 1857 annual report of the Smithsonian.

Professor Daniel Coit Gilman of Yale University included a plea for a federal map collection in an article entitled "The Last Ten Years of Geographical Work in this Country," published in the *Journal of the American Geographic Society* (vol. 3, 1872). Gilman acknowledged that "many

able officers of the government [were] engaged in investigations of the highest value to mankind, [but] much of their usefulness is impaired by the defective arrangements for gathering up, presenting and distributing to the public the results thus ascertained. They likewise point to the importance" Gilman continued, "of having established in Washington, or elsewhere, as a department of the general government, a bureau of maps and charts and geographical memoirs, where all these vast accumulations may be stored, classified and rendered accessible, like the books in the library of Congress . . . so that persons who have the right may make inquiry respecting them."

Regrettably, the successive recommendations of Hunt, Kohl, and Gilman were not acted upon, and several more decades passed before a separate map department was established in the Library of Congress. Nonetheless, during these years the cartographic collections of the Library continued to be augmented through various acquisitions. The volume of accessions, in all formats, increased greatly following passage of the Copyright Act in 1870, which required mandatory deposit in the Library of Congress of two copies of all copyrighted publications.

Several noteworthy collections of maps were acquired by purchase before 1897. The earliest such accession was the Faden Collection which includes 101 manuscript and printed maps relating to the French and Indian War and the American Revolution. The maps, many of which were drawn by British military engineers, had formed part of the working collection of William Faden, foremost English map publisher during the last quarter of the eighteenth century. A special congressional appropriation of $1,000 was voted on July 2, 1864, to purchase the Faden Collection from Edward Everett Hale.

In 1867 the Congress purchased for the Library, at a cost of $100,000, the notable collection which had been assembled by Peter Force, distinguished archivist and Americanist. In addition to extensive and valuable holdings of books, pamphlets, manuscripts, journals, and newspapers, the Force purchase included more than twelve hundred maps and views. The maps greatly enriched the Library's cartographic holdings. After more than a century of collecting and growth, Force items are still among the rarest treasures in the map collections.

Before the establishment of federal mapping agencies, maps prepared under official authorization were included as supplements in published congressional document series. The maps were printed on contract by various engravers and lithographers. In 1843 some hundred and fifty congressional series maps were assembled and bound in a large folio volume, now in the Geography and Map Division. Although an inscription states that "this is not a complete collection of maps, charts &c., published by order of Congress," the volume provides an excellent cross section of U.S. official mapping over a period of more than two decades.

In 1875, Philip Lee Phillips joined the staff of the Library of Congress as a cataloger. The youngest son of a prominent Washington, D.C., lawyer and one-time member of Congress, Phillips had been enrolled briefly as a student at Columbian College of Law but had displayed little interest in legal studies. The elder Phillips arranged for him to work at the Library of Congress and, in fact, for almost four years supplied the funds to pay his salary.

Phillips's duties apparently included servicing books and general maintenance of the collections, in addition to cataloging. Early in his career he became painfully aware of the disorganized state of the Library's cartographic materials. In such time that he could spare from his regular duties, Phillips began to organize and catalog the Library's maps and atlases. Because

of these efforts and his growing knowledge of maps, their history, and their makers, Phillips came to be recognized as the cartographic specialist. By the time the Library's new building opened in 1897, he had compiled an extensive *List of Maps of America in the Library of Congress,* which was published in 1901. The volume also included a comprehensive bibliography on the literature of cartography. These evidences of his specialized interest and knowledge strengthened Phillips's candidacy for the position of superintendent of the newly created Hall of Maps and Charts, to which he was appointed in 1897.

After the maps were transferred from the Library's rooms in the Capitol to the new building, Phillips estimated that the collection included 47,000 maps and almost 1,200 atlases. The new superintendent initiated various projects to stimulate accessions. In 1902, for example, he sent letters of solicitation to postmasters in the administrative cities of some 2,867 counties. The same year he wrote to official mapping agencies in various foreign countries requesting that their publications be deposited in the Library of Congress on a regular basis.

A year later he recommended to the Librarian "that permanent special agents, whose interest and experiences qualify them, shall be retained to look at and report on the latest map publications in Europe and in South and Central America. An ordinary agent or bookseller is not satisfactory. A cartographer or map dealer who will not only act as agent but as a bureau of cartographical information is needed. Map publications, even when issued for governments, frequently escape our attention for a time, because so little is published concerning maps. An agent such as recommended should make use of his business not only to execute orders, but to keep the Division informed on matters related to cartography." There is no evidence that this recommendation was heeded. Some forty years later, however, the Library's Map Division, in cooperation with various federal mapping agencies and libraries, established a cooperative foreign map procurement program along the lines proposed by Phillips.

During Phillips's tenure, the cartographic collections were also augmented by transfers of noncurrent maps and atlases from various federal libraries. Of particular note is a large collection of nineteenth-century county maps and atlases which were transferred by the Coast and Geodetic Survey in 1900. Phillips was also instrumental in acquiring a large number of sheets of large- and medium-scale map series published by Great Britain's Ordnance Survey.

Perhaps Phillips's greatest contribution to the Library's strength in Age of Discovery holdings came in the form of his efforts toward increasing the collection of rare maps and atlases. To achieve this goal he maintained contacts with major European dealers in out-of-print publications. In 1907, 1908, and 1909 he made summer trips to Europe, at his own expense, for the purpose of visiting antique dealers and bookshops. On these expeditions he purchased for the Library's collections many distinctive items at prices which represent but a minute fraction of their present monetary value.

During his entire professional career, Philip Lee Phillips's interests were primarily American and antiquarian, and this is reflected in the Library's early cartographic acquisitions. He was, in short, more concerned with quality than quantity. In his 1907 report, for example, he noted that "while the accessions show an extensive increase in number, the value of the material is not as great as in former years, especially the last year as the opportunity offered of gathering material was helped considerably by a trip to Europe. The Map Division, from its collection and recent accessions," Phillips observed, "is reaching that condition of completeness when only very rare material is needed."

Phillips's successor, Col. Lawrence Martin, was a professional geographer, with specializations in the physical and military aspects of the discipline. Martin's personal interests were in boundary studies and political geography, and he was also seriously concerned with strengthening the Library's holdings of official set and series maps. Martin's experiences in World War I had introduced him to European map series, many of which he subsequently acquired for the Library. He also established contacts with officials in U.S. mapping agencies and greatly increased the influx of maps and charts from these sources. Martin's studies of boundaries and of several maps utilized in international treaties stimulated an interest in historical maps. This was reflected in successful projects to obtain photocopies of manuscript maps relating to America from various European and American libraries and archives.

During World War II all federal mapping agencies, as well as most commercial map publishers, were engaged in preparing military maps and charts. Moreover, distributions of many cartographic publications were rigidly restricted during the war years. These conditions were reflected in decreased accessions in the Map Division from 1940 to 1944.

With victory won, military agencies deposited in the Library of Congress selected issues of World War II maps. Map accessions for fiscal year 1945 accordingly passed 58,000 as compared with 7,000 in 1942. Following V-E Day (May 8, 1945) and V-J Day (September 2, 1945), there was rapid contraction of various wartime offices and agencies. Some map libraries, assembled to support various military and intelligence programs, were deactivated, and the Library's Map Division fell heir to their collections. Large military cartographic libraries weeded their holdings and transferred large quantities of maps and charts to the Library. More than seventy-five thousand sheets were accessioned in fiscal 1947, and additional volumes of transferred material, which could not be processed by the small staff, were stored in the unfinished attic of the Adams Building.

Wartime demands had revealed significant gaps in the division's cartographic holdings, particularly in large- and medium-scale foreign topographic series. With the objectives of filling such gaps and reestablishing and expanding foreign exchanges, the Map Division joined with the Department of State and other federal cartographic agencies and libraries to establish a cooperative foreign map procurement program. The Interagency Map and Publication Acquisitions Committee (IMPAC), organized in 1946, is still functioning. The cartographic acquisitions program, coordinated through the Department of State's Office of Map and Publication Procurement, supports geographic attachés in several American embassies, as well as a number of Washington-based cartographic specialists, who make periodic procurement missions to selected countries. For the past quarter century more than 90 percent of the Library's foreign cartographic accessions, both exchanges and purchases, have come via IMPAC channels.

Most of the maps, charts, and atlases in the Geography and Map Division (G&M) are in the general cartographic collections. Some of the more distinctive and valuable holdings are preserved in a large, 5,000-square-foot masonry vault, which is equipped with independent temperature and humidity controls. Among treasures in the vault are a number of cartographic groups which are maintained as special collections. Of particular interest to researchers concerned with Age of Discovery maps are the Kohl, Lowery, Harrisse, and Vellum Chart Collections.

▪ VELLUM CHART COLLECTION

The Library's collection of nautical charts on vellum is a modest but important one. It includes representative works of a number of the major schools of chartmakers and allows opportunity for an evolutionary study of European navigation through a period of some four centuries. All of the charts are filed together in G&M's vault and are available for study by serious researchers. The collection includes the following charts from the fifteenth and sixteenth centuries:

1 *Mediterranean Sea.* Francesco and Marco Pizigano, Venezia, 1367. (Ms, copy made in 1802)

2 *World.* Abraham Cresques, [Majorca], 1375. (Modern facsimile on vellum and hand colored)

3 *Mediterranean Sea.* Anonymous, [Genoa?, ca. 1320–50?]

4 *Europe and Mediterranean.* Arnaldo Domenech, [Siena?], 1484.

5 *World.* Battista Agnese, ca. 1544. (Portolan atlas)

6 *Mediterranean and western Europe.* Jaume Olives, Marseille, 1550.

7 *Mediterranean and western Europe.* Mateo Prunes, Majorca, 1559. (Facsimile with notes available from the Library of Congress)

8 *World, Europe and Mediterranean Sea.* [Joan Martines?], [Messina?], [ca. 1560]. (Attributed to Juan Oliva; available in facsimile from the Library of Congress)

9 and 10 Two charts of *Central and South American Pacific Coast.* Anonymous, unknown, 16th century.

11 *Mediterranean Sea, northwest Europe, northwest Africa.* Giacomo Scotto, [Civita Vecchia?], [ca. 1590?].

12 *Mediterranean Sea.* Anonymous, [Messina?], 16th century.

13 *Mediterranean Sea.* Anonymous, [Italian], 16th century.

14 *Mediterranean Sea.* Placido Oliva, [Messina?], 16th century.

The number of tentative entries, circas, and question marks included in this short list suggests the research challenges that this one small collection of original navigation charts from the Age of Discovery holds for the interested and qualified researcher. For more information about the Vellum Chart Collection consult the Library's 1977 publication compiled by Walter W. Ristow and R. A. Skelton titled, *Nautical Charts on Vellum in the Library of Congress.*

■ HENRY HARRISSE COLLECTION

Henry Harrisse (1829–1910) bequeathed to the Library of Congress in 1915 more than six hundred tracings and pencil sketches of old maps relating to the discovery and exploration of America, as well as fourteen rare manuscript maps. The tracings and pencil sketches were prepared by Harrisse when he was compiling his *Bibliotheca Americana Vetustissima,* originally published in New York in 1866. This noteworthy reference work, which is subtitled *A Description of Works Relating to America Published Between the Years 1492 and 1551,* was reprinted in 1967 by Argonaut, Inc., of Chicago.

The manuscript maps included in the bequest were part of Harrisse's personal library and include several notable treasures. Most distinctive is Champlain's original manuscript map of New England and Nova Scotia, drawn on vellum and dated 1607 (see Chapter 3 herein). It is considered to be the most important of Champlain's large maps. Along the coast are noted, in his own hand, explorations of 1604, 1605, and 1606. Clearly shown on the map is the river which Champlain called St. Croix, as well as Cape Sable and Port Royal. An anonymous vellum map in the Harrisse bequest, entitled "Description dv pais des Hvrons, 1631," is based on one of the very early surveys of the country between Georgian Bay, Lake Simcoe, and Lake Ontario, including the Saugeen Peninsula and

part of Lower Ontario. The map may have been made to show the extent and location of established missions. It reflects characteristics which may indicate Native American input in its original compilation. Also in the bequest were manuscript maps of parts of North and South America, drawn in 1639 by Joan Vingboons, cartographer to the Prince of Nassau. Of particular interest is Vingboons's so-called Manatus map of 1639, which is the earliest cartographic representation of Manhattan Island. The maps bequeathed by Harrisse are not yet cataloged but plans are underway for them to be listed in the Harrisse Collection finding aid mentioned in the Rare Book and Special Collections Division discussion above.

In the custody of the Rare Book and Special Collections Division are some two hundred and twenty volumes and pamphlets, as well as several boxes of charts and notes, which also came to the Library with the Harrisse bequest. Information about Harrisse and his bibliographical methods is given in Randolph G. Adams's *Three Americanists* (Philadelphia, 1939) and in Frederick R. Goff's "Henry Harrisse: Americanist" published in the *Inter-American Review of Bibliography* (vol. 3, no. 1, 1953); and in Richard W. Stephenson's "The Henry Harrisse Collection of Publications, Papers, and Maps Pertaining to the Early Exploration of America" published in *Terra Incognitae* (vol. 16, 1984).

■ JOHANN GEORG KOHL COLLECTION

The Kohl Collection consists of a series of skillfully executed manuscript copies of maps significant in the history of cartography up to 1834. The 474 maps, with descriptive notes in Kohl's fine hand, are mounted on acid-free paper backed with muslin. Names, legends, drawings, and symbols are, for the most part, in black ink. On some maps a blue wash has been applied to large rivers and along the coasts. The plates vary considerably in size. The maps were prepared by Johann Georg Kohl, nineteenth-century German historian, librarian, and Americanist, who brought his valuable collection of maps to the United States in 1854. The U.S. Congress made a grant of $6,000 to Kohl in 1856 to prepare copies of his maps for American scholars as the basis for a catalog of early maps of America. Kohl's drawings were originally deposited in the Department of State but were transferred to the Library of Congress in July 1903. Justin Winsor's detailed description of the collection was published in 1886 by the Harvard University Library as its "Bibliographic Contribution No. 19." Winsor's monograph was reissued by the Library of Congress in 1904 as *The Kohl Collection (now in the Library of Congress) of Maps Relating to America,* with an index by Philip Lee Phillips. Many of the maps, which were so laboriously and carefully hand copied by Kohl, have subsequently been published in facsimile editions. The Kohl copies are, therefore, less in demand today, although his annotations are still of interest and value. The Kohl Collection is briefly described in Walter W. Ristow's "Recent Facsimile Maps and Atlases," in the July 1967 issue of the *Quarterly Journal of the Library of Congress,* and in John Wolter's "Johann Georg Kohl and America" in the December 1981 issue of *The Map Collector.*

Among other Kohl manuscripts in the custody of the Geography and Map Division are *Chart of the Gulf Stream, Map of the Progress of the Discovery of the Gulf of Mexico,* and notes and sketches relating to his studies of the U.S. coasts and bordering oceans. For two examples of Kohl's facsimile cartography see Chapter 5 herein.

■ WOODBURY LOWERY COLLECTION

The Lowery Collection was acquired in 1905 through the bequest of Woodbury Lowery, who had made an extensive study of early maps of the Spanish settlements within the present limits of the United States. Lowery's research, carried on over a long period of years, resulted in a two-volume publication on the subjects. The list of maps compiled by Lowery includes 740 titles, of which some 300 were in his personal map collection. Approximately two hundred additional maps on the list were in the collection of the Map Division in 1906. All but fifty or sixty of the remaining maps on Lowery's original list have subsequently been added to the collection, either as originals or in photoreproductions. In 1912 the Library published *A Descriptive List of Maps of the Spanish Possessions Within the Present Limit of the United States, 1502–1820* by Woodbury Lowery, edited by Philip Lee Phillips.

■ ATLASES

The atlas collection numbers about 42,000 titles (50,000 volumes) and increases yearly by about 1,000 volumes, representing the largest collection in the world. If the average atlas contains about 150 maps, the atlas collection makes available another 7.2 million individual map sheets to the scholar. Atlases are also classified according to the G schedule and all have been cataloged, although all titles do not appear in the MARC data base. In addition to the catalog shelflist and MARC records, some twenty thousand atlases acquired before 1973 are described in Clara Egli LeGear's *United States Atlases* (Washington, Library of Congress, 2 volumes, 1950–53) and Philip Lee Phillips and LeGear's *A List of Geographical Atlases in the Library of Congress with Bibliographic Notes* (Washington, Library of Congress, 8 volumes issued between 1909 and 1974). A comprehensive author list to the eight-volume work was published by LC in 1992.

The collection includes general geographical atlases of the world or individual regions, countries, states, and counties, as well as thematic or special purpose atlases that display aeronautic, climatic, ecclesiastic, economic, ethnographic, geologic, historic, linguistic, military, oceanographic, physical, and other data.

All periods and publishers are represented. An examination of the atlas shelf list reveals that 1246 atlases were published before 1799, including six atlases issued between 1475 and 1499, 133 during the sixteenth century, and 325 during the eighteenth century. For the period before 1599, the following cartographers and publishers are represented: Battista Agnese; Giulio Ballino; Benedetto Bordone (3); Giovanni Botero (6); Maurice Bouguereau; Georg Braun (2); Giovanni Camocio (2); Antoine Du Pinet; Hugo Favolius; Nicolaus Gerbel; Lodovico Guicciardini (3); Pieter Heylyn (3); Gerard de Jode; Jacob de La Feuille; Antoine Lafrery (5); Barent Langenes; Conrad Low; Gerard Mercator (10); Abraham Ortelius (39); Tomaso Porcacchi (3); Claudius Ptolemaeus (34); Matthias Quad (3); Adrianus Romanus; Christopher Saxton (2); Francesco Valesio; Lucas J. Waghenaer (4); and Corneille Wytfliet (2).

While the majority of atlases in G&M are printed, there are a small number in manuscript. Noteworthy examples include João Teixeira's secret maps of the Americas and the Indies from the Portuguese Archives, 1630; Agnese's atlas of portolan charts of the world on vellum, 1544; Giacomo Scotto's portolan atlas of Northwest Europe, circa 1590; a Chinese atlas of the world, Ming Period (1368–1644); a Korean atlas of China, circa 1721; an atlas of plans of military fortifications in Guadeloupe, 1768; Alexandre Gonzales's maritime atlas of the coast of Peru and Chile, 1787–1797; an atlas of maps of cities and ports made during the Portuguese occupation of Ceylon, circa 1620; two atlases of "running charts of the upper course of the Yukon River," 1913–1923; and a large-scale atlas of an English rural estate, 1767; and William Hacke's "A Description of the Sea Coast,

Rivers . . ." drawn about 1690 (see Phillips, no. 162 for particulars on this atlas that covers the Indian Ocean and the East Indies). The atlas collection also includes facsimiles and photocopies of rare atlases from other repositories. Some representative examples are: a photocopy of Ptolemaeus's *Geographie*, 1440, from the John Carter Brown Library; a collection of reproductions of twenty-four Agnese portolan atlases from various European repositories, 1563–1564, the English Pilot, 1689, from the Massachusetts Historical Society; and a photocopy of a manuscript atlas of Brazil by João Teixeira, 1631, from the Mapoteca of the ministerio das Relacoes Exteriores, Rio de Janeiro.

- GLOBES

Original and facsimile terrestrial globes 1543–1980s (185 globes), celestial globes, 1816–1964 (25 globes), thematic globes, chiefly topographic, 1938–1976 (31 globes), and globe gores are included in the division's collection. Particularly noteworthy are Caspar Vopell's manuscript globe with armillary spheres depicting the Ptolemaic concept of the universe, 1543; and unmounted globe gores prepared by Vincenzo Maria Coronelli, 1688, and Jodocus Hondiüs, 1615. Large terrestrial (1692) and celestial (1693) globes, each approximately 110 cm. in diameter and hand painted by Vincenzo Coronelli, are on permanent display in the sixth floor lobby of the Madison Building.

There are also many individual maps in the collections which have significance for the discovery and exploration period. A number are described in Clara E. LeGear's "Maps of Early America," published originally in the November 1950 issue of the *Library of Congress Quarterly Journal of Current Acquisitions* and reprinted in *A la Carte, Selected Papers on Maps and Atlases* (Library of Congress, 1972).

Of major interest to the early history of Mexico is the "Oztoticpac Lands Map of Texcoco, 1540," a hand-drawn pictorial plan of an Aztec estate in the Valley of Mexico (see Chapter 3 herein). A detailed study of the map and its significance by the late Howard F. Cline, former director of the Library's Hispanic Foundation, was published in the April 1966 issue of the *Quarterly Journal of the Library of Congress*. Dr. Cline's article has also been reprinted in *A la Carte*.

Among other noteworthy early American maps described in *A la Carte* are Capt. John Smith's "Map of Virginia, 1612" (see Chapter 3 herein), Augustine Herrman's "Map of Virginia and Maryland, 1673," and a series of manuscript maps based on boundary surveys made by Spanish commissioners in accordance with provisions of the Treaty of San Ildefonso, signed by Portugal and Spain on October 1, 1777.

Supplementing the original manuscript and printed maps of the discovery and exploration period are photoreproductions of manuscript maps preserved in various European archives. Of particular note is the Karpinski Collection, which includes photocopies of unique manuscript maps in French, Spanish, and Portuguese archives which bear upon the early history of the American colonies. The 750 photoreproductions were secured through the efforts of the late Louis C. Karpinski, student of cartographical history and one-time professor of mathematics at the University of Michigan. The Karpinski photocopies are not retained as a unit, and the individual maps are filed with the appropriate administrative or geographical units. A list of all the Karpinski reproductions is available for consultation in the Geography and Map Reading Room. Duplicate sets of the Karpinski series are preserved in the William L. Clements, Henry E. Huntington, New York Public, and Newberry Libraries. A note by Dr. Karpinski describing the collection was published in the January 1928 issue of *American Historical Review*.

Also in G&M are reproductions of manuscript maps relating to North America preserved in the Archivo General de Indias in Seville, Spain. The original maps are described in Pedro Torres Lanzas's *Relación de los Mapas, Planos, &, de Mexico y Floridas Existentes en el Archivo General de Indias, 1900*.

Before closing this discussion of G&M attention should be directed to the division's comfortably appointed reading room located on the basement level in the green quadrant of the Madison Building. On open stacks and easily available to researchers are some eight thousand books, serials, and pamphlets relating to cartography, surveying, and geographical discovery. Of particular interest for researchers interested in the Age of Discovery are the current and back issues of the journals *Terrae Incognitae* and *Imago Mundi*. The first is the journal of the Society for the History of Discoveries and the second is published by the International Society for the History of Cartography. Information on both of these groups can be obtained from the G&M staff, many of whom are members of one or both organizations. Open stack materials are listed in the division card catalog, while vertical file materials are included in the seven-volume G. K. Hall publication, *Bibliography of Cartography*, found in most research libraries. A number of other card catalogs and published finding aids are available to help the researcher find the materials he or she needs. The G&M Reading Room is staffed with trained map librarians and is open to the public from 8:30 A.M. to 5:00 P.M. on weekdays and from 8:30 A.M. to 12:30 P.M. on Saturdays. Coin operated copy machines are available and scholars may take photographs of maps and other materials with their own cameras and available light.

A general introduction to the division and its resources is Walter W. Ristow's *The Geography and Map Division: A Guide to Its Collections and Services* (Washington: Library of Congress, 1975).

A list of the division's publications is available upon request. It describes almost seventy monographs, exhibit catalogs, checklists, short lists, article reprints, map facsimiles, microforms, and computer tapes issued by the division. Information regarding the maps online data base is provided in *MARC Formats for Bibliographic Data*, which is available from the Cataloging Distribution Service, Library of Congress, Washington, D.C. 20541. The G&M Reading Room telephone number is (202) 707-6277 (707-MAPS).

MANUSCRIPT DIVISION

The Manuscript Division of the Library of Congress is housed in the James Madison Memorial Building and it has custody of more than forty million items organized in from ten to eleven thousand collections. The division traces its roots back to the handwritten seventeenth-century records of the Virginia Company which were included among the materials acquired from Thomas Jefferson in 1815. Since that time the division has become "a major repository of the nation's memory."

The manuscripts in the collection are almost by definition unique, extraordinarily valuable, and essentially held in trust for the nation; they must therefore be used with care. Most are available, however, to anyone engaged in serious research. When you come to use the materials, you will be asked to register and to present proper identification, preferably with a photograph attached.

As you use the collections, the Library requests that you take unusual care that the existing order and arrangement of unbound materials be maintained, that sheets be handled by their margins (to avoid fingerprints and natural oils affecting the handwritten text), and that you use microfilm copies of collections when such editions exist.

In addition to the rare manuscripts, since 1905 the division has been accumulating copies of materials in other institutions around the world. In the early decades it sent copiers to duplicate by hand materials that bore on the progress of American history. With the development of microfilm copying techniques, photographic technicians have taken the place of the hand copiers, and between the two the division has great quantities of duplicated documents from such depositories as the Archives of the Indies in Seville (which record the Spanish colonization of America), early British colonial reports from the Public Record Office in London, records of the Society for the Propagation of the Gospel (minutely detailed reports sent to England from each parish on the American frontier in the seventeenth and eighteenth centuries), war reports from Hessian officers to their home governments during the Revolution, to cite just a few examples. All of these materials were collected to be used; they are in the division to help American scholarship achieve a better understanding of our past.

Manuscripts are arranged, as a rule, either chronologically by the date they were written or alphabetically by the name of the person who wrote them. While there is no general card catalog or index to all forty million manuscript items in the Library's holdings, descriptions of individual collections of manuscripts are available. For some fifteen hundred or so larger collections, the staff of the Manuscript Division has prepared individual "registers" or typed (and sometimes printed) narrative descriptions, which give details about the "provenance" (or source) of the collections; literary rights or copyright interests, when known; biographical information about the principal individuals whose papers are included; the scope and content of the collection; and lists of folder titles, containers, or other descriptions of the manuscripts which are included. For some collections—especially smaller collections and collections of presidential papers—catalogs or indexes of individual manuscript items are available; and, in addition, many subject guides to special fields of research interest have been prepared to help guide readers to rich sources of information in the manuscript holdings.

The Manuscript Division has a professional staff of historians who are available for consultation with visiting researchers. These scholars' specific areas of expertise are as follows: early American history to 1825; the National period to 1861; Civil War and Reconstruction to 1900; twentieth-century political history; cultural and scientific history; and Afro-American history and culture. Appointments can be made at the registration desk for individual consultation with these specialists.

In addition to the catalogs and registers, the division has special indexes to individual collections; a bound master record which provides current bibliographical data on all the collections; and an inventory, arranged by country, repository, and archival file, of the collection of foreign reproductions. The reading room also maintains a reference collection of materials relating to the individuals and periods represented by the manuscripts in the division's custody.

The Library has prepared published finding aids which, of course, are available in the reading room, but are also commonly in college and public libraries, and you may wish to examine them before coming to Washington. Among these are *National Union Catalog of Manuscript Collections* (annual since 1959) and *Manuscripts on Microfilm: A Checklist* (1975).

Unbound manuscripts may be photocopied, and there are coin-operated copy machines and microprinters in the reading room. Bound manuscripts can be copied through the Library's Photoduplication Service. Reproductions of manuscripts in foreign repositories and manuscripts on microfilm can usually be borrowed on interlibrary loan, and therefore can be consulted in the researcher's home community. Typewriters, tape recorders, and cameras are permitted.

The reader may have noted that the professional staff of historian-consultants available to provide specialized assistance in using the Manuscript Division's collections does not include anyone with expertise in the period of the Age of Discovery. This omission reflects the philosophy that has guided the division's development since its inception. It is a philosophy that emphasizes but does not restrict acquisition policies to those manuscripts forming "the papers of those men and women who, throughout the centuries, have most profoundly influenced the lives and destinies of their countrymen." Note the hint of a nationalistic bias in this quotation from David Mearns in *Guide to The Library of Congress,* published in 1988 (p. 101).

In spite of being skewed toward papers and collections created by Americans influential in the historical shaping of the United States, the Library of Congress has several manuscript collections containing masses of material of direct concern to researchers investigating aspects of the Age of Discovery. Much of that material can be found in the following manuscript collections.

■ PETER FORCE COLLECTION

Peter Force was a distinguished American historian and architect living in the first half of the nineteenth century. During the 1840s and 1850s Force began collecting manuscripts and other materials for a major publication project. Had his plans materialized, Peter Force would have published these materials in the first series of the projected *American Archives* which were to cover the period from the discovery and settlement of the American Colonies to the Revolution in England in 1688. This series was never published.

In 1867 Congress authorized a special appropriation of $100,000 for the purchase of the Library of Peter Force for the Library of Congress. In his Special Report to Congress's Joint Committee on the Library, then Librarian of Congress Ainsworth R. Spofford wrote of "the largest private collection ever brought together, having been formed by Mr. Force with special reference to assembling the fullest materials for editing his American Archives . . ." Spofford continued, "His library embraces an immense collection of the early American voyages in Latin, French, Italian, Spanish, German, Dutch, and English, while in books and pamphlets relating to the politics and government of the American colonies, it stands unrivalled in this country. In the field of early printed American books, so much sought for by collectors, and which are becoming annually more scarce and costly, this library possesses more than ten times the number to be found in the Library of Congress . . ."

The Force Library was, through necessity, dispersed, but the most important manuscript documents are in the care of the Manuscript Division at the Library of Congress. While Peter Force's eighteen portfolios of personal correspondence covering the period from 1812 to 1868 and other papers are of considerable interest, it is the group of manuscripts identified as the Force "Hispanic Collection, 1527–1811," that will be of most immediate interest to those doing research on the Age of Discovery. In the Manuscript Reading Room the researcher should refer to the two large three-ring binders that were compiled in 1964 by Howard F. Cline and titled, "Reference Guide to Hispanic Manuscripts in the Library of Congress." In Cline's "Reference Guide" the Force materials are found under "Series 8." The collection consists primarily of transcripts of various early Spanish writers concerning the New World. The transcribed works span the period from about 1527 (the early writings of Bishop Bartolomé de Las Casas) to 1811

(the trial of the revolutionary priest Miguel Hidalgo y Costilla). The guide lists the works alphabetically by major author except for those works where the author is unknown. Since many of these transcriptions were made in the eighteenth century from European originals, they are documents worthy of study in their own right as well as for the accounts and descriptions they contain. Particularly noteworthy are the illustrated Force transcriptions such as entry number 11, "Relacion de las ceremonies y ritos y poblacion y gobernacion de las Indios, de la Provincia de Mechoacán" (see illustrations in Chapters 3 and 5 herein).

■ HARKNESS COLLECTION

Widely considered one of the Library of Congress's most valuable and important gifts of Spanish American manuscripts and documents, the Harkness Collection was presented by the American philanthropist Edward Stephen Harkness in two installments, December 4, 1925, and October 15, 1929. The manuscripts are chiefly from the first two centuries of Spanish American history and fall into two groups: one relating to the early history of the Spanish in Peru, and the other to their early history in Mexico.

Two works on the Harkness Peruvian manuscripts were published by the Library of Congress in 1932 and 1936 respectively. They are: *The Harkness Collection in the Library of Congress, Calendar of Spanish Manuscripts Concerning Peru, 1531–1651* (Washington, 1932), and *The Harkness Collection in the Library of Congress: Documents from Early Peru, the Pizarros and the Almagros, 1531–1578* (Washington, 1936). As a perusal of these guides will quickly reveal, there are few aspects of the early history and life of Spanish Peru which are not illuminated in one way or another in these thousand and more documents dating from 1531 to 1651. With the exception of a number of cedulas of Charles V and Philip II, the documents originated in Peru. Most of them are originals, preserved by notaries, while notarial copies were sent to Spain. They come from persons in all walks of life, from the Pizarros and Almagros, the viceroys and bishops, to secretaries and merchants, pilots and sailors, schoolmasters and widows. They include decrees and proclamations of viceroys, orders and instructions of officers to subordinates, contracts and agreements, commercial accounts and letters, minutes of municipalities, manumissions, and many other varieties of documents.

A few specific instances may illustrate the richness of this collection and how it touches on the Age of Discovery beyond Peru. For example, besides the long series of documents of the Pizarros and Almagros which show the processes of conquest in Peru from 1531 on, there is the claim put forward by Diego Almagro the younger on account of the killing of his father. There is the imposing tailor's bill of Hernando de Soto. There is the long protest (1554) of some sixty of the chief notables among the conquerors against the new ordinance restricting personal services from the Indians which had been promulgated by Charles V, under the influence of Bishop Las Casas. There are the record books of two frontier municipalities, begun in 1538 and 1539, respectively. There are provisions regarding protection against the "Lutheran corsairs" of Francis Drake and the service of Indian runners to give warnings of his approach. There are announcements of royal endowment of the University of San Marcos at Lima and of provision for a chair of Indian languages, with injunction that priests and missionaries must learn the language of their flocks. In short, all the round of human life in old Peru finds illustration in the collection.

The greater part of the Mexican group of manuscripts relates to the conquistador Hernando Cortés and his sons. Approximately two-

thirds of the Cortés documents concern the proceedings before the Audiencia of Mexico and a special commission (1566–68) in twelve criminal suits against alleged participation in the so-called Avila-Cortés conspiracy to overthrow the government of New Spain and crown the second Marqués del Valle. These twelve proceedings have been published, in part, by Manuel Orozco y Berra in his *Noticia histórica de la conjuración del Marquéz del Valle, años de 1565– 1568* (Mexico, 1853).

Although Orozco y Berra stated that the Avila-Cortés documents were in the collection of José Maria Andrade in 1853, it is clear that the papers in the Harkness Collection relating to Cortés were owned at that time by one of the heirs of the conquistador, the Duke of Terranova y Monteleone, and later by his son, Prince Antonio Pignatelli. The prince was a patron of the Hospital de la Immaculada Concepcion y de Jesús Nazareno in Mexico City, and his private archive was housed there for many years. In 1926 the two royal grants now in the Harkness Collection were returned to Prince Pignatelli.

The Mexican portion of the Harkness Collection of manuscripts falls into three principal categories, with a smaller, fourth group of unrelated items. The earliest group of documents concerns the affairs of Don Hernando Cortés and his family and the lands in Oaxaca that formed the basis for his title of Marqués del Valle. The oldest of these manuscripts is dated 1525, when the Habsburg Emperor Charles V, who was also King Charles I of Spain, granted a special coat of arms to Don Hernando Cortés. The latest is dated 1565, when Don Martin, the second Marqués del Valle and son of Don Hernando, asked for permission to present evidence to counter a distinctly unfriendly attitude toward him that was becoming apparent in the Council of the Indies.

The second large group of documents, accounting for the largest volume of pages, concerns the purported Avila-Cortés conspiracy, sometimes referred to as the Encomenderos' Revolt of 1566. These were previously published in part in Spanish, but the questionnaires that bring out most of the evidence put forth in the lawsuit against Don Martin Cortés, Marqués del Valle, are included in this guide in full transcription and translation. The calendar entry for this manuscript gives in greater detail the names of witnesses on the side of the Marqués and of the audiencia. Some of the records in this group are fragmentary, but they nevertheless shed a great deal of light on this real or suspected plan to rebel against the Spanish king.

A third group of the manuscripts includes the denunciations and judicial proceedings of the Holy Office of the Inquisition. These records date from the third quarter of the sixteenth century. They reveal the close church-state relationship in the Spanish Empire in America and show how ideas and behavior were controlled through such devices as the regulation and inspection of imported books and the suppression of religious nonconformity.

The remaining miscellaneous manuscripts range in date from 1557 to 1609 and include such unrelated items as a ledger of contributions to a church in Barcelona, the granting of marriage licenses, and a report of an Indian insurrection in Tlapa. In their own way, they add to the broad range of information to be found in the Harkness Mexican manuscripts.

The most visually magnificent items are in the first group of manuscripts, which includes the beautifully illuminated royal grants to Cortés and the Harkness 1531 Huejotzingo Codex (see illustrations in Chapter 3 and 5). Both of these items have been published with translations in *The Harkness Collection in the Library of Congress: Manuscripts Concerning Mexico, A Guide* (Washington, 1974). Apart from their intrinsic value as rare and authentic instruments, these manuscripts are rich in source material about the events and the social, economic, and political aspects of life in sixteenth-century Mexico. The symbolism of the coat of arms of a conquistador and the detailed ordinances on the treatment and conversion of the Indians furnish a wealth of information; the Indian paintings reflect the Mexican way of perceiving and recording events.

In view of the Spanish legalistic tradition and propensity for bureaucratic procedures, it is fitting that most of these manuscripts should owe their existence to lawsuits or some other form of judicial proceeding. The career and legal affairs of Hernando Cortés are similarly recorded in many other papers that are in the Archivo General de la Nación in Mexico and the Archivo General de Indias in Seville.

A brief statement of the institutional framework and the narrative of events will help to place these manuscripts in their historical setting. The Spanish were at first represented in the New World by the conquistadors, but as the need to protect royal prerogatives became evident, offices and administrative bodies were created and filled. In New Spain or Mexico the audiencia, usually composed of a president and several judges, was the first of these arms of royal authority; it held both judicial and administrative powers within the kingdom of New Spain. The members of the first audiencia, not now considered to have been men of exemplary character, were in conflict with Hernando Cortés, who had claimed and been assigned special powers. The king appointed him Governor and Captain General of New Spain but refrained from giving him the greater powers that Cortés probably coveted. During Cortés's visit to Spain in 1528, when he set out to repair his rights and reputation, the first audiencia tried to take over his lands and powers. The second audiencia, composed of men of higher caliber, was less hostile, but Cortés still felt out of favor when he left on his expedition to Lower California in 1535. In that same year, Don Antonio de Mendoza was sent by Charles V as the first Viceroy of New Spain, a post he was to hold until 1550, when he was followed by Don Luis de Velasco.

It was in the context of wavering allegiances, in Spain as well as in New Spain, that informers came forth to report plans for a conspiracy to the members of the audiencia. As the detailed provisions in the royal grant indicate, the Spanish system of justice permitted that informers be paid and that the property of criminals be used to pay costs and enrich the royal exchequer. Fear, malice, or a desire to curry favor could have motivated the informers and the *oidores* in their accusations that treason against the king was contemplated.

■ JOHANN GEORG KOHL COLLECTION

Johann Georg Kohl was mentioned above in the discussion of the Geography and Map Division's holdings. Kohl was a German geographer who spent several years delving into the history of the discovery of North America. He visited many of the important libraries and museums across Europe in the midnineteenth century to collect material on this topic. Operating as he was in a period lacking photographic copying technologies, Kohl arranged to trace many of the original early maps that documented the history of North American discovery. After devoting about five years to these efforts, Kohl came to America in 1854. In the course of his sojourn he came into contact with one of the leading scientists in the United States, Dr. Alexander Dallas Bache, first president of the National Academy of Sciences and Superintendent of the U.S. Coast Survey.

Bache was impressed by the depth of Kohl's knowledge of the discovery and early exploration of the coasts of the United States. He hired Kohl to undertake a series of detailed historical coastal reports to be used as the basis for deciding what names would be given to the bays, harbors, channels, inlets, coves, and other features shown on the survey's printed charts.

While the voluminous Bache-Kohl correspondence is in the National Archives, Kohl's original maps and manuscript coastal studies and study of the exploration of the Gulf Stream are in the Library of Congress. In the Manuscript Division's Kohl Collection are his comprehensive study on the coasts of the Gulf of Mexico, a catalog of books dating from 1519 to 1855 used in his East Coast study, and finally a listing of the names of Atlantic coastal features.

Writing in 1974, the late doyen of the History of Discovery Samuel Eliot Morison observed, "Kohl, while in the United States (1854–1857), worked out a method of reproducing the essential features and toponymy of old maps for modern printing that, in my opinion, has never been surpassed; and his originals are accessible in the Library of Congress." Clearly, the researcher utilizing the Kohl material will be required to find his way to both the Manuscript and Geography and Map Divisions. Fortunately, both are conveniently housed in the James Madison Memorial Building of the Library of Congress.

■ KRAUS COLLECTION OF HISPANIC AMERICAN MANUSCRIPTS

The generosity of Hans P. Kraus and his wife Hanni was outlined above in the discussion of the magnificent Sir Francis Drake Collection they presented to the Rare Book and Special Collections Division in 1980. Twenty years before that presentation, in 1960, Hans P. Kraus gave the Library of Congress "the most important acquisition of Hispanic materials since the gift in 1929 by the late Edward S. Harkness of his collection of Spanish manuscripts from the early years of the colonial history of Mexico and Peru."

Significant not only for the wide range of information it contains about Spanish colonial history, the Kraus collection also sheds historical light on territories now within the limits of the United States. Among the manuscripts are contemporary colonial writings that document exploration of the New World, the government of New Spain, the workings of the Inquisition, taxation, economic conditions in the colonies, Spanish relationships with the Indians and the French, and the loss of part of the Spanish Empire to American encroachment.

Four years after receiving the collection the Library of Congress published a superb guide by J. Benedict Warren titled *Hans P. Kraus Collection of Hispanic American Manuscripts* (Washington: 1974). This catalog-guide forms a rich descriptive and analytical overview which forms in itself "a significant contribution to scholarship in this field," to quote the words of Librarian L. Quincy Mumford's Foreword.

A recitation of the bibliographic entries of just a few of the many items that are described in detail by Warren should whet the research appetites of a host of Age of Discovery scholars:

117 [*Fernando Alvardo Tezozomoc*] . . . *La corónica Mexicana.* [*Mexico, ca. 1600 (i.e., between 1598 and 1609)*]. 158 leaves.
The author, who lived from circa 1520 to 1609, was a descendant on both sides from Aztec emperors. On his father's side he was a great-grandson of Axayácatl, the sixth emperor, and his maternal grandfather was Montezuma II, emperor at the time of the Spanish invasion. In his writing he was able to draw upon the oral traditions of his people to give a fuller interpretation of the hieroglyphic histories which had been preserved.

121 *Giovanni da Verrazano and the Verrazano family. Collections of letters, documents, and transcripts relating to Giovanni da Verrazano and the Verrazano family. Florence, 15th–18th centuries.* 49 manuscript items; 100 leaves, bound in two volumes.

141 [*Gerónimo de Ipori(?)*] *Del Rio Marañon y de su descubrimi[ent]o y sus nazimi[ent]os y de otras muchas particularidades del, y de la Jornada q[ue] hizo P[edr]o de orsua.* [*ca. 1580–1600*]. 62 leaves.
This manuscript traces the history of the exploratory expedition down the Amazon [Marañon] under Pedro de Ursúa.

In concluding this discussion it should be pointed out that our understanding of the transcriber of Christopher Columbus's *Diario* or log of his first voyage, Bartolomé de Las Casas, has been greatly enriched through recent use of the Kraus Hispanic Collection in the Library of Congress. I refer to Helen Rand Parish's *Las Casas As a Bishop: A New Interpretation Based on His Holograph Petition in the Hans P. Kraus Collection of Hispanic American Manuscripts* (Washington: Library of Congress, 1980). In this handsome volume Parish structures a new interpretation of an important phase of Las Casas's career from a document in his own handwriting found in the Kraus Collection.

▪ WOODBURY LOWERY COLLECTION

In his report for 1908, the Chief of the Manuscript Division mentioned "the transcripts and notes from Spanish sources received under the will of the late Woodbury Lowery of Washington, D.C." The eighteen volumes of transcripts and notes had been assembled by Lowery in the course of his research for the book he published under the title *The Spanish Settlements Within the Present Limits of the United States, 1513–1561* (New York, 1911). Ten of the volumes relate to Florida, five to New Mexico, and the balance to miscellaneous matters and to California, Texas, and Louisiana.

Lowery was a Washington-born lawyer who practiced law there until 1897. In addition to his practice of law, Lowery published a number of legal digests and abstracts for the legal profession. After the publication of his *Spanish Settlements*, Lowery travelled to the archives of Mexico, Madrid, Seville, London, and Paris hunting for "maps and books that could throw light upon his work."

Lowery's map collection, like the Kohl map collection, is to be found in the Geography and Map Division. Researchers interested in examining the materials he left to the Library of Congress will be wise to spend time in both the Manuscript and Geography and Map Divisions.

As mentioned in the opening paragraphs, the Manuscript Division has been accumulating copies and facsimiles of historical manuscripts from other repositories around the world for a century. The serious researcher should certainly take advantage of these materials as they apply to her or his Age of Discovery investigations at the Library of Congress. One of the photocopied collections includes important materials bearing on Christopher Columbus that are in the Duke of Veragua's library in Spain. A sampling of the Duke of Veragua Collection includes:

A Letter from the King of Portugal to Columbus dated March 20, 1488.

More than fifty decrees, orders, letters, instructions and royal letters patent to and concerning Columbus from the monarchs Ferdinand and Isabela dating from 1492 to 1498.

Columbus's original codex "Book of Privileges," 1502.

These and several other Columbian treasures from the Duke of Veragua's collection were exhibited at the World's Columbian Exposition in Chicago in 1893. The photographs in the Library's Manuscript Division were printed from glass plate negatives originally made by the famous Civil War photographer, Mathew Brady.

Of course the Age of Discovery researcher interested in Columbus's career need not rest content with the Duke of Veragua, or other, photo copy of his "Book of Privileges." Among the

truly distinguished treasures of the Library of Congress is an original vellum Columbus Codex of 1502. It is one of four copies that Columbus made of his Book of Privileges for safekeeping in monasteries (see Chapter 4 herein).

Probably the easiest access to the Manuscript Division's Hispanic manuscripts is through the set of two large three-ring binders compiled in 1964 by Howard Cline. These form the "Reference Guide to Hispanic Manuscripts in the Library of Congress" and are available in the division's reading room. For manuscripts copied from other overseas collections the researcher should consult the division's finding aid printout titled "Manuscript Collections Copied from Foreign Repositories." Staff members in the reading room can quickly assist in the use of these guides.

A researcher interested particularly in Native American questions would be wise to study the multivolume *Handbook of Middle American Indians*. Volume 14 was edited by Howard Cline and is in the series "Guide to Ethnohistorical Sources" (Austin: 1975). Included among the many codices and Native American pictorial manuscripts discussed in that source are a set of large colorful manuscript maps of the Mexican village of Puebla-Tlaxcala. What makes these twenty-four artistically colored and illuminated maps fascinating is the fact that they are falsified. While the maps purport to date from the sixteenth to the nineteenth centuries, they are nineteenth-century forgeries prepared for a land litigation. The artists, who forged both the maps and the official seals some of them bear, were convicted in a Mexican court. It is possible, however, that the forgers may have copied old maps and that the forgeries may contain accurate landscape data such as architectural details, field layouts, and road alignments. When used with appropriate caution these stunning forgeries may be of value. They represent an interesting research challenge in any event. For further information see item no. 937 in part 3 of Cline's guide mentioned above.

The Manuscript Division Reading Room is conveniently located adjacent to the atrium on the first floor or street level of the Madison Building, a few steps from the building's main entrance. As might be expected, the division's security precautions are of the highest order. On entering the well-appointed reading room you will be expected to provide proper identification—preferably something like a driver's license bearing your photograph—and complete the division's registration form that outlines the rules for using rare materials. Lockers are available so that you can leave your coat and briefcase or notebooks in a secure place before entering the reading room proper. Paper, file cards, and pencils for your use are provided so plan to leave your usual note-taking materials in your locker upon entering. Typewriters and personal computers may be carried in and used in the reading room. There are coin operated copying machines available so that quick copies can be made of suitable unbound materials. Be sure, however, to check with the staff for approval before you copy manuscripts. The Manuscript Division Reading Room is open to the public on weekdays and Saturdays from 8:30 A.M. to 5 P.M. Information booklets are free and the reading room telephone number is (202) 707-5387.

HISPANIC DIVISION

The Hispanic Division is the Library's center for the pursuit of studies in the cultures of Latin America, the Iberian peninsula, and related areas. The division guides the development of the Library's Hispanic collections; assists scholars, government officials, and the general public in the use of those materials; and describes and interprets Hispanic library resources through the preparation of guides, bibliographies, and other publications of scholarly interest. Needless to say, much, if not most, original research on Age of Discovery topics requires some use of Hispanic materials.

An unusual aspect of the Hispanic Division is to be found in the fact that most of the Library's vast Hispanic collections are actually maintained and serviced by other divisions. In the Manuscript Division of the Library, outstanding Hispanic items include the sixteenth-century Columbus Codex, the Book of Privileges granted to Columbus and produced in Seville, a 1547 Mexican treatise on the native languages, and a 1542 letter written by Hernándo Cortés to Charles V, recommending that the Indians of Mexico be put under the protection of the crown. In addition to such important individual items, the Manuscript Division holds major groups of Hispanic materials: the already described Harkness and Kraus Collections, as well as a collection of Portuguese manuscripts.

Microform copies of Hispanic manuscripts far outnumber original collections and include hundreds of thousands of pages of documents copied from the Archivo General de Indias in Seville, the Archivo General de Simancas, the Archivo Histórico Nacional, and the Ministerio del Estado at Madrid, as well as material from major Latin American countries such as Mexico and Argentina. Among other major microfilmed collections are unpublished fifteenth- to seventeenth-century documents relating to the history of Spain, unpublished documents relating to the discovery and colonization of America, pre-1800 Latin American imprints selected from the bibliographies of José Toribio Medina, the Hidalgo del Parral Archive, 1631–1821, OAS technical reports, Spanish drama of the Golden Age, nineteenth-century Spanish plays, and among recent acquisitions, the personal and professional papers of the Spanish philosopher,

José Ortega y Gasset, and of the Chilean poet, Gabriela Mistral.

Important groups of Hispanic materials can also be found in the Law Library, the Music Division, the Prints and Photographs Division, and the Geography and Map Division. The outstanding strength of the Library's Hispanic collections lies, however, in their general coverage of printed Hispanic materials produced over the last 100 years. Presently there are an estimated 1,750,000 volumes in the Library's Hispanic collections, and more than 20,000 books and 90,000 journal issues are being added each year. The Library of Congress has long pursued the policy of obtaining complete sets of official gazettes, debates of parliamentary bodies, and all other significant official publications of national agencies, as well as selected provincial or state imprints. As a result, its collection of official Latin American documents is among the strongest in the world. Its collection of Hispanic newspapers is also outstanding. There is complete coverage for many of the major newspapers.

Although most published Hispanic materials are housed in the general collections, bibliographic activity and reference services are housed in the Hispanic Room and its ancillary space. In addition to special bibliographies and guides, the Hispanic Division of the Library prepares an annual, annotated *Handbook of Latin American Studies*. First published in 1936, the handbook is recognized by scholars as the basic reference and acquisitions tool for the area and has long been a cooperative enterprise. More than one hundred contributing editors, each a distinguished specialist in his or her own discipline, collaborate to provide descriptive and evaluative comments for the more than six thousand books and periodical articles listed in each volume.

The primary roles of the Hispanic Division continue to be the development of the Spanish and Portuguese collections of the Library of Congress, the facilitation of their use by the Congress, other federal agencies, and scholars, and the explanation and interpretation of their nature and content through published guides, bibliographies, and studies. Since its establishment, the Hispanic Division has published some of the more basic research tools for the field. As a study center, it continues to work to improve communication among scholars interested in Spanish, Portuguese, Caribbean, and Latin American affairs. It welcomes all such scholars to use its facilities.

In a word the Hispanic Room in the historic Jefferson Building is the nerve center for a truly enormous segment of the Library of Congress. In it the researcher will find more than three thousand reference works on open stacks. Here are the earliest Spanish and Portuguese dictionaries, lexicons, and glossaries that are so vital for understanding the original documents covering so much of the Age of Discovery in the Americas. Biographical dictionaries and linguistic studies are also to be found here. Equally important gazetteers and geographical dictionaries are to be found in the Geography and Map Division.

If, by some remote chance, the Iberian materials you require are not in the Library in some form, the staff specialists in the Hispanic Room can tell you where they may be found. This is because the division serves as the U.S. bibliographic center for Luso-Brazilian and Hispanic materials. Chances are that immediate efforts would be made to obtain copies of such absent but worthy research materials for the Library. In 1980 the Library of Congress published a particularly valuable guide to the Portuguese manuscripts which date from the fifteenth through the nineteenth centuries. Age of Discovery researchers whose interests may focus on Portuguese sources should consult *The Portuguese*

Manuscripts of the Library of Congress: A Guide. Over five hundred manuscripts and groups of manuscripts receive treatment in this guide.

In addition to the Hispanic Division's own indexes and other finding aids, the serious researcher should keep in mind a number of online data bases that can be searched by using a computer terminal. A reference librarian can advise you on the availability of computerized search services in your area; remember, however, that there may be a fee for use of the data base searched.

Under preparation in the Hispanic Division's Reference Section is a "Guide to Sources for Latin American Studies," which serious Age of Discovery researchers should consult. Since it is an ongoing project it may be advisable to mention to Hispanic Room staff that the guide you wish to see is being compiled by the Head of their Reference Service, Dr. Everette E. Larson.

In the words of one bibliographic specialist on the Age of Discovery, the Library of Congress "has one of the most superb collections of chronicles, original editions of printed reports and polemics from the exploration and conquest of America of any library in the world . . . It possesses in one form or another—in original imprint, photostat, old-fashioned facsimile or modern edition on the one hand, or in photographic form on the other—almost every imprint of colonial South America ever recorded, and a number of basic works on the continent of other origins." Needless to say the keys to most of this bibliographic bonanza are found under Paul Philippe Cret's artistically painted stainless steel rendering of the Columbus Coat of Arms that dominates the Library's Hispanic Room.

Located on the second floor of the Jefferson Building the Hispanic Room is staffed by professional reference librarians who will provide orientation to researchers interested in Iberian, Caribbean, and Latin American studies. Computer terminals, the already mentioned reference collection, and various pamphlet files contribute to the division's facilities for a maximum of approximately thirty working scholars. The Hispanic Room is open and the reference staff on duty weekdays from 8:30 A.M. to 5:00 P.M. Telephone queries are received at (202) 707-5397.

PRINTS AND PHOTOGRAPHS DIVISION

The Library's Prints and Photographs Division (P&P) has custody of more than fifteen million photographic prints and negatives, posters, fine prints, cartoons, drawings, documentary prints, and records relating to the disciplines of architectural design and engineering. While international in scope, the collections focus on the history and cultures of the United States. They provide a visual record of people, places, and important events in the United States and throughout the world. A large portion of these holdings are in the public domain and can be reproduced for researchers.

To gain some better idea of the holdings of P&P and how they might contribute to research agendas directed to the Age of Discovery, the following descriptive publications are available for study. (Not surprisingly, there is no single comprehensive published catalog of the more than fifteen million items held by the Division.)

Guide to the Special Collections of Prints and Photographs in the Library of Congress. Compiled by Paul Vanderbilt. 1955. 200 pp. Available on microfilm, $14, or electrostatic copy, $19, from the Photoduplication Service, Library of Congress, Washington, D.C. 20540 (Microfilm no. 79589).

The Prints and Photographs Division in the Library of Congress. Brochure. 1983. Available from the Prints and Photographs Division, Library of Congress, Washington D.C. 20540 (out of print).

Treasures of the Library of Congress. By Charles A. Goodrum. (New York: Harry N. Abrams, 1991).

Available from Harry N. Abrams, Inc., Publishers, 100 Fifth Avenue, New York, N.Y. 10011.

Pictorial Americana: A Select List of Photographic Negatives in the Prints and Photographs Division of the Library of Congress. Compiled by Milton Kaplan, 1955. 68 pp. Free. Available from the Prints and Photographs Division, Library of Congress, Washington, D.C. 20540.

"Architectural Collections of the Library of Congress," by C. Ford Peatross. Reprinted from the July 1977 *Quarterly Journal of the Library of Congress.* Free. Available from the Prints and Photographs Division, Library of Congress, Washington, D.C. 20540.

The Poster Collection in the Library of Congress. Brochure. 1979. 16 pp. Free. Available from the Prints and Photographs Division, Library of Congress, Washington, D.C. 20540.

Historic America: Buildings, Structures, and Sites Recorded by the Historic American Buildings Survey and the Historic American Engineering Record. Checklist compiled by Alicia Stamm, essays edited by C. Ford Peatross (Washington: Library of Congress, 1983), 208 pp.

A Century of Photographs 1846–1946, Selected from the Collections of the Library of Congress. Compiled by Renata V. Shaw (Washington: Library of Congress, 1980).

America's Yesterdays: Images of Our Lost Past Discovered in the Photographic Archives of the Library of Congress. By Oliver Jensen. New York: American Heritage, 1978 (out of print, check your library).

Posada's Mexico. Edited by Ron Tyler. (Washington: Library of Congress, 1979) (out of print, check your library).

Bernard Reilly, *American Political Prints 1766–1876: A Catalog of the Collections in the Library of Congress* (Boston: G. K. Hall, 1991).

A few collections are easily identified as promising sources of materials bearing on the Age of Discovery issues raised in this book and can be discussed briefly here. They include the following:

■ MEXICAN INDIAN PICTORIAL DOCUMENT COLLECTION

The Mexican Indian Pictorial Document Collection consists of approximately one thousand mounted black-and-white photo prints of Middle American Indian pictorial manuscripts. They are cataloged according to the numbers employed to describe the original manuscripts in the *Handbook of Middle American Indians.* The photos were assembled between 1960 and 1971 from seventy-five collections around the world by Dr. Howard Cline and were transferred to P&P in 1973. This large file of Mexican pictorial documents was gathered together by Dr. Cline when he served as editor of four volumes of the *Handbook of Middle American Indians.* The collection was described and inventoried by Dr. John B. Glass. The description and inventory are available in the P&P Reading Room and form an excellent finding aid and guide to this amazing collection. The six major components of the collection are:

1 Numbers 1–434 (over 900 photographs). Pictorial manuscripts in the native tradition. These documents are described under the same numbers by John B. Glass and Donald Robertson, "A Census of Native Middle American Pictorial Manuscripts," HMAI, volume 14, article 23.

2 Numbers 701– (approximately 30 photographs) Techialoyan manuscripts. Described under the same numbers by Donald Robertson, "Catalog of Techialoyan Manuscripts," HMAI, volume 14, article 24.

3 Numbers 801– (approximately 7 photographs). Testerian manuscripts (pictorial catechisms). Described under the same numbers by Glass, "A Census of Middle American Testerian Manuscripts," HMAI, volume 14, article 25.

4 Numbers 901– (approximately 33 photographs). Falsified pictorial manuscripts.

Described under the same numbers by Glass, "A Catalog of Falsified Middle American Pictorial Manuscripts," HMAI, volume 14, article 26.

5 RG numbers 1– (approximately 16 photographs).
Maps of the relaciones geográficas, 1579–1585.
Described under the same numbers (without the RG prefix) by Robertson, "The Pinturas [maps] of the Relaciones Geograficas, with a Catalog," HMAI, volume 12, article 6, pp. 265–278.

6 Supplementary series ("Sup." numbers 1–16) (16 photos)
Miscellaneous documents not described in the articles cited above although some are cited or mentioned therein. The numeration employed was created for the purpose of the present listing.

■ FRANCES BENJAMIN JOHNSTON COLLECTION

While this collection clearly does not contain materials of Age of Discovery vintage, it does deal with a topic of considerable interest to anyone concerned with the observation of the Columbian Quincentenary. Johnston was a photographer who provided a visual record of the 1892 World's Columbian Exposition in Chicago. Included are photographs of the Exposition site under construction and after completion, showing buildings, monuments, and grounds including the many canals. Asian participants such as Javanese musicians and cockfight onlookers, exposition visitors and staff, exotic animals, and crowd scenes were among the many subjects for Johnston's recording lens. A detailed finding aid for the collection is filed under "Johnston" in the P&P Reading Room.

■ PRENTICE DUELL COLLECTION

Prentice Duell was a scholar and a collector whose interests included the Spanish missions built in the American Southwest in the wake of the Age of Discovery. Many of the mission buildings represented in his collection were built in the seventeenth century and photographed in the late nineteenth century before large-scale restoration projects took place. The Mission San Xavier del Bac is probably the best known of Duell's subjects. In addition to many photos of the famous mission church, this collection includes measured drawings and blueprints as well as a large collection of notes devoted to this striking complex near Tucson.

■ EDWARD S. CURTIS COLLECTION

Many of the photographs published by Edward S. Curtis in his award-winning, twenty-volume work *The North American Indian* came to the Library of Congress through copyright deposit. Curtis traveled extensively to remote regions over Canada and the United States to capture the images of Native Americans during the last century. The Curtis images in P&P are original photoprints and include examples from each of the regions documented in *The North American Indian:* the Plains, the Northern Pacific Coast, Northern and Central California, and the Central Plateau. A copy of the original edition of *The North American Indian* should be consulted in the Rare Book and Special Collections Division before searching the files in P&P. In the divisional catalog, cards are filed under names of specific tribes as well as under "Curtis."

Many of the portraits contained in the Curtis Collection lots are indexed in the Indian Biographical Index which can be found in the far left corner of the P&P Reading Room as one enters. Should the Curtis photographs you need not be found in the Library of Congress, it may be worthwhile to extend your search to the Smithsonian Institution. During the 1950s many Curtis photographs were transferred to the Smithsonian's Department of Anthropology, and in some instances duplicates were not retained by the Library of Congress

■ HISTORIC AMERICAN BUILDINGS SURVEY

Known familiarly as HABS, this is the largest and most widely used architectural collection in P&P. The survey was begun in 1933 "as a work relief project under the Civil Works Administration to aid unemployed architects and draftsmen and at the same time to produce a detailed record of such early American architecture as was in immediate danger of destruction." Reaching its peak in the period 1934–1940, the HABS project was discontinued during World War II and resumed in the fifties. The project records buildings in all fifty states, the District of Columbia, Puerto Rico, and the Virgin Islands. The National Park Service administers the program, the American Institute of Architects serves in an advisory role and the Library of Congress receives the HABS records and makes them available to the public.

The collection includes photographs, measured drawings, and written historical documentation on close to twenty-one thousand structures and sites surveyed by HABS since 1933. During the last thirty years the original focus on individual structures has come to include a broader interest in historic districts and complexes. One category of buildings certain to be of interest to Age of Discovery researchers would be the "Missions and Spanish Churches." These were the foci of an important facet of the religious, cultural, and economic interaction that took place between Native Americans and Catholic missionaries in that era. A printed listing titled "Missions and Spanish Churches Recorded by the Historic American Buildings Survey" is one of many similar HABS finding aids that are available from P&P upon request, free of charge.

A type of historic settlement included in HABS is the Indian Pueblos of the far Southwest. The Spanish gave these prehistoric settlements their word for town, and it is common knowledge that their classic period was contemporaneous with the construction of Europe's great cathedrals in the thirteenth century. A study of the black slave-explorer Estevan and the entrada leader Coronado might be, for example, enriched through the inclusion of detailed knowledge of these important settlements.

With an eye toward the interest in likenesses of Columbus that the Columbian Quincentenary promised to stimulate, the division prepared a helpful illustrated broadside titled "Columbus: Selected Pictures from the Library of Congress," for free distribution. The broadside contains ten images of the Admiral of the Ocean Sea with full details on how to request photographic prints from the Library's Photoduplication Service.

In P&P's Graphics File, Age of Discovery researchers will encounter a number of topical headings of potential interest. For example, the file Latin America and Islands is broken down as follows:

A Latin America and Islands—Misc.

B Cuba

C Chile

D Mexico

E Explorers and Discoverers

F Indians of Central and South America

Under Early Illustrations of N. Am. Indians the breakdown is:

A Misc. Sources

B John White—Virginia

C De Bry engravings

Several of these are squarely on target for the Age of Discovery. The Graphic File is an access tool for original collections/items in the division, rather than a collection in itself. Due to space limitations and time constraints, a number of pertinent collections have not been described. These include the McKenney and Hall Indian portraits, the photographs of the Columbian Exposition, the Berryman collection of Jamaica drawings, and the Archive of Hispanic Culture.

The Prints and Photographs Reading Room occupies a large well-lit area on the third floor of the Madison Building's blue quadrant. Upon entering, the researcher will be expected to register and produce a picture identification such as a driver's license. Personal belongings, coats, bags etc. can be left in the registration area or in a locker room. One of the unusual items of furniture in the P&P Reading Room is a centrally located camera stand for do-it-yourself photocopying with available light. Photocopying and change-making machines are available for copying, but be sure to get staff approval. Transparencies, slides, and negatives can be viewed in a light box with staff approval also. Microform readers for studying P&P film and microfiche are also on the floor in the reading room.

One of the helpful handouts P&P has prepared for use in the reading room is a map of the facility. It is extremely useful in finding one's way to the catalogs, indexes, and files that are available. Be sure to obtain a copy of it as you begin your research in this archive of graphic materials.

As mentioned, there is no comprehensive written catalog describing the enormous holdings in P&P's collections. A list of current and out-of-print publications relating to material in the division and other finding aids will be sent or provided on request. The telephone number for the P&P Reading Room reference librarians is (202) 707-6394. The reading room is open on weekdays from 8:30 A.M. to 5:00 P.M.

MOTION PICTURE, BROADCASTING, AND RECORDED SOUND DIVISION

At first glance it might seem strange to include a discussion of this division in a guide to researching the Age of Discovery. It is, however, no stranger than including the many tens of thousands of books, engravings, manuscripts, maps, and illustrations that can tell us about that age, its events, places, and personalities, even though they were written or created long after the age had passed. The Age of Discovery and the exploration of the Americas that followed inspired filmmakers and broadcasters from the late nineteenth century onwards.

Fortunately the Library of Congress began collecting the earliest filmmakers' products as they were deposited for copyright. Because there was no provision in the copyright law for registering motion pictures, these and other early films were deposited as photographs printed on rolls of paper. These early deposits became known as the Paper Print Collection. In 1912 new copyright legislation permitted the registration of motion pictures as a distinct form. During the next thirty years, however, because of the difficulty of handling the flammable nitrate film of the period, the Library retained only descriptive material related to motion pictures. This practice changed in 1942 when, recognizing the importance of motion pictures and the need to preserve them as an historical record, the Library resumed collecting the films themselves. From 1949 on, films made for television were included. Today the Motion Picture, Broadcasting, and Recorded Sound Division has responsibility for the acquisition, cataloging, preservation, and service of the Library's motion picture and television collections, including items on film, videotape, and videodisc. The division has similar responsibilities for the Library's collections of sound recordings and radio programs.

The film and television collections contain over seventy-five thousand titles, with several thousand titles being added each year through copyright deposit, purchase, gift, or exchange. Items selected from copyright deposits include feature films, short works of all sorts, fiction and documentary, exemplifying the range of current film and video production and reflecting the diversity of American thought and experience. The collections also include some three hundred thousand stills.

It should come as no surprise to find that Christopher Columbus and his exploits came to the attention of filmmakers more than any other figure from the Age of Discovery. The earliest extant theatrical motion picture about Columbus known to be in an American film archive is a 1910 French production by the Gaumont Company entitled *Christopher Columbus.* A copy is in the collection of the Library of Congress. It was imported and released in America by George Kleine, a Chicago-based film distributor.

The first feature-length American motion picture about Columbus was the three-reel production *The Coming of Columbus,* released by the Selig Polyscope Company of Chicago in May 1912. The scenario was written by C. E. Nixon and the starring roles were played by Charles Clary, Thomas Santschi, Bessie Eyton, and Herbert Rawlinson. The film is of special interest because the producer, William N. Selig, filmed many scenes on board replicas of the *Niña, Pinta,* and *Santa Maria* that had been presented to America by the Queen Regent, Christina of Spain, for display at the World's Columbian Exposition of 1892. In an effort to achieve authenticity and publicity, Selig also secured the use of Columbus's original log book as a prop in the film.

The most widely distributed English-language, sound-era feature film on the life of Co-

lumbus in the collection is the 1948 J. Arthur Rank production of *Christopher Columbus,* starring Fredric March. Though the Gaumont, Selig, and Rank productions span almost forty years, they depict the identical dramatic events of Columbus's life in the same reverent and conventional manner that characterized mainstream commercial biographical films until the 1960s.

Short subject productions from the same period created humor by incorporating Columbus's name into their titles. Examples include the 1911 Thanhouser one-reeler *A Columbus Day Conspiracy;* the 1933 Vitaphone short *Double Crossing of Columbus,* starring the vaudeville act "Vanessi and The Maxellos"; the 1934 Walter Lantz cartoon *Chris Columbus, Jr.,* with animation by Tex Avery; and the 1939 Terrytoon *Chris Columbo.* As with the majority of important historical figures whose lives have been dramatized in motion pictures, Columbus has also been the target of occasional satires, as in Chico Marx's fine cameo burlesque in the otherwise forgettable *The Story of Mankind* (Warner Bros.), produced in 1957.

Motion pictures have been directed to purposes other than feature entertainment films since the making of narrative films began in the early 1900s. The Library has, for example, the 1923 Yale University Press Film Service production of a biographical film entitled *Columbus,* based on Irving Berdine Richman's book *The Spanish Conquerors.* This film, along with others in a series known as "The Chronicles of America Photoplays," was produced partly as a rebuttal by the academic community to the often factually incorrect costume melodramas of commercial producers in New York and Hollywood. The series was also intended to promote the use of film as an educational medium.

One of the more interesting noncommercial applications of motion pictures was made by the historian Samuel Eliot Morison in 1939, who used the medium for recording scientific information during his effort to retrace the voyages of Columbus. The Library of Congress is particularly pleased to have this intimate filmed record of Morison's field research for his Pulitzer Prize-winning study on Christopher Columbus titled, *Admiral of the Ocean Sea.*

Numerous short educational films about Columbus and other explorers have appeared, especially in the post-World War II era. Productions of this type, relating to Columbus, that continue to be circulated by distributors of educational films include: *Christopher Columbus* (BBC/ Time Life, 1976), *Christopher Columbus* (Churchill Films, 1982), and *Christopher Columbus—the Voyage of Discovery* (American Films, 1989).

Two notable television productions on the life of Columbus have appeared in the past twenty years. First is the 1971 CBS Television News broadcast *You Are There: Columbus and Isabella,* which was hosted by Walter Cronkite. The second is the six-hour TV miniseries entitled *Christopher Columbus,* also broadcast by CBS. Produced by Radiotelevisione Italiana with international financing, the series was widely seen throughout Europe and the Americas. Both programs are but preludes to the many others that doubtless will be broadcast in the period of Columbian Quincentenary observations.

Though Columbus, Cortez, Balboa, de Leon, Champlain, Drake and the other famous explorers may not have inspired, collectively speaking, as many biographical motion pictures as other generic groups—i.e., generals, cowboys, authors, and composers—all have either been the subject of at least one feature film or have been depicted at various times as historical characters in fictional melodramas set against the exploration and colonization of the Americas. No one knows the total number because of the lack of overall documentation relating to worldwide film production since the industry began. However, it is probable that all the important discoverers have been portrayed in films at least

once in the past ninety years in productions made in the countries of their origin. Many, but by no means all of these, are represented in the Library of Congress's collections.

Christopher Columbus was of interest to early filmmakers because of his obvious link to the origins of America. But there was another more direct reason why Columbus was regarded by the first film producers as an historical figure of particular interest to contemporary audiences. The age of commercial development of motion pictures began the year after America celebrated the quadricentennial of Columbus's discovery in 1892. During this period of precinematic cultural activity, an enormous output of amateur and professional plays, novels, songs, poems, etc., were produced on the life of Columbus. The outpouring of these works actually began to appear before 1880 and carried on throughout the early part of the twentieth century. In the decade of the 1890s alone, the U.S. Copyright Office registered over forty dramatic compositions based on the life of Columbus, and many biographies, historical novels, and other written and graphic works as well.

The Motion Picture, Broadcasting, and Recorded Sound Division (M/B/RS) maintains a reading room with extensive card catalogs of its film and television holdings. Primary access to the materials is by title. The published catalog *Early Motion Pictures: The Paper Print Collection in the Library of Congress* by Kemp R. Niver is available on the premises along with the following pertinent publications: *The Theodore Roosevelt Association Film Collection, A Catalog; The George Kleine Collection of Early Motion Pictures in the Library of Congress, A Catalog;* and *Three Decades of Television: A Catalog of Television Programs Acquired by the Library of Congress 1949–1979.*

Also available in the reading room is a basic collection of reference books on cinema and television, along with distributors' catalogs, yearbooks, reviews, and trade periodicals. Fuller collections of published reference materials are included in the Library's general and periodical collections, and can be consulted in the larger reading rooms.

M/B/RS also has custody of descriptive materials (pressbooks, plot synopses, continuities) for motion pictures registered for copyright after 1912. The division's catalogers are experimenting with ways to computerize all cataloging information in order to replace the various card catalogs with a data base from which bibliographic information can be retrieved in a variety of ways.

Most of the sound recordings in the collection have not been fully cataloged. The Recorded Sound Reference Center houses the Library of Congress printed card catalog for sound recordings and a card index for many of the uncataloged recordings held by the division. The Recorded Sound Reference Center also services, in conjunction with the Music Division in the Performing Arts Reading Room, manufacturers' published catalogs, trade catalogs, discographies, books and periodicals on sound recordings, finding aids, reference books, subject folders, and lists. Many materials on sound recordings are included in the Library's general and periodical collections and can be consulted in the general reading rooms.

The Library of Congress Film and Television Reading Room is located in Room 336 of the Madison Building and is open to serious researchers on weekdays from 8:30 A.M. to 4:30 P.M. When you arrive sign the register before beginning your work. Research in sound recordings or radio is conducted in the Recorded Sound Reference Center of the Performing Arts Reading Room located in Room 113 of the Madison Building. It is open for use on weekdays from 8:30 A.M. to 5:00 P.M. The telephone number in the Film and Television Reading Room is (202) 707-1000 and in the Recorded Sound Reference Center (202) 707-7833.

AMERICAN FOLKLIFE CENTER AND ARCHIVE OF FOLK CULTURE

One of the Library's more recently established divisions, the American Folklife Center, came into being as a result of the American Folklife Preservation Act of 1976. The center is charged with "preserving and presenting American folklife" through programs of research, documentation, archival preservation, exhibition, publication, dissemination, training, and other activities involving folk traditions in the United States. A couple of years later the Library's long-established Archive of Folk Culture became an important part of the center. Established in 1928 the archive represents one of the world's most significant collections of folklife materials. Its holdings include audio recordings of folk songs, folk music, folk tales, oral history and other forms of traditional expression. It also holds over eighty thousand pages of manuscript materials as well as a collection of periodicals and books dealing with folk music and folklore carefully selected from the Library of Congress's collections.

Like some of the divisions already discussed, the Folklife Center does not hold materials that date from the Age of Discovery. Its holdings may, however, contribute to our understanding and appreciation of the human echoes still to be heard from the cultural encounters set in motion in that age. A few of the collections possessing such promise seemed worthy of mention in this guide. In some cases these collections owe their existence to efforts designed to commemorate the 400th anniversary of Columbus's momentous first crossing of the Atlantic, the World's Columbian Exposition in Chicago.

■ BENJAMIN IVES GILMAN COLLECTION

Benjamin Ives Gilman recorded on wax cylinders at the 1893 World's Columbian Exposition in Chicago to provide a sound record of musicians performing at the Samoan, Javanese, Turkish, and Vancouver Island Indian Villages. Students of North American Indian cultures will be particularly interested in the eighteen cylinders containing the songs and ceremonies of the Kwakiutl Indians from Vancouver Island on the Pacific Northwest coast of Canada. Franz Boas made important use of some of these recordings in his 1897 (1970 reprint) publication titled *The Social Organization of the Secret Societies of the Kwakiutl Indians.*

■ HORNBOSTEL DEMONSTRATION COLLECTION

This collection comprises 120 pressed wax cylinders made from original wax field recordings of ethnic and tribal music at the Berlin Phonogramm-Archiv. Erich Moritz von Hornbostel compiled several slightly different anthologies of music from around the world for scholarly use. This set came to the Library in 1943 as the gift of Walter V. Bingham. Greenland and North American Native people from many areas as well as Central and South American Indians are recorded on these cylinders.

For a more detailed listing of the recordings in the Benjamin Ives Gilman and Hornbostel Collections consult Dorothy Sara Lee (ed.), *The Federal Cylinder Project: A Guide to Field Cylinder Collections in Federal Agencies,* volume 8, *Early Anthologies* (American Folklife Center, 1984).

■ EDGAR LEE HEWETT COLLECTION OF NAHUATL INDIAN MUSIC AND SPOKEN WORD

This collection includes six cylinders of Nahuatl Indian music and spoken word recorded by Edgar Lee Hewett in Tepoztlan, Mexico, in September 1906. Hewett was an archaeologist who made the recordings on the occasion of the annual pueblo fiesta during which mock battles took place at the temple, on the cliffs, and in the

plaza. Concerning the ceremony Hewett wrote, "It is entirely in the Nahua idiom and is said to consist of a series of recitals of ancient combats etc. (all pre-Spanish) between the Tepoztecos and Xochicalos." For a further discussion of these recordings and their contents refer to volume 5 of *The Federal Cylinder Project* edited by Judith A. Gray, an ethnomusicologist on the staff of the American Folklife Center.

A major focus of the observance of the Columbian Quincentenary by the Library of Congress in 1992 is the American Folklife Center's innovative program "Italian Americans in the West." Research on this theme began in 1978 in a remote community in central Nevada and continues in California, Washington, Colorado, and Utah. In 1992 the project will culminate in an exhibition that will help inaugurate Catholic University's Italian-American Heritage Center in Washington, D.C. A major component of the project is devoted to the festivals celebrated by Italian Americans. Particularly important among these are the Columbus Day celebrations and pageants which provide opportunities for Italian Americans to celebrate their heritage in a uniquely American way.

Probably the best guide for an Age of Discovery student wishing to employ folk materials in his research effort is a creative imagination. The Archive of Folk Culture has prepared for free distribution on request *An Inventory of the Bibliographies and Other Reference and Finding Aids.* It is probably the best place to begin to apply your creative imagination. A recent edition of this inventory started with "Bibliographies and Discographies of *African* music," and ended with "Wisconsin Field Recordings". A sample of the intervening entries that seemed to hold promise of particularly relevant materials were:

Music of the *California Indians* Culture Area
Music of the *Cherokee Indians*
Eskimo Music

Bibliographies in the Field of *Ethnomusicology*

Huron (Wyandot) Indian Music

Music of the *Incas* and Early Peru

American *Indian* and Eskimo Music

Composers Utilizing American *Indian* Music

Music of the *Nez Perce* Indians

Music of the American Indians on the *Northwest Coast*

Seneca Indian Music

Shawnee Indian Music

Zuni and Eastern Pueblo Indian Music

Peruvian Field Recordings

Latin American and Caribbean Recordings

The American Folklife Center and Archive of Folk Culture are located on the ground floor of the Jefferson Building where a reading room open to the public offers the following services:

a 4,000-volume reference collection of books and periodicals on American and international folklore and ethnomusicology; a set of the Library's pub-lished documentary folk music and folklore recordings, with listening facilities; tape and cassette machines for research listening (by appointment); microfilm and microfiche readers; self-service photocopying; card catalogs for most of the recorded, manuscript, and microform collections processed by the archive; terminal access to the Library's computerized catalogs; a special author card file of books and articles published in the last twenty years in the field of ethnomusicology; and full-time reference assistance by the archive staff.

The archive staff provides direct reference assistance to readers, telephone inquirers, and correspondents, addressing general questions about folklore and ethnomusicology as well as inquiries about specific items in the Library's collection. The archive also acts as a referral service to other sources of information in the United States and elsewhere. Reading room hours are from 8:30 A.M. to 5:00 P.M., Monday through Friday. Mail queries should be addressed to: Archive of Folk Culture, Library of Congress, Washington, D.C. 20540. The reading room telephone number is (202) 707-5510.

INDEX

Dates are in italics.

Page numbers for illustrations are in boldface.

Norumbegue

pen tegoet

Isles perdues

Mont desert

Isle haute

Dorsenes Isles

norumbegui

la tertue

baye de marchen

Isle de boeus

chouacoit

Pau x
Isles

la ronde Ile

bene longue   Isles getées

cap aux Isles

por du cap aux Isles

baye des Isles

Cap S. Loüis

S. Loüis

Cap blanc

baye blanche

po aux huitre   Malle bare